Remembering Ezra Vogel

HARVARD EAST ASIAN MONOGRAPHS 455

Remembering Ezra Vogel

Compiled by
Martin K. Whyte and Mary C. Brinton

Published by the Harvard University Asia Center
Distributed by Harvard University Press
Cambridge (Massachusetts) and London 2022

The Harvard University Asia Center publishes a monograph series and, in coordination with the Fairbank Center for Chinese Studies, the Korea Institute, the Reischauer Institute of Japanese Studies, and other facilities and institutes, administers research projects designed to further scholarly understanding of China, Japan, Vietnam, Korea, and other Asian countries. The Center also sponsors projects addressing multidisciplinary and regional issues in Asia.

Front cover: Ezra in Hong Kong just prior to delivering a speech, 1991. Courtesy of the *South China Morning Post.*

Back cover: Caricature of Ezra by artist David Levine, inspired by the success of Ezra's book, *Japan as Number One.* The caricature was featured on T-shirts distributed at Ezra's retirement party in May 2000. © Matthew and Eve Levine.

Cataloging-in-Publication Data is on file at the Library of Congress.

ISBN 9780674278271 (paperback)

♾ Printed on acid-free paper

Last figure below indicates year of this printing

31 30 29 28 27 26 25 24 23 22

Contents

Illustrations

Preface

Ezra F. Vogel (1930–2020) was one of America's foremost experts on Asia, mastering the Japanese and Chinese languages and contributing important scholarly works on both countries and on their relationship with each other and with the world, as well as on multiple other topics. Although he lived to the age of ninety, he remained so healthy and vigorous (publishing his last major book, *China and Japan: Facing History*, at age eighty-nine) that his sudden death following a medical procedure came as a shock to his many friends around the world. In the wake of the sad news of his passing, the outpouring of gratitude and grief from those his life had touched was overwhelming and stimulated discussions about how best to honor Ezra's legacy. The present volume is one result of those discussions.

A familiar way that prominent academics are honored, either in the closing stages of their lives or after they have died, is to hold a symposium in which colleagues and former students present academic papers demonstrating how their work was influenced by the person being honored. Often a set of such papers is published in a volume referred to by the German term *festschrift*. After discussions among Ezra's colleagues, family members, and friends, we felt that this was not the best way to honor him. During his lifetime Ezra made contributions on so many different fronts and developed such a wide network of grateful and loyal friends around the world (many of them outside of academe) that no standard academic volume would suffice.

Fortunately, we were able to take advantage of the fact that Ezra had followed in the footsteps of two towering figures in Asian studies at Harvard, John King Fairbank (on China) and Edwin Reischauer (on Japan). When Fairbank died in 1991, his colleagues at what would eventually be renamed the Fairbank Center for Chinese Studies devised a novel way to honor him.[1] They invited a wide range of colleagues, former students, friends, and family members to write brief reminiscences of particularly memorable interactions they had had with Fairbank. The resulting volume, *Fairbank Remembered*, compiled by Paul Cohen and Merle Goldman, was published by the Fairbank Center in 1992. We decided to use that volume as a template to produce a set of similar reminiscence essays honoring Ezra Vogel.

Each person we contacted was asked to focus on a particularly memorable experience they had had with Ezra (rather than recounting their entire history together) and to describe what that experience revealed about Ezra's character. We instructed contributors to describe that experience in 1,000 words or less. The result is the 155 brief essays contained in the following pages. These essays are affectionate, insightful, revealing, deeply personal, and sometimes very funny. Cumulatively they form a portrait that is unusually intimate and honest, not only in what the authors say about Ezra, but also in what they say about themselves and the significant impact Ezra had on their lives.

Since the contributors were given free rein to say what they wanted, certain themes, and even particular incidents, crop up again and again, and we have not attempted to eliminate this repetition. (We could have created an entire section of accounts by people who describe having breakfast with Ezra at the International House in Tokyo.) But on occasion the accounts about incidents involving Ezra differ somewhat, and here again we have not tried to eliminate those differences. In general we have confined our editorial role to correcting factual inaccuracies, spelling errors,

1. The Center has a history dating back to 1955, with John King Fairbank as its first director, and in subsequent years it went by a series of names. In 1961 it became known as the East Asian Research Center, and in 1977, following John Fairbank's retirement, it was renamed the Fairbank East Asian Research Center. During William Kirby's directorship, shortly after the Center celebrated its fiftieth anniversary in 2005, its name was changed to the Fairbank Center for Chinese Studies. Contributors to the present volume are referring to the same entity even if they use somewhat different terms in doing so.

incorrect dates of publications, and so forth, as well as standardizing the format of the essays. For example, all authors are identified simply by their name and either their place of residence or their organizational affiliation, without any of the titles they may have earned during their lives. In some cases we also assisted authors in cutting down the length of their essays in order to stay within our firm 1,000-word limit. As a general rule we made strenuous efforts as editors to preserve each author's voice. We see the resulting collection of essays as a mosaic portrait from which a reader may gain a clear view of what an extraordinary human being Ezra Vogel was.

Creating a coherent volume out of 155 disparate essays was no small challenge. We created thirteen categories, combining both chronology and thematic content, and placed each essay into the part that seemed most appropriate to us. However, since many of the essays (despite our request for sharp focus on a particular experience with Ezra) cover long time periods and recount many aspects of Ezra's impact on the author, we often had to be quite arbitrary about where in our categorical scheme to place a particular reminiscence. We beg the indulgence of the reader, and of our authors, if our sorting logic seems obscure and the resulting placement of an essay differs from where the reader (or author) would have located it.

The essays in this volume are preceded by two short documents. One is the chronology that summarizes the major events in Ezra Vogel's personal life and career and the years in which they occurred. The document that follows is the Harvard Memorial Minute that Whyte and Brinton were invited to draft to honor Ezra (also in 1,000 words or less). This is a ritualized document peculiar to Harvard that will be read out in a future meeting of the Faculty of Arts and Sciences (delayed due to the COVID pandemic) to honor Ezra. The Memorial Minute is a summary of the major benchmarks in Ezra's life and career, so it substantially duplicates the events listed in the chronology. Together these two short documents are intended to help readers anchor the many events and incidents described in the individual essays with which they may not be familiar.

This volume came together through the efforts of many people. The news of Ezra's unexpected death in December 2020 was followed by an outpouring of messages mourning his loss. Among these messages were many exchanged among his former students, colleagues, and other longtime friends. The suggestion to publish a volume of brief reminiscences in Ezra's honor was first raised by two former students included in this volume—Perry Link and Melinda Liu. Whyte and Link exchanged emails when they realized that they had both attended Ezra's class on contemporary China together in 1965, a coincidence that prompted Link to nominate Whyte to take the lead in assembling such a volume. Charlotte Ikels, Steven Vogel, and Michael Szonyi all joined in the remote exchange of ideas for such a volume, with Charlotte getting a copy of *Fairbank Remembered* out of the library and realizing the close similarity of that volume to the ideas the group had begun discussing. Paul Cohen supplied copies of the original letters he and Merle Goldman had sent out to authors for that earlier volume, which we used to help draft invitations to the authors of the current volume. Whyte's reluctance to play a leading role was overcome when Mary Brinton agreed to sign on as his partner in assembling this volume, particularly to take the lead in working with authors in Japanese and Korean studies.

The initial lists of names and email addresses of the many "friends of Ezra Vogel" who were invited to contribute reminiscences were assembled by Charlotte and Steve, with many other names suggested by others and added later. James Robson signed on for the Asia Center and provided sage advice on how to prepare a book proposal to submit to the Center's Publications Program. The Asia Center, Fairbank Center, Reischauer Institute, and their staffs all played enthusiastic supporting roles, and Jess Viator (Mary's staff assistant in Sociology) assisted Mary and assembled a full set of the draft essays so that Charlotte and Steve could check dates and facts for accuracy. The few essays submitted in a language other than English were translated by Shinju Fujihara and Steve Vogel (Japanese) and by Gao Hui (Chinese). Finally, Bob Graham and the Asia Center Publications Program Executive Committee enthusiastically approved the publication of *Remembering Ezra Vogel* and efficiently saw it through to publication, with Bob working with the photographs selected by Charlotte to add the visuals that grace the final volume. We also extend our thanks to Deborah Del Gais for her very patient and skillful copyediting of the entire manuscript. We could not have completed the job without the efforts of so many, whose love for Ezra resulted in their deep commitment to making this volume in his honor a success.

Finally, we echo the sentiments of so many contributors to this volume by saying that this has been a labor of love for a man who meant so much to each of us.

M.K.W.

M.C.B.

Postscript: The † symbol has been inserted after the names of two of the contributors to this volume, Fred Hiatt (1955–2021) and Marshall Murphree (1931–2021), who died after production of the book had begun.

Chronology

1930	Born July 11, in Delaware, Ohio
1947	Graduates from Willis High School, Delaware, Ohio; enrolls in Ohio Wesleyan University
1950	Graduates Phi Beta Kappa from Ohio Wesleyan University with a major in sociology; enrolls in the MA program in sociology at Bowling Green State University
1951–53	Serves in the United States Army
1953	Enrolls in the doctoral program in the Department of Social Relations at Harvard; marries Suzanne Hall
1956	Birth of son David
1958	Completes Harvard PhD in sociology, with a specialization in family sociology
1958–60	Accompanied by Suzanne and son David, lives in Tokyo to study Japanese and conduct fieldwork on middle-class families in a Tokyo suburb
1960	Publishes *A Modern Introduction to the Family* (co-edited with Norman Bell; revised edition 1968)
1960–61	Assistant Professor, Department of Psychiatry, Yale University
1961	Birth of son Steven
1961–64	Postdoctoral fellow, Harvard, studying Chinese and beginning research on China
1963	Publishes *Japan's New Middle Class*, based upon fieldwork in Tokyo

1963–64	Conducts in-depth interviews in Hong Kong with refugees from China
1964	Begins teaching in the Department of Social Relations at Harvard; birth of daughter Eve
1967	Promoted to professor with tenure in the Department of Social Relations
1969	Publishes *Canton under Communism*, which receives the Harvard University Press Faculty Book of the Year Award
1972–91	Chair, East Asian Studies AB program
1972–77	Director, East Asian Research Center
1975	Publishes *Modern Japanese Organization and Decision-Making*
1977–80	Chair, Council on East Asian Studies
1978	Divorce from Suzanne Vogel
1979	Publishes *Japan as Number One: Lessons for America*; marries Charlotte Ikels
1980–87	Director, Program on U.S.-Japan Relations
1985	Publishes *Comeback, Case by Case: Building the Resurgence of American Business*
1986–90	Clarence Dillon Professor of International Affairs
1987	With Charlotte, spends seven months doing fieldwork in Guangdong Province to examine the launching of China's market reforms
1989	Publishes *One Step Ahead in China: Guangdong under Reform*
1990–2000	Henry Ford II Professor of the Social Sciences
1991	Receives Japan Order of the Sacred Treasure, Gold and Silver Star
1991	Publishes *The Four Little Dragons: The Spread of Industrialization in East Asia*
1993–95	Serves as National Intelligence Officer for East Asia at the National Intelligence Council in Washington, D.C., on leave from Harvard
1995–99	Director, Fairbank Center for East Asian Research
1996	Receives the Japan Foundation Prize
1997	Publishes *Living with China: U.S.-China Relations in the Twenty-First Century*
1997–99	Founding Director of the Asia Center at Harvard
1998	Receives the Japan Society Prize

2000	Retires from teaching at Harvard; publishes *Is Japan Still Number One?*
2008	Receives the Harvard Graduate School Centennial Medal
2011	Publishes *Deng Xiaoping and the Transformation of China*; co-editor of *The Park Chung Hee Era: The Transformation of South Korea*
2012	Deng Xiaoping book is awarded the Lionel Gelber Prize as the best book in English on foreign policy
2019	Publishes *China and Japan: Facing History*
2020	Dies in Cambridge on December 20

Various years: recipient of eleven honorary degrees from U.S. and foreign universities

Harvard Memorial Minute

EZRA FEIVEL VOGEL

Born: July 11, 1930

Died: December 20, 2020

E zra Vogel, Henry Ford II Professor of the Social Sciences, *Emeritus*, was one of America's foremost authorities on East Asia. In a career spanning sixty years, he published groundbreaking works on Japan and China based upon detailed fieldwork, in-depth interviews, and documentary research.

Ezra grew up in the small town of Delaware, Ohio. His father ran a men's and boys' clothing store where Ezra often helped out; his mother was a homemaker and part-time bookkeeper at the store. He graduated from Ohio Wesleyan University, and, after serving in the army, he enrolled in the doctoral program in Social Relations at Harvard. He intended to become a family sociologist, completing his Ph.D. in 1958.

Ezra's transformation into a researcher on Japan, and then on China, occurred as a result of chance conversations and a willingness to take risks (on the part of both Ezra and his wife, Suzanne, a trained social worker, whom he married in 1953). One of his doctoral advisors, Florence Kluckhohn, asked Ezra how he could generalize about American families if he did not have anything with which to compare them. Accepting this challenge, Ezra obtained funding to spend 1958–60 living in Tokyo, where he studied Japanese intensively and then conducted weekly interview sessions with six suburban families over the course of a year. The result was *Japan's New Middle Class* (1963).

Ezra returned to a position at Yale. Opening the door to a second transformation, the anthropologist John Pelzel told Ezra that Harvard had received a grant to fund social scientists willing to retool for careers studying contemporary China. Despite having no background on China, Ezra was intrigued by this opportunity, and Pelzel arranged for him to meet with John King Fairbank. With Suzanne's support, Ezra declared himself willing to transform into a specialist on China as well as Japan, provided he received a three-year post-doctoral fellowship to enable him to learn Chinese and begin research on contemporary China, to be followed by a teaching position in Social Relations. This package was quickly negotiated, and Ezra left Yale in 1961 and spent the remainder of his career at Harvard.

After Ezra's intensive Chinese lessons, the Vogels spent 1963–64 in Hong Kong, where he conducted in-depth interviews with individuals who had once lived in the People's Republic of China (PRC). These refugee accounts of daily life, augmented by Chinese press accounts, became *Canton under Communism* (1969), detailing how the Chinese Communist Party had transformed the institutions and social patterns of the province adjacent to Hong Kong.

Ezra's subsequent research shifted between China and Japan. The difficulties American auto companies experienced in competing with Japanese carmakers stimulated Ezra to write his provocative book, *Japan as Number One* (1979), which argued that, in certain respects, Japan was becoming a more successful modern industrial society than the U.S. By the 1980s China's nascent economic boom drew Ezra's attention back to the PRC. In 1979, divorced from Suzanne, Ezra married Charlotte Ikels, an anthropologist of China, and in 1987 they spent seven months living in Guangzhou. That fieldwork became *One Step Ahead in China: Guangdong under Reform* (1989).

Ezra was concerned about America's ability to compete on the world stage but was also deeply committed to cooperation between America and Japan and China. *Comeback* (1985) conveyed his ideas about how the U.S. could respond to the Japanese challenge. In 1993–95 he took leave to serve under the Clinton administration as the National Intelligence Council officer for East Asia, and over the years he published numerous essays analyzing America's relations with rising East Asia.

Ezra continued writing and publishing after retiring from teaching in 2000. He spent more than ten years on research for his masterful book, *Deng Xiaoping and the Transformation of China* (2011), which described how Deng, a lifelong communist, was able to steer China into a successful post-socialist economic transition. His last book was *China and Japan: Facing History* (2019), a detailed historical investigation of the relations between the two great Asian powers over many centuries.

Ezra's reputation for honest, knowledgeable, and sympathetic scholarship on the societies he studied earned him widespread praise and respect on both sides of the Pacific. The translation of *Japan as Number One* became a bestseller, and a Chinese translation of his book on Deng likewise became a bestseller in the PRC. He traveled to Japan at least once a year starting in 1958. After a first visit in 1973, he visited the PRC annually starting in 1980. He lectured frequently in Asia, giving public lectures and media interviews in fluent Chinese and Japanese.

In addition to his impressive scholarship, Ezra was an academic institution builder. At Harvard he directed the East Asian Research Center, the Council of East Asian Studies, the Fairbank Center for East Asian Research, the Asia Center, and the Program on U.S.-Japan Relations, and he was the founding chairman of the East Asian Studies concentration, continuing in that role from 1972 to 1991. He was also active in numerous external organizations devoted to Asian studies and U.S.-Asia relations.

Ezra earned multiple book awards, was given honorary degrees by eleven universities, and received Japan's Order of the Sacred Treasure, Gold and Silver Star, in 1991 and the Centennial Medal of the Harvard Graduate School of Arts and Sciences in 2008.

None of these honors conveys the characteristics of Ezra Vogel that earned him such gratitude and affection from those whose lives he touched. His boundless optimism, utter lack of pretentiousness, generosity, intense curiosity, eagerness to exchange ideas, and devotion to promoting the careers of young scholars generated an extensive network of friends and admirers around the world. Ezra cherished these ties, maintaining contact partly through his annual Christmas card list, which eventually included more than 600 names. His was a full and rewarding life on a large stage for a modest youth from a small town in central Ohio.

Ezra is survived by his wife, Charlotte Ikels; children, David, Steven, and Eve; sister, Fay Vogel Bussgang; and five grandchildren.

Respectfully submitted,
Mary C. Brinton
Martin K. Whyte, Chair

ONE

Family and Early Years

Fay Vogel Bussgang

Dedham, Massachusetts

I believe I have the distinction of being Ezra's first student. When we were children growing up in Delaware, Ohio, one of our favorite games was to play "school." Ezra, two and a half years older than I, was always the teacher, and I was his willing pupil. As he learned something in real school, he taught it to me. Thus, with his help, I learned to read at an early age, and later, while other children in my class were struggling with multiplication, I was already doing long division. In addition to being eager for knowledge, I think I was also motivated by a strong desire to "catch up" to my big brother, which, of course, proved to be impossible.

Even in high school, Ezra coached me in debate and oratorical declamation. When it came time to go to college, I might have gone somewhere close by had Ezra not been impressed with two Wellesley girls he met one summer. I thus ended up at Wellesley College, fell in love with Massachusetts, and settled in the Boston area. Ezra came to Harvard a few years later and did the same, one of the few times he followed me.

In 1987, my husband, Julian, and I and our three children all benefited from Ezra's well-honed teaching skills. Ezra and Charlotte were spending seven months working in Guangzhou, China. Ezra offered that if we came to visit in December during our children's college vacation, he and Charlotte would give us a personal tour—ten days in China, ten days in Japan. Who could resist the opportunity to have such expert guides? As expected, we had a wonderful trip, both enjoyable and educational. Every time we went to a restaurant, lots of servers would hover about us, all very curious who we were and why Ezra and Charlotte spoke Chinese so well!

Ezra, more than I, was always interested in the backgrounds of our parents. I am very grateful that during visits with our ailing father before he died, Ezra encouraged him to talk about his boyhood in Poland, asking questions about his family and taking notes. These notes became invaluable to me years later when, after a trip to Poland with my Polish-born husband and our children, I became interested in genealogy and tracing our family history.

It was a great gift to have Ezra's family and ours both living in the Boston area all these years. Every December, for the past twenty years or so, Ezra gathered his and our growing clans, along with a few cousins and their families, for a holiday party at his home that helped keep family members in touch with each other.

I have been very proud of what Ezra accomplished—as a teacher, author, scholar, and mentor. Our immigrant parents would have been doubly so. We miss him terribly.

Derwent Suthers

Green Valley, Arizona

On the cover page of his book *Japan as Number One*, I have this inscription: "To Derwent, fondest companion from our tender years of youth—with best wishes, Ezra."

We were best friends through high school in Delaware, Ohio. We were debating partners, and I was in his home many times. We took bike trips around the county, and I visited the Jewish temple in Columbus with him. One summer he visited us at our cottage in Canada, and we canoed together on the lake.

He helped his father, Joe Vogel, at The People's Store, a clothing shop in our town. I asked him which was the best underwear to buy and he told me: "Hanes." I still wear them today!

We saw one another over the years at our class reunions—the last in 2018. We walked around to see our old home sites. I also visited him in Cambridge when my grandson was in the hospital in Boston.

Dear Ezra was a good friend—intelligent, communicative, and friendly. I miss him!

Dick Johnson

Bradenton, Florida

Ezra was an outstanding student. As such, he did not often participate in many current high school class activities. Ezra's scholastic endeavors took him elsewhere. Although I knew Ezra, I really did not know much about him until later in life. He was always cordial and responsive, and quite likable as a friend. He was very responsible in promoting our class reunions and always mixed well with all of the class members. Ezra and his wife, Charlotte, visited Jean and me many times, along with other classmates, at our home in Bradenton, Florida. By then, we were all retired from our separate careers. Ezra's Harvard career and his many scholastic achievements, along with his Chinese studies and publishing, speak extremely well for Ezra. Ezra's life was very productive, and he was an outstanding citizen example for all of America and the world.

Ezra exemplified the very best!

Marshall Murphree†

Harare, Zimbabwe

The establishment of the MUSUVO Stamp Company (Murphree, Suthers, and Vogel) at Willis Jr. High in Delaware, Ohio, in 1943 was certainly my oldest venture, and Ezra was my oldest friend. After high school we both became social scientists, but our specific subject matter was so diverse that there was little intellectual exchange between us, our contacts being those of old friends. (I was trained in social anthropology and did research on the human and natural environment in sub-Saharan Africa.) Usually we met in the New England area, although Ezra did meet with me once in Zimbabwe. We spent a delightful Christmas together in the Bahamas in the 1980s.

Ezra did, however, have a subtle influence on my scholarship, and this was in pushing me away from the laziness which pursues me. Ezra was a dedicated scholar who had little time for other things, and I shall always remember the vignette of the Vogel/Murphree families frolicking in the azure waters of Elbow Key . . . except for Ezra, sitting in the shade of a palm tree with his tape recorder, polishing up on his Chinese.

I join with a host of others in celebrating the acuity of his scholarship and the dedication that he had to those he studied and the world in which we now live.

Paul Dietterich

Chicago, Illinois

Ezra Vogel was one of my dearest and closest friends. Here are two distinct memories of him:

BETA SIGMA TAU

Ezra and I met in 1947 when we were classmates at Ohio Wesleyan University in Delaware, Ohio. World War II had just ended and a large number of veterans were on campus completing studies they had initiated while serving with the U.S. Navy. Their presence, coming from a variety of backgrounds and faith traditions, enlarged the university's cultural outlook. What had been primarily a sectarian Methodist college for white, Methodist youths was now something different. Ezra and I were two wet-behind-the-ears seventeen- to eighteen-year-olds in this incoming class of twenty-five- to thirty-year-olds.

Ezra was a local boy from a Jewish family. His father owned Delaware's only men's clothing store. My father was a Methodist minister in Olean, New York. We found ourselves on a campus with fifteen national fraternities, all of which had discriminatory clauses restricting their members to white and Protestant only. Many freshmen like Ezra and me, and many returning veterans too, found these clauses offensive and repulsive. A world war had just been fought against racial and religious prejudice. Why was this university, through its fraternity system, promoting it? In 1946 these fraternities provided nearly all the housing for male students. The university had little housing to offer male students. So if you weren't a member of a fraternity, housing would be a problem for you. Also acceptance. Unless you were a fraternity member, you were outside the informal social system of the university. What were the two incoming black guys and six Jewish guys to do? About a dozen of us, including Ezra, decided to form our own interracial and interreligious fraternity. It took many meetings with each other and with university administrators, soul searching, and even fundraising from university alumni with a kindred spirit, but within that first year we launched the Beta Sigma Tau fraternity, joined the interfraternity council, and began searching for a suitable fraternity house. Our little group joined with similar groups on other campuses and formed a national organization of interracial and interreligious fraternities with chapters on about a dozen campuses across the nation. We were an early expression of the Civil Rights Movement, but we didn't know it. It was in this fraternity that our deepest friendships were formed.

Ezra was one of the very creative voices as the fraternity came into being. He was also one of the brightest students, with a straight four-point academic record. In 1950, the year most of the founders graduated, not only had the fraternity won the university scholarship cup for three consecutive years, but when the Omicron Delta Kappa honorary men's leadership fraternity tapped nine new members, six of the nine were from Beta Sigma Tau. Typical of Ezra, warm, friendly, and gregarious as he was, he not only helped form the fraternity but he populated it. He actively sought out and brought into the fraternity men who did not meet or accept the discriminatory clauses of the dominant fraternities. They became creative and productive members and good friends.

FRIENDSHIP BONDS

Lewis M. K. Long, PhD, had a ninetieth birthday. Lew was the widowed husband of my sister Barbara and lived in Arlington, Virginia, where Lew had been research director for the National Institute of Mental Health and my sister had been a high school teacher. His children and extended family and friends gathered on the big day at Lew's church in Arlington. The party had only begun when in the door walked Ezra Vogel. He had flown down to Arlington from Boston especially to help Lew celebrate and to see Phil Dietterich and me, two friends and fraternity brothers from the past. What a treat that was! At the party Ezra spoke warmly of Lew, whom he knew from previous associations in Lisle Fellowship. The high point for me was being able to share some time with Ezra, catching up on each other's lives. We had not seen each other since 1950 and it was now 1998, so we had a grand reunion. We made plans to meet at Ezra's home on Thanksgiving. We did this on four occasions, along with several fraternity brothers from the past whom Ezra invited. Ezra's warm hospitality helped us remember former bonds and create new ones.

Joseph Stavenhagen

Belmont, Massachusetts

Ezra and I first met in our late teens in 1948 as students at Ohio Wesleyan University. We have lived in close proximity to each other ever since and followed one another's personal and professional lives until his recent death. Ezra, ever interested in others and quick to compliment, remained the same amiable, down-to-earth comrade I had known as a youngster. He never condescended nor put on airs despite his eminence and renown as a scholar, author, and high government consultant. He demonstrated that one can make huge contributions to society without seeking self-aggrandizement or losing one's humility—a stunning legacy.

David Folkman

San Mateo, California

Ezra Vogel and I grew up in central Ohio communities that were close in distance and social connections. I came to know Ezra when he and his family spent time with my father, a well-known congregational reform rabbi in Columbus. My father had a deep appreciation for Hebrew language and literature, the Torah, and the history and principles of Judaism. Ezra often came to our home, where my brother, sister, and I got to know him and his sister, Fay Vogel. Ezra would often share with us what he was learning from my father and demonstrated clearly that he was already becoming an excellent teacher.

I followed Ezra's career and especially his writing about Japanese culture. A few years later, when I was in Cambridge, taking an undergraduate degree at Harvard and an MBA from Harvard Business School, I called Ezra and he immediately extended a welcoming hand. If my memory serves, I believe my (now late) brother Judah, then at Harvard Medical School, went out with Fay, who was at Wellesley, where my sister Joy was also in college. We all continued to admire Ezra as his academic reputation was beginning to soar and he became the quintessential teacher and humanitarian.

Rock Jones

Ohio Wesleyan University

Countless Ohio Wesleyan University (OWU) students and alumni say that this beautiful, tree-lined campus situated around a core of nineteenth-century academic buildings feels like home. Perhaps that feeling of belonging was truer for no one more than for Ezra Vogel.

A member of the Class of 1950 and one of OWU's most esteemed and beloved alumni, Ezra grew up just a short walk from our Delaware, Ohio, campus, and while his career and lifelong scholarship carried him around the world, he continued to return to this community. And he was always welcomed with open arms. His hometown and his alma mater were overwhelmingly proud of the vast accomplishments of this Harvard professor, eminent scholar, and trusted adviser to world leaders. Yet, we were even more delighted to welcome him back to our campus as a kind, humble, generous, and engaging friend.

While he was building bridges between the Far East and America, Ezra continued for nearly seventy years to reach out and create a vast web of connections with generations of OWU faculty, alumni, administrators, and students. He advised alumni in leadership positions at global organizations such as IBM, he helped OWU leaders expand their reach in Asia, he personally inspired students to see a wider world and a greater potential in their future. And he backed up his words with generosity, establishing a permanent endowment to support OWU students engaged in international study, including research and travel involving East Asia.

The endowment continues to grow because Ezra donated to Ohio Wesleyan all the proceeds from the mainland China printing of his critically acclaimed book *Deng Xiaoping and the Transformation of China*. That gift was classic Ezra—smart and spot-on—helping prepare our students for the global stage.

Ezra was a consummate teacher who could weave fascinating stories—in print and from the podium. He always said that his goal in writing was to challenge his most-educated readers with profound ideas while simultaneously telling a story—using what he called "plain English"—that a child could understand and learn from. He demonstrated this talent in his books and in the many lectures he delivered to OWU students over the years.

I especially remember the final time he spoke at Ohio Wesleyan in September 2019. Speaking on the topic "From Delaware to Deng Xiaoping," Ezra mesmerized the audience with his stories of growing up in Delaware in the 1930s, working in his father's downtown clothing store while young men headed to war in Europe, and studying at Ohio Wesleyan in the postwar years.

He spoke of his high regard for a generation that appreciated the sacrifices people made during the Great Depression and World War II. He said this generation understood that we had to get along with other nations around the world to avoid war again. This outlook continued to serve as the lodestar for Ezra's brilliant career and his rich and fulfilling life.

Ezra's love for Delaware and for Ohio Wesleyan led him years ago to endow an annual lecture focusing on some aspect of local history. Ezra wanted to cement the connection between town and gown and to use this lecture to bring the town to the campus and to engage the campus with the town. He established the lecture in memory of his parents. Longtime residents of Delaware revere the Vogel family name, remembering how Ezra's parents generously extended credit during the Great Depression, allowing families to acquire the dry goods needed when resources were scarce and times were hard. This generous spirit, so evident in Ezra's own life, is well known in our community as the character of the Vogel family.

Each year, Ezra returned to Delaware for the Vogel Lecture, and each year members of the local community, including Ezra's former classmates, would join Ezra for dinner and spirited storytelling prior to the Vogel Lecture. Among my favorite personal memories of Ezra are seeing him engaged with lifelong friends, mixing stories from childhood with reflections on a lifetime of curiosity, scholarship, and care. Whether on the global stage as a preeminent scholar, or back home as a lifelong friend with people from all walks of life, Ezra reflected the best of the human spirit and the ultimate example of a life well lived.

I am proud to have known Ezra, and I will always cherish our conversations and friendship.

Steven Vogel

University of California, Berkeley

I have been asked occasionally what it is like to be the son of Ezra Vogel. This is one of those questions that seems perfectly natural to the person asking the question, and yet quite strange for the person who is supposed to answer. For me, it is kind of hard to imagine an alternative. If the alternative is not to have been born at all, then I am certainly grateful to have been my father's son. But let me try to consider this question more in the spirit in which it was asked. Then I would have to say: well, it wasn't so bad. If I were to construct a kind of crude cost-benefit ledger, then the benefits would be many: travel to faraway places, meet interesting people, and garner insights from a wise scholar. On the cost side, it all really boiled down to just one item: embarrassment.

For example, sometimes when we were walking through the airport, Dad would suddenly dart off after an Asian-looking person. Maybe it was someone he knew. Or maybe he just wanted some language practice. And I would think to myself: "Why can't we just check in like the other families?" This happened often enough that I once asked my father: "Don't you ever find that one of those people you accost is really born and raised in Kansas and doesn't speak a word of any Asian language?" "Yes, that sometimes happens," he conceded. "But then aren't you embarrassed?" I charged. "No," he replied calmly, "but *they* sure are."

Or there were those times when we were at a Chinese restaurant, and Dad would insist on practicing Chinese with all the waiters. This could get tiresome. But even in those cases, there was sometimes a silver lining. Occasionally I would lean over to my neighbor at the table and whisper softly: "Now he is asking where the waiter's parents came from in China; now he is asking what his parents did for a living. . . ." And then my neighbor would be really impressed: "I knew you spoke Japanese, but I had no idea you speak Chinese so well!" And then I would confess: "Well, actually I don't. But I know the questionnaire."

As I grew older, I reached an epiphany of sorts. What I had found embarrassing about my father as a child is precisely what everyone else admired so much. Where I would see "goofy," they would see "unpretentious." Where I would see "overly friendly," they would see "charming."

So eventually I came to appreciate my father most for what I used to find embarrassing. He brought the humility, the boyish enthusiasm, and the community spirit of a kid from small-town Ohio to the most unlikely of places, Harvard University. And he brought that same joyful spirit to his interactions with those of us who were fortunate enough to have been born into his family. We miss you, Dad.

Charlotte Ikels

Cambridge, Massachusetts

As many people know, Ezra's father owned and ran a boy's and men's clothing store, The People's Store, in Ezra's hometown of Delaware, Ohio. From an early age Ezra was expected—and delighted—to work in the store. One of his special tasks was to keep tabs on the sock inventory.

Working in the store shaped Ezra's attitudes toward his own clothing. As an adult he was meticulous in hanging up his clothes. No clothing ever remained on the floor or tossed on the bed. Every morning he tucked his pajamas and sleeping cap behind his pillow—at the ready for bedtime. This neatness was in direct contrast to the treatment of his books and papers, which were scattered and stacked every which way in his study—on the floor, on the sofa, on each other.

Another legacy of his work in the store was the belief that one wore one's "good" clothes only when outside the house but old clothes when inside. After attending some meeting in suit and tie, Ezra would return home directly to the closet and change into a worn shirt and some old baggy trousers. After retirement, when he went to fewer meetings and spent more time at home, he became more and more accustomed to wearing his old clothes all day—even outside when we took our daily walk.

One day we decided to combine our walk with running errands in Harvard Square. After a stop at the bank, I needed to go to the CVS pharmacy next door. This would entail a climb up a hefty set of stairs to the second floor, so Ezra decided to sit on a bench outside to wait for me. When I returned, he had a funny look on his face and said, "You'll never guess what happened while you were away. Some young woman came over and asked if I wanted a lunch voucher." She had mistaken him for one of the homeless people who frequent Harvard Square during the day when the local homeless shelters are closed!

I would like to be able to say that this incident led Ezra to change his sartorial practices, but sadly it did not.

POSTSCRIPT

On hearing this account of Ezra's alleged neatness, Ezra's sister, Fay Bussgang, exclaimed "No way! Our mother was always picking his clothes up off the floor." How then to explain his adult transformation if it was not a legacy of working in the store? On hearing this account of Ezra's sister's response, the husband of a friend of mine asked a simple question: "Did Ezra serve in the military?" "Yes." "There's your answer. Nobody else is going to pick up your clothes in the military."

TWO

Friends and Colleagues

Padraic Burns

Brookline, Massachusetts

I must say that I do remember Ezra with great affection. How could anyone forget him? He played a long and interesting role in my life, a very personal, non-academic role. Our friendship over the years began with his first experience in the role of *nakōdo* (matchmaker) at Ikuko's and my Tokyo wedding in 1959.

In the spring of 1959, I was in Japan and engaged to my wife-to-be, Ikuko Kawai. We had scheduled our Tokyo wedding for the coming November. I had resigned from my position as an Army psychiatrist that June, returning to the U.S. after my two years, which were spent mostly in a psychiatric outpatient clinic in Yokohama. I planned to return in September or October to complete our wedding plans and to have a last vacation with Ikuko before November 3rd, our scheduled wedding date. This included a pre-wedding or "civil wedding" at the U.S. Embassy in Tokyo. We had agreed that she would ask a favorite professor from her four years at Yamagata University to be the matchmaker for the wedding ceremony. With that accomplished, I purchased two cases of American champagne to be delivered to the wedding reception.

Before my return to Japan, Ikuko informed me that our *nakōdo* had come down with a serious illness and would not be able to attend and officiate. I had remained in touch with my psychiatry professor at Yale (Eugene Brody). I told him my news, and he responded with interest from his new position as Professor and Chairman of Psychiatry at the University of Maryland. He told me that a friend who had spent time in the Yale Department of Psychiatry would soon be coming with his new Japanese wife to conduct their second wedding in Japan. He offered to arrange an invitation for me, which I eagerly accepted.

At that wedding event, I met Ezra and Suzanne Vogel, who were the only other native English speakers. I introduced myself and the circumstances that brought me to Japan and that party. They had come to Japan on a grant to study postwar family structure. Their studies included parental roles in the family and work life. Several years down the road Ezra would leave Yale to return to Harvard with a continued focus on Asia with a sociological perspective. As Ikuko and I had settled in Boston, this allowed us to continue our family friendship—a relationship which encompassed, due to Ezra's sometimes lengthy sojourns overseas, the care of the Vogels' dogs; first Snooks in 1963/64 and then Didi in 1975/76.

When we first met at that wedding, Ezra and Suzy had been in Japan for about one year, organizing themselves, recruiting Japanese families with children to interview, and studying Japanese so they could communicate with the couples. I quizzed Ezra on whether he could give a brief talk, in Japanese, for the assembled guests at our upcoming wedding. Perhaps it was due to our common midwestern roots, but I believe that he and I both felt that despite our lack of earlier acquaintance, his position as an American academic scholar, and mine as a medical professional, made his being our "go-between" appropriate. I consulted with Ikuko, who was very positive about my initiative—she was then, and throughout our marriage, always positive about novelty and adventure. The date was set on a national holiday called Culture Day, November 3rd, to facilitate attendance. Many years later, after Ezra and Suzy divorced, Ezra asked if he could marry Charlotte on that very same day, so we then had the opportunity to celebrate our shared wedding anniversaries together over several eras.

Through the years Ikuko and I maintained our close family ties and mutual interests with Ezra. Ikuko established herself as a major individual in Boston's Japanese community, socially, artistically, and even sociopolitically, with ongoing assistance from Ezra. He helped introduce important Asian visitors, building friendships and connections with people such as the Japanese psychiatrist Takeo Doi (whom I had met previously in Tokyo) and social psychologist Sumiko Iwao. Ikuko was very impressed by Ezra's son David's work with Burn Survivors of New England and made sure we never missed their fundraising dance parties. Ezra and I shared midwestern origins, his in Ohio and mine in Iowa, and similar undergraduate educational experiences, his at Ohio Wesleyan and mine at University of Chicago, leading to his graduate degree at

Harvard, PhD in Sociology (Family Studies), and mine at Yale School of Medicine, with a focus on Psychiatry and Child Development. Though there was academic and cultural overlap, the major aspect of our relationship was friendship. It was in our New Hampshire farmhouse that Ezra composed his first book. That summer following our wedding, Ezra asked if he could occupy our vacation home to work on his Japanese family research. He brought his substantial research notes and a carton of diet protein shakes, working steadily there for several weeks to complete his first draft of *Japan's New Middle Class*.

That chance meeting in Tokyo many years ago forged a long and close relationship in which we shared each other's work and interests. My interests were in psychiatry and his in sociology, focused on Asia. My focus on Asian culture has been influenced by my fifty-plus-year marriage with Ikuko, and by our three children and theirs, who continue to enrich my life following Ikuko's October 8, 2017, death from lung cancer. Ikuko appreciated the deeply romantic gesture, an unquenchable thirst for adventure, an infectious joy that drew people together. Ezra had a dynamic intellect and curiosity. He was truly interested in people, an ever-interesting conversationalist. In recent years I have enjoyed small moments, reminiscing with him at his eighty-ninth birthday cookout at his son David's house in Cambridge as well as at my ninetieth birthday party here at my Brookline home. Reconnection constantly deepened and enhanced our already profound friendship.

William C. Hsiao

Harvard School of Public Health

In 1955, Ezra Vogel became a legend to me when I pledged Beta Sigma Tau, an interracial fraternity at Ohio Wesleyan University. Ezra had graduated a few years earlier, but stories about his efforts leading the fight against racial prejudice on campus were already legend. For example, in his sophomore year Ezra led a delegation to see the president of the university to hotly protest the discrimination against Blacks, Asians, and Jews. I did not meet Ezra in person until 1972 when I came to Harvard. We did not have much contact, since we were in two very different fields of study, but this changed when China opened up and I began to do field research there in the mid-1980s.

Over our shared interests, Ezra and I developed a decades-long friendship. While I am engaged in the economic study of China's health reforms, I am no sinologist. Ezra encouraged me to explore the history of Mao's mobilization campaigns to deliver healthcare to the peasants, something I knew little about. He patiently explained the importance of historical context to understand how past lessons might impact future developments. He was fascinated with my social experiments in poor rural Western regions of China, where I lived with peasant families, and deeply interested in their living conditions and my conversations with them.

Ezra taught me the meaning of genuine friendship. Annually, he made the effort to plan a dinner reunion of Beta Sig brothers and our wives. Ezra delighted in reminiscing about his college years; he laughed loudly as we sang our fraternity's anthem. Ezra also hosted informal dinners at his home and introduced my wife and me to his friends, which expanded the circle of sinologists I got to know. At these small dinners, Ezra always showed his humility, expressing his inquisitiveness, his doubts, and the limits of his knowledge and analyses. Later, to my complete surprise, Ezra gathered information from my younger colleagues and quietly nominated me for an honorary doctoral degree at Ohio Wesleyan. I only learned of the nomination from the university president.

Ezra's thirst for knowledge and his open-mindedness were exemplified by his invitation to me in 2015 to co-lead a weekly Harvard forum on Critical Issues Confronting China. I told him I was not qualified, since I am not an expert on Chinese affairs. Ezra replied: "I want your views as a Chinese-American who spent your childhood in China and has close personal contacts with the peasants through your research." All credit is due to Ezra for making the forum the vibrant and impactful event that it became. Throughout his lifetime, I believe Ezra manifested the old Chinese saying: 学无止境—there is no limit to learning. His attitude prompted others to speak honestly and listen to each other.

There is not much for me to add to the many accolades for Ezra's scholarly contributions. Ezra had a gift for taking his academic research on Japan and China and making it interesting and relevant to readers in both the United States and Asia. Like many, the foundations of my understanding about Japan and China came from reading Ezra's seminal works, *Japan as Number One: Lessons for America*; *Deng Xiaoping and the Transformation of China*; and *China and Japan: Facing History*. He has undoubtedly enhanced the mutual understanding of these cultures and nations for millions of Americans and others around the world, and that will be his lasting contribution to all of us.

Gerald Curtis

Columbia University

I first met Ezra Vogel in the early 1970s, shortly after I began teaching at Columbia University. Ten years older than I, Ezra was already a well-known figure in the Japanese studies community. His book on *Japan's New Middle Class,* published in 1963, had in particular established his reputation as the leading Japan-specialized sociologist of his generation. We quickly struck up a professional relationship and a personal friendship that grew deeper and closer over the decades that followed. In a conversation a few years before his death, we agreed that one of the things that initially drew us together was that temperamentally we were rather kindred spirits, social and political anthropologists at heart, interested at that time in the lives of Japanese salarymen in his case and of professional politicians in mine.

Over the course of his career Ezra wrote any number of important and influential books on Japan and China, including writing what remains to the present day the number one bestselling non-fiction book in Japanese by a foreigner, *Japan as Number One*. In many of his writings it was the individuals who made things happen—or who had things happen to them—who were at the center of his concerns. Ezra was a social scientist who believed in the importance of listening carefully—in Chinese and Japanese as well as in English—to people whose behavior he was interested in studying. In doing so, he suspended judgment while he put together the pieces of the puzzle he was out to solve. Though out of fashion in present-day American university social science departments, where students are expected to specify their dependent variables before knowing much about the object of their research and to eschew anything that,

God forbid, smacks of "area studies," Ezra's participant-observer approach and his eclectic methodological style resulted in an impressive oeuvre of insightful and eminently readable books and articles about China, Japan, and America's relations with both.

The last time I was with Ezra was in November 2019. Having been invited to be on a panel at Harvard's Reischauer Institute of Japanese Studies, I went up to Boston a day early to spend time with him. Little did I imagine that this would be our last encounter. Ezra was his usual self, warm, enthusiastic, interested in getting my take on recent developments in Japan, telling me about what he was writing on China, and anxious to discuss U.S.-Asia policy and what we might do to encourage more young people to study East Asia.

After a couple of hours, the doorbell rang, pizza arrived, and Ezra, Charlotte, and I gathered around the kitchen table. Charlotte reminded Ez that he had a plane to catch at 1 a.m. that night for Hong Kong. Yes, then eighty-nine-year-old Ezra Vogel was off that rainy, cold evening for a flight to Hong Kong, embarking on a trip that I believe included a stop in Tokyo on the way back. Ez just refused to let age slow him down.

After dinner the three of us piled into their car. Charlotte drove me to my hotel and I said my goodbyes, taking it for granted that sometime over the following months I would once again be knocking on Ezra's door in Cambridge or would see him in New York or Washington or Tokyo. I was stunned, and still am, to learn that he had died.

Ezra, as I am sure everyone contributing to this volume would attest, was a special person. He loved his students, and he nurtured and cherished his friendships. He had a deep and abiding affection for China and for Japan and did what he could to contribute to having them improve relations with each other. Ezra was realistic about the challenges that face China and Japan and that confront the U.S. as its policies toward East Asia continually evolve, but his innate optimism never waned. I got back to my hotel that rainy evening in Cambridge feeling, as I felt on so many occasions when I met with Ezra or had long phone conversations with him, uplifted and more cheerful. He was a wonderful man whom I feel very fortunate to have had as a friend for so many years.

John Berninghausen

Middlebury College

It was the best of times, it was the worst of times, it was the age
of wisdom, it was the age of foolishness. . . .
—Charles Dickens, *A Tale of Two Cities*

Late April 1972 at the Universities Service Centre (USC) in Hong Kong—
a first meeting with Prof. Ezra Vogel. The times were indeed turbulent.
For foolishness there was this country's disastrous Americanization of a
distant war in Vietnam. It was, however, in other ways arguably *the best
of times*—a tremendously exciting time to be immersed in studying
modern China.

Ezra, at forty-two already an eminent professor at Harvard and author of seminal books on *both* Japan and China, had recently returned
to the USC for further research. I, one of eighteen to twenty "new generation" China scholars affiliated with USC that year doing doctoral research, was delving into Mao Dun's early fiction from the 1920s and 1930s
for a Stanford PhD in modern Chinese literature. Less than two months
before meeting Ezra, Nixon and Kissinger's historic trip to China had re-
shuffled the world's geopolitical deck.

In March I had finally gained entry into the People's Republic of
China, as that nation had been inaccessible to Americans and most
foreigners. The Cultural Revolution was still going strong. One of thirty
anti–Vietnam war activists from the Committee of Concerned Asian
Scholars selected for a month-long visit, we all felt extremely fortunate to
have been invited to form a friendship delegation. With ill-contained excitement we boarded a Chinese train in the drowsy, rural border town of
Shenzhen—nowadays a megalopolis of high-rise buildings and 12.5 million urbanites—and commenced a fascinating and eye-opening thirty-five-
day tour through several provinces. Our nine days in Beijing concluded in
the early-morning hours of April 11th with a four-hour meeting with Zhou
Enlai and two members of the infamous "Gang of Four."

Five of us on the trip were from the USC, so we were tapped to speak
about the experience and our observations. When presenting our comments

to a packed room at the USC days later, unbeknownst to me, Prof. Vogel was in the audience. To no one's surprise our five reports mainly "accentuated the positive." I broke ranks to some degree by voicing a few criticisms. Among other things, I described my distaste for the Maoist cult of personality, revealing a bit of disillusionment provoked by the deification of Chairman Mao. To me the incessant obeisance to Mao Zedong thought had seemed rote, obnoxious, and frequently ludicrous.

Prof. Vogel came up afterward, introduced himself, and suggested we should soon take a meal together. I was surprised and not a little flattered—this established "big name" scholar was interested in conversing with me? Needless to say, I agreed. Days later, over a simple but delicious Cantonese meal, I found myself gradually loosening up and the conversation flowed. Although I was unable to foresee it, that two-hour conversation marked the beginning of a close and enduring friendship, one that within six years would be expanded to include his new wife, Charlotte, and my new wife, Alice.

First impressions are still vivid half a century later: 1) Ezra was a really good listener. A skillful interlocutor, his friendliness and curiosity soon put me at ease. 2) Ezra's powerful intellect, broad erudition, and prodigious memory were well balanced by an innate courtesy and empathetic nature, to say nothing of his self-deprecatory humor and open-mindedness. He was not at all haughty, elitist, or pedantic. 3) Eventually he inquired about my childhood and family background; upon hearing that my mother had grown up in Columbus, Ohio, he reciprocated with details about having himself grown up in the nearby small Ohio town of Delaware. Although implicit, I sensed some private pride in his own background—he and his younger sister had grown up in a Jewish family in an overwhelmingly gentile milieu. As a young man their father emigrated from Poland to Ohio before 1920. Eventually Joe Vogel established The People's Store, selling dry goods in Delaware. I can still hear the fondness in Ezra's voice as he recalled for me his parents' pride over their son excelling at Ohio Wesleyan, the hometown college. 4) It was highly gratifying to discover that Ezra had read and was much taken with Mao Dun's lengthy novel from 1932, 子夜 (*Midnight*); he in turn seemed pleasantly surprised to learn that I greatly admired George Orwell's writings. 5) The fact that starting as an adult learner he had attained such high-level proficiencies in *both* Japanese and Chinese linguistic/cultural skills was downright amazing. 实在了不起!

Over subsequent decades, as we became closer friends, I much appreciated his unwavering support for dedicated teaching/mentoring and commitment to rigorous standards of excellence. Upon numerous occasions Ezra selflessly contributed time, energy, and astute observations by serving as an external consultant or evaluator in order to assist programs in East Asian studies across the country, including many at undergraduate colleges such as Middlebury. Eventually he was to donate all the proceeds from the People's Republic of China translation of his 2011 magisterial biography of Deng Xiaoping to his alma mater, Ohio Wesleyan.

An inspiring role model in various ways to many—as someone who steadfastly strove to promote increased understanding between the U.S., Japan, and China; for his service to the nation as a senior adviser on East Asia in the Clinton administration; for a prodigious scholarly productivity that continued long after "retiring" at age seventy; for the students he inspired and mentored. As just one example of his manifold post-retirement activities and contributions, I would cite the central role he played over the past fifteen years in guiding and assisting the very successful National Committee on U.S.-China Relations Public Intellectuals Program, an enterprise combining interdisciplinary expertise with educating the public that was very close to his heart.

Ezra was 蓋世無雙,無與倫比, one of a kind, a 君子, a *mensch*, a great scholar/teacher, a pillar of the East Asian studies profession, and a loyal friend to so many.

Andrew Gordon

Harvard University

I first met Ezra Vogel during my freshman year at Harvard, when I took his sociology course titled Japanese Society. It was February 1971, a short fifty years ago.

I enrolled in that course both for its topic and the reputation of its instructor. I had had the serendipitous good fortune to travel to Japan as a rising high school senior in 1969, on a summer study program led by a teacher at my high school. After that, I decided that I wanted to study Japan and Asia in depth in the future. That teacher, Wayne Altree, had earned an MA degree in Harvard's Regional Studies East Asia program with a focus on Chinese history. As I was heading off to college, he told me: "You really should switch from studying Japan to China and take courses with Fairbank. But if you insist on Japan, look into courses taught by Ezra Vogel. I hear he's an emerging young scholar." When I took his course as an eighteen-year-old, Professor Vogel struck me as having already emerged, and at over twice my age, not *that* young.

But Mr. Altree's advice was sound. The course was fascinating, both the lectures, the sections taught by Rick Dyck, and the readings—including of course *Japan's New Middle Class*, published less than a decade earlier. But even more important was coming to know Ezra personally. As I best recall, he was the only tenured faculty member to whom I spoke in person that first year of college. That is no coincidence. His accessibility and openness to all comers were extraordinary. His advice to me was wise, even when negative: "The origins of permanent employment is too ambitious a topic for the term paper in my course"; "It is better you tackle that in the future, maybe for a senior thesis" (well, it ended up as my PhD thesis); and "While studying Japan and Asia is great, you shouldn't forget to obtain a rounded liberal arts education that includes the study of other places and spans various disciplines."

Those conversations (probably just two conversations over the course of one semester, but vivid in memory still), were the start of a relationship that continued to the end of Ezra's life. He served as wise mentor, and in later years as a colleague and friend. In my sophomore year we crossed paths one day as I was walking toward a class. He stopped to say he was hoping to launch a new concentration (major) in East Asian Studies (EAS), if the faculty approved his proposal. He encouraged me to think of enrolling. A few months later, I happily followed his suggestion. In my senior year, although he was not my honors thesis adviser, as head of the EAS program he took the trouble to read and comment on a rough draft and send me a letter with his comments for final revision. Only in later years did I realize how unusual it is for the director of undergraduate studies to give that sort of attention to student work. He did the same for my classmates.

Over the following years, as I studied in Harvard's PhD program in History and East Asian Languages and then joined the faculty at Duke, we were less closely connected. But on occasions when I was in Japan for research, I would join the annual reunions of Ezra's Japan-based students. Thinking back on those gatherings, it was simply extraordinary how effectively Ezra cultivated a network of students, scholars, and those out in the "real world." More striking is that his irrepressible networking aimed not so much to help him as to enable all of the rest of us to thrive.

On joining the Harvard faculty in 1995, Ezra became a close colleague, as well as friend and supporter, and later a model for what an active life in nominal retirement might look like (now a less distant matter than it once was). But with that support came a strong opinion: it was important even for historians to engage big topics and address contemporary issues in ways that might reach an audience outside the academic world. I'm not sure I have done that to his full satisfaction, but I've tried.

Ezra's was a long and full life, to be sure, rich in achievements. I join many others in feeling sadness at the loss of such a warm and generous teacher and friend.

Paul A. Cohen

Harvard Fairbank Center

In fall 1965 I accepted an offer to teach at Wellesley College, which brought me back to the Boston area, where I had done my graduate training. Since the town of Wellesley was only a thirty-minute drive from Cambridge, this meant that I could spend part of every week at Harvard, taking advantage of Harvard's Chinese library resources but also enjoying the opportunity to have close contact with an outstanding collection of scholars devoted to the study of China. Ezra Vogel was one of those scholars.

I had the good fortune, over the ensuing years, to work closely with Ezra. Although I was never one of his students, I did attend the roundtable in his honor shortly before his retirement from teaching in 2000 and was much moved by the praise showered on him by his former students. This was a side of Ezra's career that I hadn't seen (we were of course much too close in age). But there were many other sides to which I had been direct witness over the years. At the time of his retirement, which happened to come in the same year as my own retirement from Wellesley, I wrote Ezra the following: "I won't ask you, as friends and relatives not part of the academic world have been asking me with growing frequency in recent months, 'So what are you going to do after you're finished?' A perfectly reasonable question, yet one that I was mystified by when I first heard it, since I had never assumed that after my teaching career was over I would be 'finished.' I'm sure, Ezra, that this applies to you also. So let me take this opportunity to offer you, along with my congratulations, my wishes for a long and productive 'afterlife.'"

My wishes certainly bore fruit. Already, during his teaching years, Ezra had published widely in both the Chinese and Japanese fields. (I should add here that he was one of a very small number of American scholars who were equally at home working with Japanese and Chinese materials.) After his retirement he came out with two large and very important books, *Deng Xiaoping and the Transformation of China* (2011) and *China and Japan: Facing History* (2019). Both of these volumes, although written by a scholar trained in sociology, incorporated a very strong historical sense. I may have made a very minor contribution to this since Ezra asked me to read both books from beginning to end at the manuscript stage, making comments as needed, which I then conveyed to him. But the truth is that Ezra was not obliged to accept any of my suggestions, and the fact that he accepted a good many of them leads me to suspect that he himself embodied a good bit of the historian's consciousness.

In addition to being an outstanding teacher and scholar, Ezra took on more than the usual share of professional responsibilities. After Fairbank's retirement, he served for some years as director of what had come to be known as the Fairbank Center for Chinese Studies. He was the founding director of the Harvard University Asia Center (1997–99). Moreover, during the last years of his life, in addition to working on a biography of Hu Yaobang, he organized and administered a weekly noon-hour Critical Issues Confronting China speaker series. Ezra had an almost insatiable appetite for hard work. Yet, unlike a lot of very busy people, he was eminently approachable, blessed with a good sense of humor, quick to smile, and easy to talk to. A giant in the East Asian studies field in the United States, Ezra Vogel will be sorely missed.

Bill Alford

Harvard Law School

I feel both saddened and pleased to be writing this short tribute to our dear friend Ezra Vogel. Saddened in that even though he lived ninety years and did so as well as could be imagined, his sudden passing leaves a gnawing sense of loss. And pleased because I so appreciate the opportunity to repay, however modestly, his many kindnesses to me and so many others. Many examples come to mind, but I find myself fixing on a joke Ezra made some three decades ago while introducing a speech at Harvard by the late Liu Binyan (1925–2005), whom David Barboza of the *New York Times* described as "the forceful dissident writer who repeatedly exposed official corruption and openly challenged the Chinese Communist Party to reform itself before and after he was exiled to the United States in the late 1980's." In the midst of an eloquent and serious introduction of Liu, Ezra, with a sly smile, noted that commentators spoke of both Liu and himself as "journalists," adding that in Liu's case they meant it as a compliment whereas with reference to himself, it was, he suggested, not intended to be positive.

That one line captured so many of the qualities that made Ezra so singular a figure. Perhaps most obviously, there was genuine self-deprecating humor—a quality not exactly in superabundance among distinguished academics, perhaps especially so at our institution. For all his many accomplishments (including eleven honorary degrees as well as a Guggenheim Fellowship, the Japan Foundation Prize, and several other international honors), Ezra seemed always to have a wonderment about how a small-town Ohio boy ended up as a major university-wide figure at Harvard. That found expression in his openness throughout his life to new people and new ideas, his unstinting willingness to help seemingly endless numbers of students, and his quiet decision to donate all his Chinese royalties from his study of Deng Xiaoping to his hometown college and undergraduate alma mater, Ohio Wesleyan (an amount rumored to exceed a million dollars).

Ezra's warm introduction to (and implicit endorsement of) Liu Binyan evidenced another less obvious aspect of who he was. Because he tended to look on the positive side of pretty much everyone with whom he came in contact and to work toward bridging differences (between Japan, Korea, and China, and between the U.S. and China), some observers dismissed him as naive about, or unconcerned with, the abundant challenges China presents regarding human rights. But as his very public embrace of Liu at a time when that heroic figure was persona non grata in China demonstrated, Ezra was far from starry eyed about China while being willing to put himself out on behalf of many a person who earned Beijing's wrath. Indeed, there were several instances in which Ezra drew on his reservoir of goodwill with Chinese authorities to seek to help those in their disfavor—without drawing attention (which he saw as likely to complicate those efforts).

On a variety of matters I have a great deal of gratitude to Ezra for his kindness and generosity over decades. I am especially grateful to him for two notes he sent my way after a local student newspaper published a story grossly mischaracterizing my interaction with a dissident I had, in fact, gone to considerable lengths to assist. I received well over 100 comforting messages from scholars across the world in the aftermath of that article, but Ezra's stood out. In the first he spoke generously of how much, over decades, I had done to assist Chinese (and other) scholars and students, popular and unpopular. But it was the second that stands out even more—for in it Ezra wrote, "I value the moral part as much as the scholarship." Those words may have been part of a letter directed to me, but, in the end, they are a fitting description of our late friend.

May he rest in peace.

Joan Kaufman

Schwarzman Scholars Program

I first met Ezra after arriving at Harvard for my doctoral studies in public health in 1984, following a four-year stint in Beijing for the newly opened UN office where I supported the 1982 census and trained a new crop of demographers. As my first two degrees were in Chinese studies, I found myself at the Fairbank Center quite a bit, satisfying my need for

China events and colleagues. Although no longer the director while I was there, Ezra was always around. It turned out we had a separate connection through my public health world. A work colleague and roommate with no China connection was an old friend of Ezra and Charlotte's, so we got to know each other socially. I saw Ezra often over the next thirty years, back and forth between my subsequent work stints in Beijing (Ford Foundation and other jobs), or back at Harvard, where I maintained my affiliation through Radcliffe, the Kennedy School, and the Public Health and Medical Schools, continuing to hang out at the Fairbank Center while there. Ezra was always warm, always insightful, always modest, always interested in hearing what I was working on, and ever curious about my work, which overlapped with Charlotte's (with whom I also corresponded on work topics).

With Ezra, one moment stands out for me and warms my heart whenever I remember it. We were at the annual meeting of the Association for Asian Studies (AAS) in Denver in 2018. As a mother I had that particular delight of having my daughter Rosie attend the meeting in her own right as a China expert. She works at the National Committee on U.S.-China Relations, and Ezra was the longtime senior adviser to their Public Intellectuals Program, which Rosie manages with Jan Berris. Rosie and Ezra had gotten to know each other well over the previous couple of years. At the Denver AAS meeting, Rosie and I ran into Ezra together in the lobby of the conference hotel, holding court in his way for the many friends and colleagues who stopped to share a hello or a longer conversation. He greeted us both with his usual warmth and noted how proud I must be of Rosie and how exceptional she was. She was beaming, as was I. He said something delightful about our two-generation China careers which put all my regret about dragging my family back and forth to Beijing for my various jobs into perspective. Our two generations were both so lucky to have Ezra in our lives. I am forever grateful for the affection, admiration, advice, and attention he showered on me and then also showed my daughter. And I am heartbroken for her that she won't have him as a mentor and be able to bask in his kindness and wisdom in the future, as all of us did over the last few decades.

Nancy Hearst

Harvard Fairbank Center

Ezra was always conflicted about coming to the library. His "people" personality could never quite resist the temptation to stop and chat with whomever he might meet in the reading room. New friends or old, China people or not, he would always stop to say "hello" to other library users. But it seemed that a simple greeting could never end at just that—sometimes leading to long and drawn-out conversations keeping him away from the intended purpose of his visit. He would first meet his Davis Center friends as he entered the reading room, proceed along to the Japan scholars and students, and then, finally, get to the China collection at the very back of the room. Sometimes I could hear him upon entry, but usually it would be a long while before he would finally reach the China stacks. After hearing his voice, I recall numerous times looking out to see how he had gotten waylaid on his way down to the back of the library. Such distractions usually were not really a problem—as much as he enjoyed doing his research, he also enjoyed meeting up with library patrons and conversing with friends and students—really whomever he might meet.

However, before each new book project, Ezra would come into the library with the express purpose of wanting to read all the background material on the latest subject at hand. Whether it was twenty years of back issues of *Far Eastern Economic Review*, a complete run of the Foreign Broadcast Information Service (FBIS) translations, or the latest books on Deng Xiaoping, Hu Yaobang, or whatever he was working on, Ezra would go through each and every item to make sure that he had not missed even the slightest mention of the topic he was working on. But the time spent socializing would often distract him from his work. Even after he would find a seat and get settled into a carrel, this problem did not go away. As soon as he was noticed, some student or scholar would always go over to say "hello," and in most cases such a simple "hello" would lead to an extended conversation. . . .

Ezra could never say no. . . . However, it was not that he was unaware of how these efforts to socialize got in the way of his research. After a time, he started sitting in the very far-end carrel next to the wall in the reading room in hopes that he would not be sighted. But this plan usually did not work. He would always be found, and Ezra being Ezra was never one to turn away a student or friend. Finally, however, he came up with what he thought was a good idea about how to solve the conflict between his research and his fan club.

Before an intended trip to the library, he would often phone me to see how crowded the library was—not because he was worried that he would not find a seat or his materials would not be available, but rather because he was worried whether he would be able to focus on his project. Unfortunately, this strategy really did not work very well. He would no sooner gather his materials and sit down at a desk when someone new would enter the room and, upon spotting Ezra reading in a carrel, he/she would invariably go over to say a few words.

Finally, however, Ezra concocted a solution to this problem. When he wanted to engage in research, he would phone me in the library with a list of items he intended to read and then he would ask me to deliver them to his home at 14 Sumner Road, only a block away. In this way, he could have a morning or afternoon with no interruptions or distractions. At the end of the day, the library bookmobile would return to his home to retrieve the materials. This scheme seemed to work well, and, in the end, he produced a number of major books that will have a shelf life for just as long as Ezra will be remembered for being so generous and giving of his time.

Thomas Hout

Tufts University

Ezra's generous spirit took so many forms. If measured in sheer number, maybe his gift of many hundreds of thousands of dollars of royalties from China for his best-selling book on Deng Xiaoping to his alma mater, Ohio Wesleyan University in Delaware, Ohio, where he grew up, is hard to top. But my most lasting memory of Ezra is of his consistent gift of time and gracious attention to those people with whom he loved to discuss subjects nearest and dearest to him—Japan and China.

There was no encounter, either planned or random, that was not suitable for a serious exchange of information or views about these places.

I remember the occasions so well, because often either the manager or Charlotte would finally have to say time is up. International House of Japan (no pancakes though) in Roppongi. The running path along the Charles River. The front porch of an inn on Martha's Vineyard. Ezra's orientation to Japan and China was positive and constructive, while mine was neutral and skeptical, so we had lots to talk about—whether Japan's economic successes would last, whether the international trading order would survive China's growth and scale, whether Chinese state-owned companies were as good as they were cracked up to be, etc. We had the most useful arguments about all this. He once invited me to give a talk, based on my years in the field consulting and studying at the industry and firm level, at one of his midday seminars at Harvard, where I expressed the view that China's best, most consequential companies will be almost entirely non-state-owned. I am sure Ezra disagreed with much of my talk, but he graciously said afterward, "It is clear you have given a great deal of thought to this."

Ezra and I are both products of Ohio midsize towns. My father and Ezra overlapped for a year or so on the Ohio Wesleyan Board of Trustees. I always felt a real bond with him, rooted in growing up in these provincial but good communities where one had to imagine so much of what the wider world was all about, which I suppose led to our great appreciation of Asia and the Other. We both cared a lot about what we were studying. What a good way to live!

Tony Saich

Harvard Kennedy School

Everyone knows of Ezra's generosity and the time he was willing to spend helping people find resources and build connections. Like others, I benefited enormously from this. Indeed, Ezra was instrumental in persuading me to think about coming to the Harvard Kennedy School and in persuading the school to take my application seriously. However, one of his most important pieces of advice, not to me but to my wife, was to say No.

In 2016, I had decided to take my sabbatical in Japan, in part to understand the country where my wife, Junko Gentry, was born and also to better understand Japanese research on Chinese history and society.

We knew that Ezra was staying at the International House, Tokyo, and one morning we arranged to meet up for breakfast. As usual, at the buffet breakfast Ezra was in high demand from other guests who wanted to hear his ideas and find important leads for their own work. Once I had told Ezra what I was hoping to do in Japan, his Rolodex mind went into action, and he provided me with a who's who of people I should try to meet. However, there was one important unresolved question. The Japanese language. I had thought that I would spend each morning immersing myself in intensive courses at a program in Tokyo. Given Ezra's correct belief that knowledge of language was important to any serious research endeavor, I was sure that he would agree.

Breakfast at the International House was a buffet service, and as I strolled off to fill my plate, Ezra and Junko engaged in a deep conversation about the wisdom of my spending so much time studying the language. His advice to her was No. His view was that unless I intended to become a true expert on Japan, the time and effort would not be justified. He assessed that most of those with whom I wished to speak would either be conversant in English or Chinese. He was correct, of course. Further, he made the introductions for me to the Japanese China community and those dealing with international affairs. Time was saved and progress was made. Perhaps most importantly, I was able to use the extra time to complete the background reading and research for a book that I had been intending to work on for over a decade. Without Ezra saying No, I do not think that I would have found the time to complete this work. Perhaps the only downside for this is that Junko still has to act as my guide and occasional interpreter whenever we visit Japan.

Ezra's generosity and kindness to both of us will always be treasured and will never be forgotten.

Christina Davis

Harvard University

Sitting with Ezra over lunch at the Harvard Faculty Club in the spring of 2019, I asked him for advice. I was about to become the new director of the Program on U.S.-Japan Relations. Ezra had been the founding director of the program, which was created in 1980 from the vision of

Judge Hisashi Owada and Ambassador Edwin O. Reischauer to bring Japanese visitors to Harvard and build greater understanding between Japan and the United States. Ezra kicked off the program as the training ground for a future Japanese elite, using his influence to attract the best and brightest young leaders from academia, government, and private institutions in Japan to come spend a year at Harvard. He then turned the program over to Susan Pharr, who spent the next thirty-two years building an institution with a very strong reputation and over six hundred alumni. I would be starting as the third director in January 2020, as the program celebrated its fortieth anniversary. Ezra immediately launched into an enthusiastic pep talk about how he thought I would do a terrific job leading the program. He didn't offer me any roadmap to success, but urged me to find my own vision for the program and balance my investment of time in the program with my goals as a scholar.

Ezra was at his best as a cheerleader. He undoubtedly encouraged countless students before me to keep trying to find the research question or policy solution that drove their interests. His research was infused with a deeply held belief in the capacity of societies to learn from each other and to do better. Whether calling for the United States to learn from the model of Japanese society or exploring the life of Deng Xiaoping as a leader who overcame obstacles to bring development to China, Ezra saw the potential for progress and achievement in everyone. His 2019 book, *China and Japan: Facing History,* tells of exchanges among students, scholars, and government leaders that allowed Japan and China to follow the lessons of successful institutions borrowing from each other. Amidst acrimony between the two countries, he saw hope for cooperation if only they would strive hard to try to understand each other.

At the end of our conversation, I mentioned that I was preparing a course on East Asia to teach for the General Education Program at Harvard and hoped to model the course partly on Ezra's famous Industrial East Asia course (Foreign Cultures 26, part of what was then called the Harvard core curriculum). I had worked as a teaching fellow for Ezra in the fall semester of 1997 when I was a graduate student in the Department of Government at Harvard, writing a dissertation about U.S.-Japan trade negotiations. He offered to share his lecture notes. Bringing them from his home across the street, he came to my office and laid down a large, black three-ring binder full of papers. Each lecture topic included the set of updated notes used for the lectures from 1989 to 1997. Some notes were in scrawled handwriting, others were typed outlines, and many were in-between—an outline that had been amended as he continued to edit and revise his thoughts. Across each of the topics, one point was constant—the optimism for change. In his outline of December 19th, 1990, he asked how much a nation can change—"East Asian nations changed with different cultures, why can't we?"

At the back of the binder was the final lecture for 1989. He ended the class by saying, "I hope that many of you who took the course only as a core requirement and even those of you who found ways to skimp on the assignments will feel, 1 year from now, 10 years from now, and even 50 years from now, long after I am gone, that taking this course helped open your eyes, realizing not so much that you learned a body of knowledge or that you were prepared for East Asia's success, but that you had a framework for absorbing new information, for understanding what is happening, and perhaps a few more ideas from East Asian practices that can make you play your role as a worker and citizen a little better. I am sure some of you will make big money and enjoy high status selling U.S. property and U.S. companies to Japanese financiers. I do not begrudge you such opportunities or criticize your choices. But I would hope that some of you will play a role in rebuilding U.S. industry, strengthening U.S. primary and secondary education, coping with crime, drugs, play a role in helping Americans understand the challenge from East Asia, and play a role in helping the U.S. form a political consensus about dealing with these issues."

Thank you, Ezra Vogel, for opening the eyes of us all to the promise of learning from East Asia and hoping for progress.

Wladimir Ramos

Medford, Massachusetts

I've been working for Ezra for approximately thirty years. He was always kind and genuine since the first day we met, patient with me as I learned English after immigrating from Brazil.

We became friends over my years of working for him. If there was ever an issue with his house, he'd contact me for general advice and help. He always respected me, my work, and advice. Ezra was dedicated to his work and craft; I always saw him working or writing. I'm honored to have had the chance to know Ezra and happy to call him a friend. I look forward to working with his wife, Charlotte, and I will miss Ezra dearly.

Rest in peace.

Michael Szonyi

Harvard University

Ezra Vogel was a mentor, a model, and a friend to me. I vividly remember our earliest meeting, almost twenty years ago, when I first visited Harvard. Naturally I was intimidated to approach someone with such an extraordinary reputation. I still remember my surprise that he turned out to be the friendly, humorous, and gentle man that generations of students and scholars in multiple fields adored. Those first impressions have never altered. In the subsequent years and decades, I often turned to him for advice, which he offered unfailingly, thoughtfully, and generously. Indeed, when the Dean of Social Sciences at Harvard wrote to propose that I serve as the Director of the Fairbank Center, Ezra was the first person I called for advice. I will greatly miss his sage counsel in the years ahead.

Ezra and Charlotte's home on Sumner Road was effectively a second Fairbank Center. A few times each month they would host a simple dinner to welcome a visitor to Harvard. They would order take-out Chinese food, and we would help ourselves in the kitchen. You never knew who would turn up at such events—senior scholars from around Asia, major government leaders, people whom Ezra had met somewhere in his long career. Nancy Hearst and Holly Angell, who had worked with Ezra for decades and were particularly devoted to him, often came to help out. The conversation was always fascinating. I felt it was a big burden on Ezra and Charlotte to host these gatherings so often. But it was only later that I realized I did not know the half of it. Besides the ones I attended, Ezra and Charlotte also hosted regular dinners for other groups like the "Vogel Japan *juku*" (study group) and the China sociologists study group.

I would have found this life exhausting, but Ezra clearly thrived and derived much energy from being around other people.

When Ezra introduced me to the guest of honor at these dinners, he would always say "Mike Szonyi is a young scholar who studies the Ming dynasty, but he's written a book about the twentieth century and is also very interested in contemporary China." I was always touched that he remembered the details of my scholarly work. But in fact, I don't think Ezra's interest in me was distinctive. He was so interested in other people that he remembered these details about virtually every scholar he met. Among Ezra's many contributions to the China studies community at Harvard and in the Boston area was a weekly seminar series on Critical Issues Confronting China. Before the talk, we'd meet for an informal cafeteria lunch with the speakers, and there was an open invitation for other colleagues to attend. Lunch could be a bit chaotic; we constantly had to rearrange the tables as people came from class or other meetings. But each time someone arrived, whether it was a senior scholar or a graduate student, Ezra would interrupt the conversation, even if the person speaking was a very distinguished scholar or official, and introduce the new arrival, saying: "This is so-and-so, and they work on such-and-such topic." Everybody was equal in Ezra's mind.

One of the activities he enjoyed most in the past few years was serving as the senior adviser to the Public Intellectuals Program of the National Committee on U.S.-China Relations. There have been several cohorts of PIPers, and they now number more than one hundred. He seemed to know something about every one of them. At our meetings, he would ask each of them how their current research project was developing. He was genuinely interested in the work and ideas of every person he met.

The last few years have been difficult for U.S.-China relations. When I got discouraged about the situation, Ezra would remind me that there have been many times when the situation was worse. Many U.S. scholars of China, especially younger ones, have been disappointed about restrictions on travel or access to research materials. Ezra reminded us that some scholars in his generation could not go to China for decades. The important thing, he would say, is for us to take the long-term view, to recognize that the work of building mutual understanding is fundamentally important, to ignore immediate political winds, and concentrate on our scholarship.

There is a term in Chinese—*xisang*, perhaps best translated as "joyous departure"—to describe the death of a person who has lived a full life. The term certainly applies to Ezra, whose life was rich in friendship, family, scholarship, and professional accomplishments. Still, it sometimes makes me sad to think that Ezra died at a moment when the cause so dear to his heart, the U.S.-China relationship, was at such a low ebb. Thinking of his life encourages me to continue our efforts to keep open the channels of communication with our Chinese colleagues, collaborators, and friends in hopes of a turn for the better.

Mary C. Brinton

Harvard University

My first introduction to Ezra was on a camping trip in 1981. Ezra wasn't there, of course. But as reading material for that trip, I had taken along my newly purchased copy of *Japan as Number One*. Having fortuitously become fascinated by Japan during my junior year at Stanford in the mid-1970s, I had moved on to the MA program in Japan Area Studies at the University of Washington, followed by a rather agonizing year at the Inter-University Center for Japanese Language Studies (where I started—but fortunately did not finish—at nearly the bottom of the class, due to my rudimentary spoken Japanese at the time). I then entered a PhD program in sociology, also at the University of Washington. My reading of *Japan as Number One* was preceded by my consumption of Nakane Chie's *Japanese Society*, Doi Takeo's *The Anatomy of Dependence*, William Caudill and Carmi Schooler's research on Japanese parenting, Ezra's *Japan's New Middle Class*, and many other monographs and research articles on Japanese society, culture, and social patterns. I was on my way to becoming a sociologist of Japan. My overriding motivation? To try to understand as much as I could about contemporary Japanese society and the historical trajectory that had produced it.

Where was Ezra in all of this? Ezra was far away (at Harvard), as were Robert Cole (at Michigan) and other prominent American sociologists of Japan. Although a combination of circumstances had led me to the University of Washington for graduate study, there were no sociologists of Japan to read my class papers on Japan's modernization or to guide my eventual dissertation research on gender inequality. But Ezra was there nonetheless, as were Robert Cole, Thomas Rohlen, Ronald Dore, and other social scientists who were probing the mysteries of Japanese industrial organization, employment relations, and workplace dynamics. Embedded in the works of these scholars there was always a hidden question that gnawed at me: Where were Japanese women in all of this? Research extolling the virtues of Japan's "manufacturing miracles," quality control, "harmony and strength" in white-collar workplaces, and the lifetime employment system seemed to quietly elide the fact that a large portion of the workforce was female. This part of the workforce did not seem to be recognized either as a crucial feature of Japan's economic success nor as the unequal beneficiary of that success. It was time for someone to write a book about women's role in helping make "Japan as no. 1," and I was determined to be the person to do it.

So it was that I finally came to meet Ezra when I went on the academic job market in 1985. Like so many others, I met him at the International House in Tokyo (although I don't recall that we had breakfast together). I had applied for a postdoctoral fellowship in the U.S.-Japan Relations Program, which Ezra directed. He was enthusiastic about my application. As for myself? I was thrilled that a scholar of his stature wanted to meet me and hear about my research. As it happened, I ultimately turned down the fellowship (as well as a position as assistant professor in the Harvard Department of Sociology) and started my career elsewhere. Ezra and I were not in close touch until nearly two decades later, when Harvard invited me to join the faculty as a full professor. Although Ezra had retired a few years prior, we became close colleagues from the time I came to Harvard in 2003 and remained so until his passing in December 2020.

Why was the "history" of my arms-length scholarly relationship to Ezra through my exposure to *Japan as Number One, Japan's New Middle Class,* and others of his works important in our relationship? In many ways it set up the scaffolding for the nature of our ongoing scholarly dialogue with each other from the very day I arrived at Harvard. The nature of Ezra's and other male social scientists' early writings on Japan had pushed me early on to move into the study of social problems in contemporary Japanese society—enduring sex discrimination in the labor market, women's well-defined subsidiary role in employment and, in many ways, in the family, strong racist tendencies in society overall, and other sources and variants of inequality that seemed to maintain a tenacious hold in Japanese social organization. It was such social problems that fascinated me. And trained as a sociologist in a department without Japan specialists, I had been forced from the very beginning to justify why Japan was important in every paper I wrote and every presentation I gave.

My focus on social problems and my training as a sociologist, both indirect products of Ezra's influence on me from the mid-1970s on, made indelible marks on our relationship. Ezra's introduction of me at every reception, dinner, or scholarly occasion inevitably went like this: "This is Mary Brinton. She's a REAL sociologist." I interpreted this as his affectionate way of signaling that I had earned my chops. And whenever Ezra asked me about my current research (which was inevitably uncovering some underside of gender relations or employment in Japan), he would always respond with something along the lines of "But Japanese society is still amazing because of . . . , and things are changing in a positive direction, right?" As noted by so many other contributors to this volume, Ezra was ever the optimist. He looked for the best in people—not just those in his extraordinarily wide circle of friends and acquaintances, but in the people he studied. I will forever miss the moments of tender banter with a scholar and colleague whose life exercised such a profound influence on my own.

THREE

Pivoting to Research on Asia

Kaoru (Hashiguchi) Nakayama

Tokyo, Japan

My parents were old friends of Ezra's, and I have had a long friendship with him as well. The Vogel and Hashiguchi families have enjoyed a connection that continues to this day. On this occasion, I would like to contribute a simple essay on my recollections of Ezra.

First, I will explain how the Hashiguchi family met Ezra. Ezra lived in Ichikawa, a Tokyo suburb, from 1959 to 1960. At the time, he was researching Japan's middle class, and he asked the principal of an elementary school in Ichikawa to introduce him to six families. Our family was one of the six. Our household consisted of seven people: my father, a salaryman (who worked for an airline company); my mother, a professional housewife; my older brother; my older sister; my younger brother; and myself; plus my mother's father. At the time I was five years old.

Ezra returned to the U.S. after that year, but he came to Japan regularly, and on those occasions he would visit our family. I had an image of scholars as being a bit stiff, but he was very pleasant, always smiling, with a sense of humor. He always complimented my mother on her cooking. Men at that time would not publicly praise others, and the men in my family were no different. When Ezra would visit, my mother seemed a bit nervous, but also very pleased.

My mother and grandfather felt that women should put getting married first, but my father believed that women should have a chance to see the world, so he encouraged me to get a job. I had only known the confines of my own family and school, but I was able to experience the broader world through my job. Then I got the urge to go abroad, so I consulted Ezra and Suzy, and they readily welcomed me to come for a homestay.

Ezra's family in America was very different from a Japanese family. My mother went shopping every day to feed our family of seven, while my father was very busy with work. Ezra's family had a large refrigerator, and they would buy a large quantity of groceries about twice a week. They also had a dishwasher, so that made housework quite a bit easier. Even so, Suzy had her own job, so I thought it must have been hard for her to manage that plus housework. Ezra would help with cleanup after parties on the weekend. That was new to me. It was refreshing to see the family relationships, how Ezra and Suzy would go out to parties as a couple or have happy conversations with the kids. I had come to study English, but Ezra spoke with me in Japanese. I had a wonderful time, but unfortunately Ezra and Suzy divorced after that. Then Ezra's second son, Steve, decided to spend a year attending high school at Keimei Gakuen. He spent weeknights in the dorm, but he spent the weekends with us in Ichikawa. He even developed a rapport with my grandfather, who was born in the Meiji era. In that way, the Hashiguchi-Vogel family exchange continued.

Finally, I would like to touch on Ezra's character. Ezra gave a speech in Japanese at my wedding. What really left an impression on me was how he used the phrase *rōbashin nagara* . . . ("while this may be the excessive concern of an elder . . ."), which was very eloquent and natural in Japanese, almost like a Japanese uncle. He was always trying to learn new words. After he retired from university teaching, I asked him: "So what are you doing every day?" And he replied: "I am studying." In Japan most people just relax after they retire, so I was surprised by those words.

Ezra would visit my house after my parents died. Since my husband was a high school social studies teacher, Ezra always asked him about Japanese students at the time. And he also interacted with my children very warmly. My relationship with him and his family is in some ways closer than a relationship with relatives. When Ezra's passing was reported in various newspapers in Japan, it reminded me once again what a remarkable person he was.

David W. Plath

Savoy, Illinois

I probably was in the front ranks of that sixty-year-long parade of colleagues and others Ezra Vogel favored with friendship. In our early years—

the late 1950s—we were just "*ez*" and "*dave*," untitled graduate students hanging out as academic wannabees. On campus you might have glimpsed us burlesquing a Talcott Parsons lecture or talking intently with Bill Caudill about Japanese personality and psychotherapy. Off campus you might not even have noticed us: two twenty-something white guys, each convoying a wife with a toddler.

Competition can sour friendship between graduate students, but it did not erupt between us. Even in hindsight I'm not sure why. We were alike in many ways, and where we differed—"*ez*" majoring in sociology, "*dave*" in anthropology—we were judged by different faculty committees.

We had similar backgrounds. Each of us grew up in a retail merchant's household in a modest-size Midwest city. Ezra's father ran a men's clothing store, mine a furniture store. On campus we were exotics but not ethnics, from a sector of American society rarely mentioned in our textbooks or researched by our mentors.

Both born in 1930, we stood on history's sidelines watching adults around us endure the Great Depression and enact the Greatest Generation. But we were old enough to be called to active military duty during the Korean "police action" before we entered graduate school.

We took different classes, sat for different tests, reported to different mentors. The big difference was that "*ez*" had already done two years of graduate study by the time we met. He became my older brother, but being Ezra Vogel he did not become Big Brother. He cared about what I was doing but did not try to manage me; he was comfortable with our differences.

What we shared most of all was excitement from inhaling the intellectual oxygen generated by humans studying humans in 1950s Cambridge. It inspired a vision: that if historical barriers around disciplines could be dropped, then any student might discover new dynamics of human conduct—even a student who wasn't dropping LSD. That vision was institutionalized in the new Department of Social Relations, which drew faculty from the old-line disciplines of anthropology, psychology, and sociology. We audited its courses and consulted its faculty.

Both of us were part-time research assistants on a project investigating recidivism among hospitalized mental patients in Massachusetts. Discharged as healed, some never were seen again, others returned often. Might it be that the returnees were not sick individuals, but instead

that their families were sick and were trying to heal themselves by ejecting a member?

The project had no connection to Japan. But from elsewhere on campus came the idea of doing a similar study in Japan. Soon to receive his
doctorate, Ezra was a prime candidate for fielding the study, though he
didn't speak Japanese. I envied him the opportunity (I had lived in Japan for a year) but had not finished all my required courses. He received
funds for language training and for supporting his family for two years
in Japan while he and his wife Suzanne interviewed families of mental
patients.

Months later the Plaths rejoined the Vogels in the Tokyo suburb of
Ichikawa. For several weeks we lived in an inn a few minutes from their
house while "*ez*" introduced me to his network of Japanese sociologists,
who helped me scout for a community that would accept me (with family)
for a year as an inquisitive resident. We ended up living at the foot of the
Japanese Alps, a full day's journey from Ichikawa. We and the Vogels got
together far less often than we had expected.

The Vogels booked their return to the U.S. on an evening flight from
Haneda Airport on July 10th, 1960. Japanese history records that as the
day of the Hagerty Incident. For months there had been mass demonstrations against plans to revise the U.S.-Japan Security Treaty. On
July 10th, 6,000 people assembled at Haneda to protest the arrival of
James Hagerty, President Eisenhower's press secretary, coming to arrange
a visit for Eisenhower later that month. A mob battered the limousine that
was carrying Hagerty and the American ambassador away from the terminal. A U.S. Marine Corps helicopter had to rescue them. Eisenhower's
visit was canceled, and an embarrassed public forced Prime Minister
Kishi to resign. For Japan-U.S. relations it was another "date that shall
live in infamy."

None of the Plaths or Vogels had noticed the news reports about a
demonstration scheduled for Haneda on the 10th. That morning "*ez*" and
"*dave*" left for the airport taking the Vogel luggage; wives and children
were to follow later. When our taxi drove through the airport gateway,
we were stunned to be surrounded by a crowd waving signs and shouting
anti-American slogans. But we should have known better: *this is Japan.*
A demonstrator saw us, our clothes identifying us as Americans. He apologized for the disturbance and offered to escort us to the terminal on

foot, with his men carrying the luggage. Our little entourage crossed the main runway and walked a quarter mile until we were secure inside the terminal building.

Ezra had rented a VIP room in the terminal and was anxious to be there early. The families, the people who for a year had opened their inner lives to him, were coming to Haneda not to protest, but to see him off with a chorus of thanks for having cared about them.

Ez and Dave met for a last hurrah on April 6th, 2019. In Ezra's old hometown (Delaware, Ohio) on the campus of its university (Ohio Wesleyan, his undergraduate alma mater) at a meeting of the Midwest Japan Seminar, we talked about our first fieldwork in 1950s Japan. A videotape of the event is available at: https://www.owu.edu/about/follow-owu/stream -owu/special-events/april-6-2019-midwest-japan-seminar--taidan-/

Hugh Patrick

Columbia Business School

I first met Ezra Vogel in early fall 1960 when we both became new assistant professors at Yale, Ez in sociology and me in economics. Initially we came together because we were professionally and personally interested in Japan, both domestically and in its rapidly evolving regional and global contexts. We became good friends, very comfortable with each other, often socializing together—Ez with his then-wife and me with my then-wife.

As his subsequent career amply demonstrates, his return to Harvard after one year was a great loss for Yale. Luckily for me, I do not think of that as a deep personal loss, since our friendship continued unabated throughout our lives. We spoke on the phone whenever we felt like it or needed to, and of course, we saw each other when I went to Boston and when he came to New Haven and to New York after I moved to Columbia.

What I admired so much in Ez was that he worked not only so well but so hard. I was impressed by Harvard's decision to train Ez to be a China specialist with fluency in Chinese as well as Japanese and was especially impressed by Ez's decision to develop his Chinese expertise. I was amazed that he got up (to my mind) incredibly early to study Chinese for a couple of hours before beginning his regular work and family day. And it is fair to say those efforts paid off, as his friends, colleagues, and students around the world continue to speak of his work and legacy.

I look forward to the statements by his colleagues, students, and other friends describing his so long and so successful professional career.

Andrew J. Nathan

Columbia University

In my first undergraduate year at Harvard, I had to select a social science class for course distribution purposes. I chose Soc. Sci. 111, History of East Asia, because of the exotic nature of the subject at that time (1960), when China and Japan were mysterious and far away. I enjoyed the class so much that I declared a major in modern Chinese history. John Fairbank, multi-tasking as usual, not looking up from his desk, signed my major declaration form and declared, "Of course you'll start intensive Chinese next year." Being too dumb to think for myself, I followed orders and enrolled in Professor Rulan Pian's introductory Chinese language course the following year.

As I remember, there were only four undergraduates in that class of twenty or twenty-five students. The others were grad students preparing for careers in the Foreign Service or Defense Department. Except for Ezra. He was beginning his transition from Japan to China studies—or, as it turned out, to the study of both. Ezra, as everyone knows, never stood on rank and age. He was just one of the students. I had no idea he was any different from anyone else.

A couple of years later, I arrived in Hong Kong at age twenty on a post-graduate Knox Fellowship awarded by the university. There was no internet in those days and you didn't phone home because it was too expensive, you sent air letters (those blue, thin single pieces of paper that you used both sides to write on, then folded into a postcard shape for mailing). I was lonely and didn't know what to do. Somehow I found Ezra, who was in Hong Kong doing research for the book that became *Canton under Communism*. He greeted me as an old friend and an equal, introduced me to a language tutor who was one of his staff, and welcomed me to use his office suite for my lessons. He gave me a sense of home.

A few months later Ezra went to Macao to conduct additional refugee interviews. He invited me along, paid my way, and paid for an interpreter so I could do interviews as well. This was a great experience; I was still only twenty. With Ezra's guidance, the interviews became the basis of my first publication, "China's Work Point System," *Current Scene* (1964), and started me off on a research career.

A few years later, I finished my PhD in political science, went on the job market, and bombed in two job interviews. Ezra was concerned. He called his friends at the University of Michigan and got me a post-doc. (These were still the days of the old boy network.) A year later I did poorly in my job talk at Columbia. The chair of the search committee called Ezra (as the chair told me some years later) and asked why he had written a good recommendation for such a loser. Ezra promised him, "No, no, Nathan will be good." They took a chance on his say-so.

I can't count all the letters of recommendation Ezra wrote for me over the years, or the many expressions of personal interest, concern, and support. But I'll add just one more story. Sometime after Perry Link and I were banned from the PRC for publishing *The Tiananmen Papers* (among other infractions), Ezra organized a group of distinguished China types who were trusted by Beijing to urge the authorities to give us visas, arguing that we were honest scholars with some influence and it would be in China's interest to allow access. This initiative didn't succeed. But it was another example of Ezra's energy, fair-mindedness, concern for others, and concern for China. It was a quiet act of generosity, typical of this gentle, caring person and of his vision of the small things, the big things, and the connections between the two.

Charles W. Hayford

Evanston, Illinois

Many others worked more closely with Ezra than I did, but not many knew him for as long. In 1962, the fall of my Harvard senior year, I got the China bug, acquired by taking Akira Iriye's United States-East Asian relations course the spring before, the second time he offered it. The first time he offered it, Ezra helped him practice each lecture. Then I took John Fairbank's Modern China course, which somehow inspired the idea of asking him to come talk at a China Table I wanted to organize at Quincy House. Fairbank's office was on the third floor of a marbled courtyard building at 16 Dunster Street. When I sat down, Fairbank had a foot-high stack of mail and memos on his desk; I left ten minutes later, and the stack was down to the last inch, but he solved my problem. He volunteered Ezra.

Ezra and I had lunch at the dining hall to plan the China Table. He ate and talked, each with equal gusto, sometimes simultaneously. This was the Ezra I would know for nearly sixty years: genial but not light-hearted, generous, voracious, centered, with an undistracted curiosity. He suggested Stuart Schram, Jerry Cohen, and some others that I've forgotten (they all came). He asked about my life, my plans, and my family. In later years, he could flip through his mental Rolodex and remind me that I had an Ohio grandfather, from Wooster, not too far from his beloved Delaware.

I went to Taiwan and came back as a grad student. A friend who was leaving town in a hurry asked me to sell his bicycle for him, a clunker that I sold to Ezra for $10. My mind's eye sees Ezra pedaling down Massachusetts Avenue in a rumpled winter coat and a dowdy woolen cap.

A few years later, even though I was in History, he asked me to be a section leader in his course, the only time I ever taught Sociology. With the Cold War peaking and the Cultural Revolution boiling, the course neither demonized Red China nor idealized Maoist socialism. I recall one lecture where Ezra sang a ditty learned in his Hong Kong interviews, "Mao Zedong, duzi tong" (Mao Zedong, my stomach's empty), followed by a *fanshen* story. "Fanshen," as in William Hinton's book, means "turning your body over," that is, revolutionary transformation, but a refugee informant slyly resisted. Before Liberation, he said, they "treated us like turtles" (*dai women dang zuo wugui yiyang*), turtles being considered slow and dumb. After Liberation? "Fanshenle!" That is, they "flipped us on our backs."

Another lecture was published as the classic 1965 *China Quarterly* article, "From Friendship to Comradeship: The Change in Personal Relations in Communist China." It showed how friendship as a unique person-to-person relationship was undermined. When the Party could require people to divulge their friendships, people could no longer confide secrets or share doubts; they could only be comrades, equal to all but intimate with none. After the lecture—well, maybe after another one, but this makes a better story—we ran into Talcott Parsons on the street, and Ezra introduced me to the Great Man, his mentor. I dutifully read up on structure and function, which convinced me I was only an historian but allowed me to see how Ezra's stories had a Parsonian architecture whose joists and beams were invisible.

The course also read his *Canton under Communism* (1969), which he said in the preface was "one scholar's efforts to get beyond his Western academic biases to understand China on its own terms." That's what he did—understand things on their own terms and organize them for people to understand. He did not see this as a political or theoretical job. For better or for worse, not an easy thing to do.

In 1970, Ezra drove a few Committee of Concerned Asian Scholars graduate students to Washington so we could tell them to Stop The War. As I recall, we slept on Nick Platt's basement floor and the next morning Ezra took us to the State Department. The war didn't stop; nor has my love for Ezra.

Jerry Cohen

New York University School of Law

In August 1963, my wife, our three young sons, and I arrived in Hong Kong, where I intended to spend the year researching China's criminal justice system. We knew no one and had not been able to make advance arrangements for getting settled. There was then no law school in the Colony to host me. There was no research center to accommodate my scholarly aspirations. We had no family connections or friends to rely on. Fortunately, Ezra Vogel came to the rescue.

We did not know Ezra, but John Fairbank had urged me to get in touch with him. Ezra was a Harvard protégé of John's who had just arrived in Hong Kong ahead of us in order to spend the year studying Chinese society and bringing his mastery of the Chinese language up to the level of his impressive command of Japanese. I arrived in Hong Kong from my teaching post in Berkeley armed with Ezra's contact information, which Fairbank's able assistant, John Lindbeck, had recently sent me. Since I had been invited, at Fairbank's recommendation, to serve as a visiting professor at Harvard Law School for the following year, and since Ezra was my age and had a family at the same stage as mine, it seemed natural to bring us together.

Finding a place to live was our first priority. Ezra solved that immediately by telling me that there was a nice garden apartment across the street from the place he had just rented in the Yau Yat Chuen section of Kowloon that bordered on the New Territories. Ezra and his wife Suzy also helped us solve our second problem, which was to find appropriate schools for our children. They told us about Kowloon Junior School, where our oldest boy Peter was able to enroll in first grade. They also suggested that we try to register our two younger boys in an informal preschool that they had heard was operated by a British army wife named Foster on a nearby street. Since they did not know Mrs. Foster's precise address, they advised us to post ourselves at the entrance to the street between 8 and 8:30 a.m. the next morning in order to watch where young children were being dropped off. That technique worked exactly as planned and, from then on, I was able to focus on my research, which overlapped with Ezra's.

We both devoted gobs of time to interviewing refugees from the mainland. That gave me an opportunity to reciprocate Ezra's assistance by introducing him to a brilliant former public security officer from Guangzhou whom we called Edward Chan. He proved to be a splendid source for Ezra's eventual book entitled *Canton under Communism*. Characteristically, at the end of our year in Hong Kong Ezra generously arranged for our mutual informant to study in the United States, where Ezra guided his further progress for several years.

FOUR

Scholarly Contributions

Lucien Bianco

École des Hautes Études en Sciences Sociales

When Ezra Vogel offered his Deng book to me in 2011, he referred to our "half a century of kinship." Not quite then, as we first met at Harvard in 1964, but more than half a century by now. I last saw Ezra in 2015 in Hong Kong, after which we kept exchanging emails, including on such topics as Trump's 2016 victory and 2020 defeat, a bare month before Ezra passed away. On the whole we met more often in Hong Kong, especially during the time when I served under Ezra's direction as a member of the Advisory Committee of the Universities Service Centre, than in the United States, where I occasionally slept in Ezra and Charlotte's home, and Europe, where Ezra did the same in our suburban home near Paris.

I could never forget our late 2011 exchange following my reading of *Deng Xiaoping*. Ezra responded to my criticisms of that outstanding work in such a modest, humane, friendly, and serious way and sent me a copy of his letter asking the Harvard Press editor to correct half a dozen or so sentences, taking into account every minor or trivial error I had pointed out. Even when I did not convince Ezra—for instance, that he might have been overindulgent toward Deng—he conceded, "Now that the book is out, I am getting some distance from Deng and will continue to gain some distance."

To come from Deng to the most recent of his successors, I would at times have preferred Ezra Vogel adopting a firmer stand toward Xi Jinping's regime. It was of course much easier for someone like me who had no responsibility whatsoever not to condone what Uyghurs suffered in Xinjiang and democrats in Hong Kong. Ezra was dedicated to improving relationships between the U.S. and China, and he believed that former imperialist countries should treat China more fairly. Chinese officials recently extracted from American, British, and German history every supposed "evil" that might be retained against each of these three peoples. They said nothing against France only because Macron had refrained from joining overdue criticisms of China's policies.

Ezra constantly endeavored not only to obtain the best from his students and peacefully solve the most difficult issues, but also to make readers appreciate the positive lessons of history, for example, in *One Step Ahead in China: Guangdong under Reform*, 1989; *The Four Little Dragons: The Spread of Industrialization in East Asia*, 1991; and *Deng Xiaoping and the Transformation of China*, 2011. It comes as no surprise that Ezra long ago revealed the clues to the success achieved by *Japan as Number One* and took care to draw out its *Lessons for America,* in 1979.

Amy Borovoy

Princeton University

I first met Ezra at his home in Cambridge in March 2011. I was interviewing him about the book I was beginning, analyzing how six canonical studies of postwar Japan tackled the question of comparative modernity and the unexpected way in which Japan emerged as a site of reflection on American society itself. *Japan's New Middle Class* (1963) was one of the texts I was treating. As Ezra was setting out our breakfast (we'd set an early meeting because he had a busy day of writing ahead), he made me feel at home with his sense of humor, telling me that he'd extended his invitation only after vetting me with his family, to make sure "I was okay." I understood from this that he was adding me to his (already large) collection of friends and colleagues, and that perhaps this was the beginning of more conversations.

To me, *Japan's New Middle Class* is one of the more remarkable ethnographies of the postwar period. The book's intensive interviews over the course of two years painted an in-depth portrait of a postwar urban community. But I was interested in the larger sociological and comparative questions that motivated the study. Ezra was eager to discuss this. He talked about the influence of Talcott Parsons in the Harvard Department of Social Relations and his interest in the family's role in reproducing social values and institutions. Parsons was interested in "the whole picture," Ezra told me, and that had inspired him to tackle an ambitious project. Although Parsons was a towering figure, I hadn't appreciated his direct influence on Ezra. "Sure," Ezra told me. "Look at the table of contents of *Japan's New Middle Class*. You'll see that the chapter headings correspond exactly to Parsons's four social sub-systems" (economy, polity, beliefs and values or ideology, and family and education). Sure enough, the chapter titles ("The Significance of Salary," "The Role of the Citizen," "The Gateway to Salary" on entrance examinations, etc.) correspond to Parsons's breakdown.

Yet as I've re-read the book over the years, it strikes me that the conclusions Ezra reached must have been somewhat unexpected in the late 1950s and early 1960s. It was a time when many American social scientists understood modernization to imply a set of qualities that would be universally consistent, involving the transition from traditional social groups to a free-market economy and individual freedoms. Ezra observed these qualities in the white-collar families he studied, but the burden of the analysis was in elaborating how Japanese society continued to be shaped by social groups and new forms of social control: involvement with the company in ways that reached far beyond the 9–5 workday, the tyranny of the examination system, neighborhood associations, and peer groups. The observation that women and men lived largely separate lives challenged the idea that the demographic transition to lower fertility would necessarily lead to the ideal of gender equality. The book states quite explicitly that although many of the interviewees commented on the bad old days of feudalism, they did not worship individualism.

Japan's New Middle Class could have been a case study of modernity, a story of rationalization and individualization, a parallel case to the work of Riesman, Parsons, or Mills. But it was a story with a different ending.

In some ways, *Japan as Number One* was also evidence of Ezra's openness to new ways of thinking and his willingness to set aside dominant assumptions. The book is often associated with a particular moment of American fascination with Japan—a moment characterized by shortsighted obsession with Japanese management practices or approaching Japan with either superficial reverence or xenophobic fear. Ezra accepted that the book was born of a specific historical moment. "But remember," he said, holding up one finger and looking at me intently, "I was ahead of my time." The book was written in the late 1970s, before the trade wars between Japan and the U.S. heated up and before most Americans even saw Japan as a worthy object of comparison. Widespread interest in Japanese management took off only in the 1980s. (A few works were available in the 1970s, mainly focusing on labor, as did, for instance, Robert Cole's and Thomas Rohlen's.) "Most people thought I was out of touch," Ezra told me. "My voice was new. . . . Americans didn't think they had to learn from anyone. It wasn't until later that they became more humble."

In Ezra's writing and his words I have always been struck by a quality of openness to new realities, by an entrepreneurial ability to see unfolding situations, and by a kind of resolute commitment not to be swayed by existing assumptions. Perhaps his confidence in telling the story of what he saw in Japan came from his deep immersion in the country and the close contacts he maintained in Japan, Cambridge, and elsewhere. Ezra's breakfast at the International House each morning was the same: *natto* and runny egg over rice, a traditional Japanese breakfast. When I look at photographs Steve has shared with me of the Vogels in Japan during 1958–1960 as they were researching *Japan's New Middle Class*, one senses their deep sense of comfort with the place, the friends they made with whom they later continued to keep in touch, and the way in which their whole family was integrated into their research.

Although I didn't know Ezra as well as many other people did, I had a number of subsequent conversations with him after that initial meeting in Cambridge, often at the International House of Japan in Tokyo where we both spent a few weeks in early summer. He would hail me and invite me to his table or introduce me to the person he was having breakfast with. He always wanted to know what I was working on and what I was thinking. He was a scholar who was always learning from people, always gathering information, and always refining his views.

Endymion Wilkinson

Petchaburi, Thailand

I first met Ezra more than fifty years ago at the lunch table of the old Fairbank Center. Since then we have gotten together in Cambridge (Massachusetts), in Tokyo, and in Beijing to dine, to visit places, or to consult each other on this or that. I will relate two or three of these occasions to illustrate his exceptional qualities.

In the late 1970s Ezra contacted me in Tokyo to join him at a house-warming dinner party given by the political scientist Satō Seizaburō and his wife Kinko, at that time a public prosecutor. Ezra had just come from a conference in Seoul and was, I thought, overly optimistic about Korean economic development. When he said "the academic standard in Korea is fantastically high. Why, all the Koreans at the conference spoke fluent English and nearly all of them had PhD's from U.S. universities," I challenged him for using such a narrow yardstick. Ez was not the slightest bit fazed and courteously rebutted me, citing increases of productivity and other substantial measures of where Korea was headed. A couple of months later I had to do the rounds of the new Korean steelworks, automobile factories, and shipyards. I was hugely impressed and realized that Ezra's enthusiasm had not been misplaced and wrote to tell him so. Later he published on the Park era and typically did so in comparative perspective (Turkey, Japan, China).

Some months after the Seizaburōs' housewarming, Ezra was again in Tokyo and I invited him to the EU Europe Day reception. When Takeo Fukuda (then serving as foreign minister) arrived I introduced Ezra to him. Without hesitation Ezra engaged Fukuda in fluent Japanese not about U.S.-Japan relations (the default subject for U.S. academics), but about EU-Japan relations (it was the period of *bōeki masatsu*—trade frictions). After that Ezra turned the subject to Japan's relations with China. His questions were serious and respectfully put, and Fukuda replied at length, not with one of his usual opaque one-liners. It was a rare moment of sanity amidst the babble of a diplomatic reception.

Ezra was one of the very few academics in the West who was fluent in both spoken Japanese and Chinese. He achieved this distinction by receiving regular language tutoring long past middle age. Ezra was also one of the few in nearly all of his many publications who combined book research with interviews. This gave his works an immediacy sometimes lacking in those of more conventional academics.

Ezra was attracted by success. Moreover, he felt that his countrymen failed to grasp how Japan had managed to get ahead since he had first gone there for post-doctoral research in the 1950s. In 1979 he published his account of what could be learned from Japan in his brilliantly titled book, *Japan as Number One: Lessons for America*. It sold extremely well in Japan, a good deal less so in America and Europe. Tokyo Broadcasting System (TBS) turned it into a TV documentary (they had done Milton Friedman the year before), and for a while Ezra was a household name in Japan. The following year a book I had written on Japan's relations with the West was going through the same process and I phoned Ezra for his advice. Typically, he gave me a comprehensive briefing, including details of his royalty payments and his contract with the TV station. His generosity proved vital to me in negotiating with my publisher and with TBS.

His natural modesty cloaking a tough mind, his interest in hearing about what other people were working on, the wide range of his publications, and his loyalty to his students and friends ensured that his global network of admirers was unusually large. Hardworking, enthusiastic in his efforts to understand the success of the East Asian tigers and the new policies in China, he also found time in his last two decades to attempt to nurture scholarly reconciliation between the academics of the two countries in East Asia that he knew best, Japan and China. One of the spinoffs was his last book, published at the age of eighty-nine, a major study of the history of Japan-China relations from the earliest times to the present.

Ezra was a rare force, influential not only through his writing but also by the example he set.

Michael A. Cusumano

Massachusetts Institute of Technology

My first meaningful encounter with Ezra Vogel was through one of his books. I entered Harvard as a PhD student in History and East Asian Languages in 1978 and then went to Japan in 1980 to do thesis research at the University of Tokyo. I accepted a part-time job teaching English to three Japanese professors. We decided that I would record a book on cassette tapes, and they would listen chapter by chapter to the tapes. Then we would meet twice a month to talk about each chapter. What book did we choose? Of course, it was Ezra's bestseller, *Japan as Number One:*

Lessons for America (1979). I had met Ezra briefly a few times, but I did not know him or his new book very well.

My familiarity with *Japan as Number One* changed greatly by the end of 1981. I spent a full year reading aloud every word and talking with the professors slowly and carefully about each chapter. We discussed whether or not there really was a "Japanese Miracle," the role of the government versus companies, the maze of Japanese politics, and the importance of education in Japanese society and history. We pondered comparisons with the United States. Overall, I learned a lot about why Ezra believed Japan had become "Number One" and where he thought America was lacking. More importantly, I was impressed by the depth, breadth, and clarity of Ezra's arguments and his ability to link a wide range of topics together for a mass-market audience. I came away more interested in current Japanese management than in business history. After graduation, I took a postdoc position at the Harvard Business School and then joined the faculty at the MIT Sloan School of Management in 1986, where I remain today. My thesis adviser, Professor Albert Craig, was the person most responsible for my move from history to a business school, but Ezra's book helped convince me to pursue this path.

My second meaningful encounter was through one of Ezra's courses. After I returned to Harvard in fall 1983, I asked Ezra if I could work with him as a teaching assistant for his Little Dragons class, which covered Taiwan, Hong Kong, South Korea, and Singapore, with some comparisons to Japan and China. I remember fondly the weekly meetings at his house to go over readings and grade assignments. Ezra asked me to take one session and give a lecture related to my research. I chose technology transfer and adaptation from the West into Japan, before and after World War II. How this happened in one industry was the core of my dissertation and first book, *The Japanese Automobile Industry: Technology and Management at Nissan and Toyota* (1985). Japan in 1980 had become number one in automobile production, so it was a timely topic. Ezra was also kind enough to give me written comments on my thesis draft and to offer a much-appreciated blurb for the book jacket. Once I became a professor, I made sure to treat my students as Ezra (and Albert Craig) had treated me—as a junior colleague, not just as a student.

Over the next thirty-plus years, as busy as he became, Ezra always made time to invite me (and sometimes my wife, who is from China) to lunch at the Harvard Faculty Club to talk about his latest project. We also ran into each other frequently at the International House of Japan, where we both liked to stay. (I recall he once spent three months there!) In our conversations, Ezra was often looking for ideas and references for his own research, but he would always insist that I explain to him in detail what I was doing, thinking, and feeling.

It is impossible to capture the life and impact of a "professor's professor" in a few words. On the surface, I experienced Ezra as extraordinarily kind and outgoing, but deeper down, I appreciated that he was very complex intellectually and very careful about how he spent his time. I saw no limits to his curiosity or ability to navigate effortlessly through many different worlds and academic disciplines. He became a superstar professor, not only of sociology but also of history, business, politics, and public policy, as well as Asian languages and culture. The breadth and depth of his skills can be seen very clearly in the last two books he wrote: *Deng Xiaoping and the Transformation of China* (2011) and *China and Japan: Facing History* (2019).

Ezra influenced many students and colleagues in profound and subtle ways. I count myself lucky to be among those people. Yet his ambitions were always to do more than just influence individuals. Ezra wanted to shape the discourse around nations and international relations. He wanted everyone to understand what he understood about Japan and China and the rest of Asia—to see people as equals and not be so easily convinced of American and Western superiority. He wanted us all to think more carefully about how we can learn from each other's traditions, flaws, and best practices. Ezra Vogel wanted Japan, China, and the United States to coexist and prosper together, peacefully, rather than engage again in military hostilities or cutthroat, destructive competition. And he did something about it.

John Lie

University of California, Berkeley

When I arrived at Harvard in 1978, I made appointments to meet the founders of modern Asian studies in the United States, such as John K.

Fairbank and Edwin O. Reischauer. Working in their gargantuan shadow, Ezra didn't register in my inchoate intellect, save that he chaired the interdisciplinary concentration in East Asian Studies. Thinking of double majoring in it with Social Studies, I met him for the first time in spring 1979. Alas, the Coolidge Hall meeting was doubly inauspicious. The fault of neither, at the time double majors were *verboten*. The second unfortunate matter was that we ended up in a somewhat tense quarrel. Taking note of my Korean ancestry—Ezra was almost unfailingly solicitous— he began to discuss modern Korean history and lauded the beneficial impact of Japanese colonial rule on the Korean peninsula. I was skeptical of this benign view and launched into a polemic against prewar Japanese militarism and imperialism and, for good measure, militarism and imperialism tout court. It was, as I said, a bad beginning.

Four years later, Ezra kindly invited me to his house for a chat (he had been on sabbatical leave during my first year of graduate school). Like almost everyone else, I had read his 1979 book *Japan as Number One*, about which I was less than enthusiastic because of its overly optimistic take on contemporary Japanese society. He had apparently read my undergraduate thesis on Japanese labor, and justifiably suspected me of leftist sympathies. The second meeting was no less unfortunate than the first. For some reason the discussion turned to the subcontracting system, about which he stressed its harmonious functionality, and I emphasized its hidden conflicts and dysfunctions. Needless to say, our differences were overdetermined: for starters, not only was Ezra an abiding student of Talcott Parsons's structural-functionalist theory, but I was antipathic to Parsons's grand theory. The Cold War seemed to structure generational conflicts as well as political-intellectual differences into two opposing camps.

The same quarrel recurred when I enrolled in his graduate seminar on Japanese Business and Society. Recalcitrant, I pointed to conflicts and contradictions in Japanese business, including the subcontracting system, in the seminar, and he was less charitable in response to my perspective. In what I assume was a rare burst of anger, he began to dilate on the evils of the Cultural Revolution and the New Left. The third time was not the charm, and I ended up not having him on my dissertation committee.

The fourth time was, however. I had returned to teach at Harvard in 2000, and though Ezra had formally retired, he welcomed me back with his irresistible smile and we had pleasant chats whenever our paths crossed. It was not just that the Cold War was a distant memory and that we had converged in our political outlook. More important, I had come to read and admire his excellent monographs, especially *Japan's New Middle Class* (1963) and *Canton under Communism* (1969). If only by dint of having written books of my own, I came to appreciate his granular and limpid analysis of the ascent of the salaryman in post–World War II Japan as well as his bravura performance of reconstructing Guangdong from the testimonies of those who had left. That both books remain eminently readable and illuminating more than a half century after their publication—who now reads Parsons?—are testaments to his intellectual strengths: devoid of intellectual hubris, such as the vainglorious valorization of grand theory or abstracted empiricism, with a sure sense of place and context, or what one might call reality. These are undervalued virtues in the contemporary social sciences, but the very survival of his early books testifies to the enduring intellectual strengths that Ezra personified.

Needless to say, Ezra kept on researching and writing into ripe old age. *One Step Ahead in China* (1989) demonstrated that he was more than one step ahead of the horde in making sense of China's economic dynamism. *Deng Xiaoping and the Transformation of China* (2011) was as illuminating about the man as it was about the country and the times. And there was much, much more. Quite clearly, retirement was nominal, and his pan–East Asian (and, indeed, pan-global) networks of students, colleagues, and friends undoubtedly remained in awe of the man and his restless curiosity and Stakhanovite stamina. I was certainly not anywhere close to being in the inner circle—though I saw him often enough, at the International House in Tokyo, the Association for Asian Studies meetings, and Harvard—and I learned about his activities from graduate-school friends who saw him annually. To be sure, it is not as if my head had been denuded of the critical hat; thinking is perforce a critical activity. Nevertheless, it was not merely respect for the éminence grise that he had become or for the almost unfailingly pleasant person that he was that animated my feelings about Ezra, but rather a deep appreciation of his academic achievements and the intellectual virtues that they represented. He had become a latter-day *junzi* (*kunshi*).

I write as a would-be prodigal pupil, mourning for an intellectual relationship that never was. His books and articles, his many students, and even his own son who is my colleague at Berkeley, are constant reminders of my loss, and now, that of all of us. Yet I would be remiss if I didn't say that my latest book, *Japan, the Sustainable Society*, begins with *Japan as Number One*, and, as I came to realize after completing the manuscript, is something of my response to that book, albeit forty-two years later. Certainly, Ezra has come to cast a gigantic shadow of his own. *Gasshō (Añjali Mudrā)*.

Kenneth Pyle

University of Washington

There are many things I want to remember about Ezra. The most obvious is the breadth of his scholarship. He was a great East Asianist with an instinct for the big questions. There have been few American scholars about whom this can be said. He had language proficiency in both Chinese and Japanese, an astonishingly extensive network of contacts with academics and policymakers in both countries, and a record of major works on both countries. Although a sociologist by training, he was interdisciplinary in his work.

Most impactful of his works was *Japan as Number One: Lessons for America*. It was a landmark in U.S.-Japan relations. In retrospect, what was remarkable about his book was that at a time when Americans were angry that Japan was not playing by our rules of free-market capitalism, he sowed doubts about the universalism of the American path to modernity and understood that there are multiple cultural paths to modernity.

Together with his instinct for the big questions, he was tireless in his research and had a passion for detail. One small experience I had with Ezra perhaps illustrates this passion. When his biography of Deng Xiaoping (his most enduring work) was published, he came to the University of Washington to give a talk on the book. Just before his afternoon lecture, we had lunch together in the faculty club. As he writes in the preface to his biography, he never had the opportunity to meet Deng. When I mentioned that I had accompanied Senator Henry "Scoop" Jackson to China in 1979 and 1983 when the senator was the special guest of Deng and that I had sat in and kept notes on their lengthy discussions about the Sino-Soviet split and Cold War politics, Ezra wanted to hear all my impressions of Deng and peppered me with questions. How ironic, I thought afterward. Here was Ezra asking me about Deng, but it was typical of him—curious, intent on detail, and a good listener.

A notable aspect of Ezra's life was his interest in, and mentorship of, young scholars. Not only to young scholars but to others like myself, Ezra was a great encourager. He was so helpful to me over the years that I declared him to be "my patron saint." He responded that being a saint was not appropriate for him "but how about *aniki*"? So from that time on, I often referred to him in correspondence as *aniki* (elder brother).

Ezra had none of the cynicism and sarcasm so cheap in the academy. Quite the opposite. He was an optimist, a person of hope, a bridge builder. These qualities came through as a theme of his last book, *China and Japan: Facing History*, where he wrote that "As a friend of both China and Japan, I fervently hope the two countries can improve their ability to work together for their common interests." His hope was that "as a bystander sympathetic to both countries" he could help to broker mutual understanding by giving a balanced account that sees issues from the perspective of both countries. In a lengthy review of his book, I wrote, "It is a noble mission, but decidedly not an easy one." And I went on to discuss the dangers posed by the growing grassroots nationalism in China from the perspective of the same phenomenon in prewar Japan. Not long before his ninetieth birthday he made a special trip to Seattle to participate in a dialogue with me on his book in an event sponsored by a Chinese student organization on campus. Ezra agreed that demonization of Japan by Chinese nationalism posed a growing danger but remained hopeful that the two peoples could overcome their troubled past by recognizing the periods in their history when they have cooperated and learned from each other.

Shortly before he died, Ezra sent me a copy of the extensive remarks he had just made to the Chinese Student Association, welcoming them back to Harvard in the midst of the pandemic and increasing tensions between China and the United States. He concluded that "as one who considers himself a bridge builder and who enjoys many Chinese friends, I believe your role as bridge builder will be very important in avoiding conflict and promoting our common interests. The world will benefit from those of you who build and maintain those bridges. As one who is near the end of his career I salute you."

Together with his remarkable scholarship, it is Ezra's open and hopeful character that I want to remember. I do not recall a harsh word that he had for anyone. As his son Steven said, "He had an irrepressible ability to see the good in every person and every nation, while recognizing nonetheless that many of us fall short of our ideals." He was that rare human being, utterly without guile.

T. J. Pempel

University of California, Berkeley

I had long been familiar with the name Ezra Vogel from poring over his extensive writings on Japanese society in my graduate school days. I subsequently met him at several conferences after I became an assistant professor at Cornell. Not surprisingly to anyone who knew him, he was always gracious and intellectually curious toward even the most junior scholars. However, we became much more closely acquainted when we overlapped on our separate research trips to Japan during 1975–76: I was investigating Japanese foreign economic policy, and Ezra was doing research for a planned book on Keidanren, Japan's major business and lobbying association. For several months we intersected with one another at various public events and, several times, even saw one another entering or leaving interviews in the same government department. Ezra effused his usual generosity, openly sharing the ideas and plans surrounding his project, as well as providing suggestions and guidance on mine. I quickly learned to appreciate his personal warmth, his breadth of knowledge, his extensive networks, and his ability to tease insightful information out of seemingly lockjawed Japanese officials.

We subsequently ran into one another at the 1977 Association for Asian Studies conference. After exchanging the usual pleasantries, I inquired how his book on Keidanren was progressing. I was stunned when he told me that he had decided to put that book on the back burner and to write a more synthetic overview of contemporary Japan. As a young scholar I was marinated in the conviction that scholarly research should be tightly demarcated, rigorously empirical, and dedicated to turning over unplowed ground. I tried my best to keep my reactions as polite as possible, but basically my peppering questions boiled down to why he was ready to abandon serious scholarship in favor of popular superficiality. He listened with exquisite politeness and patience, leaving me hopeful that I had won him over to my way of thinking.

I thought no more about it until I received a phone call from Aida Donald, then editor for East Asian acquisitions at Harvard University Press. She had, she told me, a manuscript by Ezra that she hoped I would evaluate as part of the rigorous scholarly review process for the press. I quickly agreed. Several days later, a hard copy of the manuscript arrived and I set to work reading and critiquing. I diligently prepared eleven pages of single-spaced commentary on my typewriter. (For those too young to remember, typewriters were primitive word processing devices that lacked a computer's "cut-and-paste" function; all corrections necessitated applying a white liquid called Snopake over any desired corrections, letting it dry, and then typing over the now obliterated material. I say this only to demonstrate the seriousness of my commitment to the review.)

My comments were consistent with my social science training and expectations. The vast majority took the form of "update statistics to include the most recent six-month period, which will show a slight reversal in the trend you present"; "a valuable point on page 41, but you must qualify the emphasis on societal consensus by acknowledging Japan's periodic outbreaks of citizen protests, not to mention the pervasiveness of factional disagreements on numerous political matters"; and "yes, crime rates are low, but the author needs at least a footnote recognizing the consequent dangers to citizen privacy." Feeling very much the good academic citizen for providing so many carefully wrought and presumably valuable suggestions, I was astonished when Aida called me about five days later to say that she had received my "very helpful review," passed it on to Ezra, and that she would be bringing the manuscript before the editorial board for its approval at the beginning of the next month. How could she, or Ezra, have had sufficient time to address my many thoughtful and diligently crafted qualifications? Had I not been clear enough on the benefits of much more fine-tuning?

About six months later, of course, the manuscript I had so nitpickingly dissected hit the world to lavish praise across a wide range of media outlets as well as record-breaking sales. It appeared with what I thought was the definitely-needing-to-be-more-nuanced title, *Japan as Number One*. If nothing else, years later, I realize that Ezra knew the value of seeing and presenting the big picture. It has taken some time, but I am hopeful that this embarrassing experience with him did its part in nudging me in that same direction.

Wakako Hironaka

Earth Charter, Japan

I first met Professor Ezra Vogel at a party held by our mutual friend, Ikuko Burns. I asked Professor Vogel what he was teaching at Harvard, and he replied that he was offering a course on contemporary Japan. Since I hadn't been back to Japan for many years, I asked him if I could audit the course. With the privilege of a professor's wife, I attended his course for the whole year. Fascinated by his lectures, I asked if I could be the translator of his work in case he wrote a book on contemporary Japan. He said that he had been planning to do that. The book was published in Japan in 1985 with the title *Japan as Number One* and became an instant bestseller! At that time, the Japanese economy was booming and the United States was still feeling the aftermath of the Vietnam War and the cultural conflicts of the 1970s.

In the preface to *Japan as Number One*, Professor Vogel warned the Japanese people that Japan might commit the sin of arrogance, quoting a lesson from Greek mythology. In fact, after the bubble economy burst in the early 1990s, Professor Vogel's warning was no doubt deeply felt by many Japanese people.

Professor Vogel did not dwell on the tremendous success of *Japan as Number One*. His next interest was how China was transformed under the leadership of Deng Xiaoping. I deeply regret that he can no longer pursue his interests in how our world is being shaped, and I hope that he will be able to watch us make wise decisions.

Ellis Krauss

University of California, San Diego

I didn't know Ez very well, but I will always remember him fondly. I first met him in 1978–79 when I was a young visiting scholar at the Japan Institute (prior to its being renamed for Edwin Reischauer, who was still Director at the time). I saw him thereafter when I would visit Harvard to give a guest lecture or at International House in Tokyo or at Association for Asian Studies annual meetings.

Of course, I knew his work in the Japan field very well. *Japan's New Middle Class* was a seminal book on the sociology of *danchi* families during Japan's very early rapid growth period. And his *Japan as Number One* presciently showed the aspects of Japanese society that produced better results than America's. I used both books in my classes for years. After the bubble broke in the early 1990s and the U.S. recovered from the 1970s and early 1980s, Americans assumed the book was wrong or outdated. It wasn't, about many things. Although Japan's vaunted bureaucracy and its economic effectiveness no longer inspires, the reputation of its police is a bit tarnished, and its political leaders' abilities highly variable, the capabilities of its social institutions remain. For example, Tokyo, the world's largest metropolitan area, is still the safest in the world, and Japan one of the safest countries. Japan, and especially Tokyo, without question has the best public transportation system in the world. During the pandemic, despite the government's slow rollout of vaccinations, Japan still had only 2 percent of the U.S.'s infections, and on a per capita basis, about 6 percent!

Despite his groundbreaking and preeminent scholarship in the Japan and China fields, what I will miss most about Ez is his character and personality, especially memories from International House—sitting in the coffee shop having breakfast with him, interrupted constantly as people he knew, Japanese, Americans, and others, came in and he jumped up to greet them as they approached his table. He greeted every single one very warmly, whether old friend or acquaintance, as if each was the most important person in the world to him. After all, at those moments they were. He always showed up to my talks at Harvard, both to learn about current research but also to show his support for scholars in the field. My wife has always recalled his infinite graciousness to her on the few occasions they met.

Everyone called him "Ez"—I never heard anyone refer to him as "Ezra," as if even using his short full name was a measure of formality and distance that was inappropriate for him. And it was. His genuinely warm and open personality made even that level of distance alien. As one walked across the lobby of the International House, there Ez would sit in conversation with one of his countless friends, either with his almost-constant smile and a twinkle in his eyes, or with his ample brow furrowed and eyebrows raised in curiosity at learning something new. He was as infinitely curious as he was a warm and modest person. But I don't think in conversation with me or with others I ever once saw him frown. No wonder he was as loved as a person as much as he was respected for his stature as a scholar.

For me there will always be empty chairs where Ez once sat in the International House coffee shop and lobby, no matter who occupies them now. He will be greatly missed as a scholar and as a human being.

Andrew Walder

Stanford University

Ezra and I were colleagues in Harvard's Department of Sociology all too briefly, from 1987 to 1995, but my personal history with him began long before that and deepened in the many years afterward. After I joined Harvard's faculty, I learned firsthand that beneath the relaxed and self-effacing exterior was an intensely hardworking and disciplined individual, constantly striving to keep up his language ability, finish a new project, and keep in shape. My first inkling of this was one early Saturday morning after a major blizzard around 1991. As I braved the deserted and snowbound streets of Cambridge in sub-zero weather to work in my office at William James Hall, I noticed in the near distance a solitary figure trudging through the snowdrift-bound streets, *jogging*! Just as I was thinking to myself "what kind of fool jogs on a morning like this?" I saw that it was Ezra, making the turn from Kirkland Street to his home around the corner.

Despite his unusually strong drive to learn and succeed, Ezra never seemed distracted, hurried, or preoccupied. He was able to maintain a relaxed demeanor no matter what the situation, and when you spoke with him you always seemed to have his full attention. He remained incredibly active and productive after his "retirement" in 2000. He kept up a hectic travel schedule to Asia well into his eighties, and when I saw him on several of his recent trips to Beijing he was always eager to arrange a dinner and never seemed to suffer from jet lag. He was a real celebrity in East Asia, and I had many occasions to observe massive audiences that would turn out for his public lectures. Not long ago, I was walking to the Shaoyuan complex on Peking University's campus one afternoon and saw a long line of people wrapped around the corner from the School of International Affairs, waiting to enter the building. As I came closer, I saw a poster for that day's lecture by Ezra about his new book, *Deng Xiaoping and the Transformation of China*, which was rapidly becoming a bestseller in China. He filled their huge auditorium.

Ezra also spent time recently as a distinguished visiting scholar at the Stanford Center at Peking University, and we were fortunate to have regular conversations and meals together. He was working on a new book about Hu Yaobang, a topic that interested me greatly, promising to be a major contribution along the lines of his book on Deng. Ezra gave a lecture about his recently completed book on the history of Sino-Japanese relations, a broad overview that spanned many centuries. A capacity crowd filled the atrium of the Center. What I remember most clearly about that lecture was that Ezra, well into his eighties, gave a polished and cogent lecture for close to one hour, covering five hundred years of history, *completely without notes*.

Ezra was truly one of a kind. I can't imagine that anyone of my generation will match the scope and breadth of his knowledge and influence, or the relaxed intensity with which he pursued his curiosity about China and Japan.

Jean Oi

Stanford University

Ezra Vogel was a remarkable person and scholar who made his mark across continents in so many ways. I first met Ezra in the early 1980s as one of the lucky young scholars invited for a grand day with Charlotte and Ezra on a junk that John Dolfin had rented for those of us at the Universities Service Centre in Hong Kong—an institution that Ezra always supported. Memories of that day have stayed with me—not only for how beautiful and fun it was, but also for the fact that the host was someone whose work on Japan as well as China I had been reading since I was an undergraduate. Here was an intellectual legend extending a welcome to the next generation of China scholars.

When I was an associate professor in the Department of Government at Harvard, students would talk about how much they appreciated Ezra's mentorship and interest in their programs. While there are many great memories, here I want to highlight those from the period after I moved to Stanford, after Ezra supposedly had "retired." It was then that I saw firsthand the intellectual curiosity and energy that epitomized Ezra Vogel at work—beyond the Ezra who would run up beside your car to say hi during his daily runs, even in the slush during the freezing Cambridge winters. Ezra is my role model of what scholars can do in "retirement"—stay driven, productive, and as intellectually curious as ever.

In 2012 Stanford established its Stanford Center at Peking University (SCPKU) where, as faculty director, I would spend at least one quarter of each year. It was during those stints that I would regularly see Ezra in Beijing—this was when he was working on his China-Japan book, and beginning his work on Hu Yaobang—yes, the typical slower-paced life of retirees! It also was then that I decided that Ezra must have had some secret potion that allowed someone in his eighties not to have jet lag. Often, he would get off a transpacific flight, go straight to deliver a lecture, and then have stimulating conversations with colleagues and friends afterward. It was in the fall of 2015 when Ezra was a Mingde Visiting Scholar at SCPKU that I saw how much of a rock star he was in China. His lecture on China-Japan relations packed SCPKU with over 200 people, standing room only. Ezra, with no notes, delivered cogent remarks that kept listeners in rapture, answering questions with good grace and humor from an audience that included many high-profile Chinese intellectuals, faculty from around the city, as well as students from SCPKU, Tsinghua, and other universities.

These times, which began in 2015 when Ezra and Charlotte started to visit SCPKU regularly, are the source of many wonderful memories and more insights into Ezra, the unstoppable dynamo. One of the last times was when Ezra developed a foot problem and needed a cane (sometimes). I began to worry about his getting around, especially as it got icy, but it did not stop Ezra from doing his thing in China—he was by then heavily into his work on Hu Yaobang. He would be in the office every day unless he had interviews elsewhere. More amazing but typical is the following: That same fall SCPKU hosted a retirement conference for Marty Whyte, and Ezra and Charlotte were attending. Only later did we learn that during that summer, Ezra had undergone emergency surgery in Sichuan to fix a problem in his internal plumbing. The thought of undergoing major surgery in an unfamiliar hospital in distant Sichuan seems terrifying (even if you are not eighty-five!). But Ezra, being Ezra, took the surgery in stride, arriving in Beijing on schedule and raring to go.

It was during those visits that I got to see Ezra at work up close, when he generously invited Andy Walder and me to an interview session he was conducting with someone close to Hu Yaobang. I couldn't help myself and intervened with my own questions more than once. Ezra was very accommodating, and we made a pretty good tag team.

Over the next few years, up until the pandemic, he continued to be a frequent visitor. Even during COVID he would periodically write me to ask when SCPKU would reopen so that he and Charlotte could return. I have already mentioned how widely admired Ezra was by scholars and students, but I want to add that he also made a lasting impression on the staff at SCPKU, who remember him for his refined style, humble attitude, burning curiosity about Chinese affairs, and conscientious work ethic. After learning of his death, Peggy Zou, SCPKU Program and Administrative Coordinator, wrote a moving remembrance of Ezra Vogel that was posted on WeChat and viewed by many. Everyone at SCPKU, myself included, had so looked forward to working with him again during his planned visit in 2021.

COVID stopped us all, including postponing a talk that Ezra was scheduled to give at Stanford for the China Program right as the pandemic hit in the spring of 2020. The Zoom program that we rescheduled for the fall of 2020 may have been one of the last that he did. Up until the end Ezra was extremely concerned about the direction of U.S.-China relations, including about the implications and innuendos of some of the reports that were being issued about China. He spoke to our Stanford China and Japan Programs on the challenges to the United States posed by Japan in the 1980s and by China today. If times had been normal, we would have followed with dinner and continued discussion. But given that the event had to be via Zoom, very much in Ezra style, Ezra asked that I schedule a follow-up call so that he could hear more about our views on U.S.-China relations. I feel very fortunate to have had that extra time with Ezra and was honored to have been part of his virtual ninetieth birthday gathering in July 2020.

William McCahill

National Bureau of Asian Research

As a 1970s graduate student in the Sanskrit Department, I had often heard Ezra Vogel invoked among the pantheon of Harvard Asia scholars—an exalted polymath and reputedly genial demigod.

Later, upon joining the Foreign Service and being posted to China, I soon found numerous colleagues, journalists, and business people working in Asia whom Ezra had mentored and inspired, and who spoke of him with fond reverence.

But it was not until the 1990s, when Ezra was the National Intelligence Officer (NIO) for East Asia and I was Deputy Chief of Mission in the Beijing Embassy, that he and I met. We had several and, for me, illuminating conversations about contemporary Chinese politics before Ezra left his NIO post and returned to Cambridge to resume teaching and writing.

Several years later, after I had left the Foreign Service and started a business career in Beijing, Ezra and I became friends. Somehow—I can't remember quite how—Ezra came to lodge with me in my Beijing flat while he was writing his massive biography of Deng Xiaoping. For weeks at a time Ezra was my houseguest, making his Beijing base in my Spartan spare room with its single bed and tiny writing table.

His rhythm of research was to work several months in Cambridge, reading documents and plotting his book, then come to Beijing armed with questions to ask Deng's family members, Deng's surviving colleagues, their relatives, academics, and retired officials—anyone whom Ezra thought could shed light on Deng's character and goals and on the political context in which Deng operated. So, this is how scholars work, I thought.

Ezra began his Beijing workdays in my kitchen. While I was brewing coffee, he would pour yogurt and muesli into two bowls, then carefully slice a banana into each bowl. We'd then sit at my small kitchen table, munching the muesli and chewing over what Ezra had learned from his interviews the day before. What the French call "décanter les choses."

He sought my advice: "Should I have put this question to so-and-so another way? Is there anyone else I should ask about this? Do you remember how Deng's successors interpreted his guidance on such-and such?" Some mornings our talk ventured into "where is China headed, what might change things, how should the U.S. deal with this complex and confounding country and its leaders?"

I answered as best I could but could never quite get over my pinch-me astonishment: this is the Legendary Professor Vogel asking me, a superannuated diplomat who hadn't finished his Sanskrit PhD and had learned Chinese only in government language schools, about the Big Issues in contemporary China!

Yet here was Ezra at my breakfast table, just as genial as his reputation had foretold, chatting with me as his equal, genuinely curious to hear my thoughts, and keen to have me critique his. No wonder his "alumni association" loved and respected him as they did.

Breakfast over, Ezra would set off for his day of interviews, often far across Beijing and over long meals and much tea. A few times he asked me to accompany him on these expeditions, to meet Chinese intellectuals I would never have otherwise encountered. By nine or ten o'clock in the evening Ezra would have returned to the flat, some nights snagging a beer from the fridge before heading to his room to write up his day's findings, drafting with yellow plastic mechanical pencils until their leads and erasers wore out.

Alas, those magic moments came to an end when I moved to an even smaller flat, and Ezra lodged elsewhere on his later visits to Beijing. But we always met during his stays in the city; and when business took me to Boston, Ezra often invited me to coffee in his Sumner Road home. No matter the place, our conversations continued in the same mode as those

Beijing breakfasts: Ezra ever the keen, generous, and respectful listener, all topics fair game, him offering the occasional light touch of pastoral counseling.

The last time I saw Ezra was in the summer of 2015, and by then I was working in a Hong Kong bank. Ezra was leading two dozen of his family members on a grand tour across China, to culminate in a visit to Deng's ancestral home in Sichuan. He invited my wife and me to the group's "tour launch dinner" in a Kowloon hotel.

Arriving at the hotel, we found three generations of the extended Vogel family gathered around a huge banquet table, with Ezra presiding and the place of honor reserved for me. As the first dishes arrived, it became clear that Ezra had convened nothing less than a family seminar. He spoke of Hong Kong's unique freedoms and how Beijing had promised to respect those until 2047. To my surprise, Ezra asked me to speak. Having had business experiences and having lived in Hong Kong for several years and having watched those freedoms slowly eroding, I had become quite cynical about the Chinese regime and took gentle issue with what he had said. Never uttering a riposte, Ezra smiled kindly and declared the seminar adjourned. I've long suspected he knew what I would say and wanted his family to hear that alternative view.

After bidding Ezra and Charlotte good night, my wife and I walked to the subway to return to our flat on Hong Kong Island. Using Ezra's Chinese name, my wife said, "Fu Gaoyi has really changed."

But Ezra had not changed. He was still that kind, generous, infinitely curious, and optimistic soul who had been slicing bananas into our muesli bowls fifteen years before. For all that our views of China might have come to differ, that's how I remember Ezra Vogel.

Joshua Fogel

York University

I first met Ezra in 1974, but we only got to know each other in the 1980s when the entrances to our offices in the Fairbank Center were literally inches apart. Although twenty years my senior, he always treated me as an equal, which I have to say I treasured at a time when junior faculty at

Harvard were seen as only slightly more (or less) elevated than graduate students. And, after I left Harvard in the late 1980s, whenever we would bump into one another at the annual Association for Asian Studies (AAS) meetings, he would insist on having lunch or coffee or just a chat.

The bond was forged over our shared dual interest in China and Japan—despite the obvious disciplinary differences and overall approach to scholarship. Ezra told me once that he went back and forth: first a book on Japan, then one on China, and so on, until *China and Japan: Facing History*, in which he not only dealt with both countries but approached the topic over the longue durée, a topic much closer to my heart. More on that below.

About a dozen years ago, we both attended a China-Japan conference in Shanghai, and while the conference itself was not terribly memorable, it was wonderful to be able to spend some quality time with Ezra. As it turned out, our flights back to North America were on the same afternoon, mine a few hours before his, so he insisted we take a cab together to the airport. The cab ride was well over an hour, and then we had another two or three hours at the airport before it was time for me to board. I spent well over 90 percent of that time listening to Ezra regale me with stories about Deng Xiaoping and how much he admired the man, stories mostly elicited from discussions with Chinese at levels of government and society that I could only imagine or read about in others' work. Not only were these stories fascinating in and of themselves, but I was overwhelmed (in a positive way) by the almost joyous exuberance of this septuagenarian for the topic of his research, a model for me as I have now joined that age cadre. I should add that it was going to take considerable effort to get me to think positively about Deng, and Ezra was well aware that much of the Anglophone world was not as admiring of the late Chinese leader as he was, primarily, of course, because of the events of June 4, 1989. He later told me that the translation of his Deng book was a major bestseller in China, and that he was donating all of his PRC royalties to his alma mater, Ohio Wesleyan University.

In March 2018 at the AAS meeting, I bumped into Ezra as we always did, but this time it was different. He said he was planning the book that would become *China and Japan: Facing History*, and he asked if I would read and critique draft chapters as he completed them. He was less secure about history—and this work started back in antiquity—and sought my guidance. I of course said yes immediately. About an hour later, I ran into Charlotte Ikels, Ezra's wife, who stopped me and asked if I might have lost my mind over the last hour or so. "Do you know how long this book is going to be?" she asked, or words to that effect. Indeed, soon, meaty chapters started appearing in my email box. He read everything I suggested, added or addressed every comment I made, and was as gracious as always about it. It all made me feel as though I was in some way responsible for his being able to complete this volume, which was as ridiculous as it was wonderful.

We are all unique—there was only one Ezra.

Stephen R. MacKinnon

Arizona State University

I began working regularly with Ezra about twenty years ago. In the 1990s he was increasingly concerned about the souring of China-Japan relations. A particularly painful moment took place in the late 1990s at a wildly emotional meeting that we both attended in San Francisco; it was headlined by Iris Chang, with specially invited liberal Japanese intellectuals, friends of Ezra's. The Japanese basically were insulted, muzzled, and sent home.

Because we were working on the history of the China-Japan War, in the year 2000 Ezra enlisted Diana Lary, Hans Van de Ven, and me in a grand project. His idea was to invite senior Japanese and Chinese scholars of the war to come together with a smattering of Western scholars for an intense three days of papers and discussion of shared history. He wanted our help in identifying the right participants on the Chinese side. Ezra waved a magic wand and came up with the money to support the conferences. Most importantly, he funded simultaneous translators—the best in the business. They played a crucial role in facilitating open dialogue between the Chinese and Japanese scholars.

In the end there were five conferences, in Cambridge, Hawaii, Hakone, Taipei, and Chongqing. The intent was to map out a new more objective history of the war—from both sides. As Diana Lary has noted, the results were published in Japanese, Chinese, and English language volumes. Ezra's hope was that the bringing together of senior scholars for frank exchanges would somehow trickle down and soften the bitter divide between the two intellectual communities. The key organizer on the Chinese side was Yang Tianshi of the Chinese Academy of Social Sciences (Taiwan-based scholars also played important roles), and on the Japanese side, Prof. Yamada Tatsuo of Keio University. Both were approximately Ezra's generation and widely respected scholar/leaders.

I like to think that the resulting books and conferences had an impact at least in the scholarly realm. The edited Stanford volume on military history won a major prize. But the trickle down into better relations and feelings between China and Japan that Ezra hoped for has been elusive. Before the Xi Jinping era, there was a joint effort at textbook writing by Chinese, Japanese, and Korean scholars. And of course Ezra made a final effort in his last published work—a sweeping history of China-Japan relations (2019).

At the same time I observed firsthand another dimension of Ezra's turn to history—the writing of biography for a popular international audience. For much of 2006 we lived a mile or so away from Ezra and Charlotte in Beijing while he was in the midst of interviewing and beginning to draft the enormously successful biography of Deng Xiaoping (2011). Ezra's work ethic as we all know was legendary. At the time of his death he was in the middle of writing a definitive biography of Hu Yaobang—the quixotic reform leader of the 1980s—whose death initiated the events that led to June 4, 1989. Rumor has it that he had drafted two chapters.

One of my last prolonged interactions with Ezra came in Shanghai during the fall of 2017. We attended a small conference commemorating the 1917 Russian Revolution. It involved leading historians like Shen Zhihua and others and was organized by Chinese Russian experts, like Ezra admirer Yu Bin. One evening in a large room of the privately owned Jifeng Bookstore 季风书园, located underground beneath the Shanghai Municipal Library subway stop, Ezra held forth in Chinese to a packed audience of middle-aged intellectuals. The topic was Japan, but at the end a question was raised about his work on Hu Yaobang. As Ezra spoke, the entire audience rose to give him (and Hu) extended applause. It was an emotional and moving moment that lasted quite some time. Shortly thereafter the government forced the closure of this independent bookstore.

With the biographies and the work on the China-Japan War, Ezra was aiming at a Chinese audience, not just a Western one. He was adamant that his and our work immediately be translated into Chinese and Japanese. The outpouring around the world on WeChat and elsewhere on the internet in the weeks after his death demonstrate the sweep of his Chinese and Japanese following.

I was honored and learned so much as a participant in Ezra's final turn to history. Ezra, may you rest in peace.

Diana Lary

University of British Columbia

Ezra Vogel was a man of great charm and social grace. It was my special privilege to know him. I first met him at a diplomatic dinner in Washington when he was working at the National Intelligence Council. He was completely at home in a political world, his smile, his wit, and his intelligence breaking down the stiffness of government people. Later I saw him equally at home in a multi-ethnic academic world, at a series of trilingual (English, Chinese, Japanese) conferences that he initiated.

My fondest memory of Ezra was at one of these conferences, in Chongqing in 2009. The memory combines his humor, his urbanity, and his acute perception. Chongqing in the late summer is brutally hot, so our hosts arranged for us to see the sights of the city in the relative coolness of the late evening. We went across the river to the south bank and were dropped off at the bottom of a steep flight of steps that ascended into the darkness, apparently ending at a viewing platform. I took one look at the steps and sank down onto a chair, saying apologetically that I was too old (in my sixties) to make the climb. Gallant Ezra (in his seventies) offered to keep me company. We sat in the hot darkness—it was still well over ninety—our view of Chongqing limited, but our conversation wonderful. It ranged from China-Japan relations, to Chinese society, to Barack Obama and racial issues, to the internecine politics at Harvard, to his youthful experience in his father's store. I listened spellbound, like a country cousin, to Ezra's lucid observations and his assessments of issues, people, and tricky situations (such as the recent resignation of the

Harvard president). Some of his comments made me, as Edward Lear put it, "gasp and stretch my eyes." Two things stood out: Ezra's sense of humor, occasionally wicked, and his compassionate understanding of human frailty. When the rest of our crowd straggled down from the viewing platform, hot and grumpy, I felt I had spent one of the most stimulating evenings of my life.

Let me say a little more about the conferences. They were initiated by Ezra to try and get a common understanding among Chinese, Western, and Japanese scholars, of the war that ravaged Asia in the 1930s and 1940s. Through scrupulous academic truth-telling, Ezra wanted to reconcile the two countries, China and Japan, that he understood so well. He recruited Yang Tianshi, Yamada Tatsuo, Stephen MacKinnon, Hans van de Ven, and me to find scholars to write papers, to be published in edited volumes in each language. This was a huge undertaking. For Ezra it meant fundraising and putting in place a logistical structure, with the help of the incredibly efficient Holly Angell. We had conferences in Cambridge, Hakone, Maui, Taipei, and Chongqing—each attended by dozens, even hundreds, of scholars. Great numbers of papers were presented, with simultaneous translation; Ezra was almost always the one person who spoke all three languages fluently.

The early prospects of reaching Ezra's goal were encouraging. There was goodwill and a belief that academics could play a significant role in reconciliation by presenting an accurate narrative of the war. Yang Tianshi read his poem at the end of the first conference in 2002.

Once we confronted each other in hostility
Now we sit together and discuss our scholarly work
Scholarly battles are so much better that military ones
Like the debates at Goose Lake, we seek truth through discussion.

The elegant poem, with an appropriate reference to Zhu Xi (1130–1200), was a tribute to Ezra for bringing us together.

As the years wore on the political landscape changed. Research on the war was politicized. Even the name of the war was problematic: for Chinese it remains the Resistance War; for Japanese it is the Second Sino-Japanese War; for Europeans, Australians, and Canadians it is the Second World War (starting in 1939); for Americans it is the Second World

War (starting with Pearl Harbor). The Pacific War is an agreed-upon term, but it starts in 1941, a decade after Japan's conflict with China started.

We did not achieve a common understanding. The war is still a painful subject. Interpretations shift, and anniversaries are commemorated—or not. All the scholars who participated felt a deep debt of gratitude to Ezra for organizing a gigantic scholarly project that would have been impossible without his status in the study of both China and Japan and his unrivalled contacts. Our gratitude was tinged with regret that the time was not right to fulfill his vision.

Paula S. Harrell

Georgetown University

Ezra Vogel was exceptional among America's Asia specialists. Uniquely knowledgeable about both China and Japan, he was in his single person the worthy successor to both John Fairbank and Edwin Reischauer at Harvard. His two bestsellers, *Japan as Number One* and *Deng Xiaoping and the Transformation of China*, made him a celebrity, but he published countless other books, articles, and conference papers that in the Fairbank-Reischauer tradition sought to broaden American understanding of the East Asian experience. Highly respected for his scholarship and teaching, Ezra Vogel was more than the usual academic; he was a true public intellectual. He spoke at think tanks and universities in new media formats and advised policymakers, American, Chinese, and Japanese. And, years into his retirement, after more than half a century studying China and Japan, he turned his deep knowledge and energies to writing their joint history, hopeful that providing readers in both countries with a balanced view of their long relationship would lead to greater understanding between them.

I had known Ezra Vogel by reputation for many decades, ever impressed by his enormous scholarly output. But we met in person only in 2015 when we began a wonderful, lively conversation, mostly by email, around our mutual interest in China-Japan relations. Ezra was at the time launching the book project that ultimately became his final publication, *China and Japan: Facing History* (2019). As our emails piled up, so too did my appreciation not only of his expansive scholarship, but of his personal qualities—his unassuming manner, kindness, gentle humor—that endeared him to colleagues and former students who had known him for a lifetime. We became great friends.

Ezra took on big, unexplored topics and worked tirelessly, honestly, and collegially to research them. His project to explain 1,500 years of China-Japan relations in a single volume, as he set out to do in *Facing History*, was a singular enterprise. It required reading hundreds of sources in Chinese, Japanese, and Western languages, consulting dozens of people working on different parts of the same story, then writing, re-organizing, and re-writing again and again. Ezra managed all of this remarkably. He was fluent in both Chinese and Japanese, equipped not only to read fluidly, but to conduct interviews and give lectures in either language. He had an amazing ability to absorb huge amounts of material, then talk about it in detail before large audiences without notes. In *Facing History*, as in all of his work, he sought to get as close as possible to the truth of the matter at hand through open-minded, evidence-based research, leaving no stone unturned. Understanding of individuals' lived experience took precedence over demonstrating grand theories. Ezra was a generous listener, and exceedingly generous as well in giving credit to others for their insights and suggestions.

Along with a busy schedule of online talks about *Facing History*, Ezra at ninety had resumed work on a project long on the drawing board: writing a biography of Hu Yaobang, the liberal-minded, pro–Japan Party leader whose death in April 1989 triggered the protests leading to the Tiananmen crackdown two months later. This was another big topic that offered the opportunity to reach a new understanding of China's "opening to the outside world" and the supportive roles of Japan and the U.S. in the process. Yet "understanding" and "closer ties" were not the operative words in 2020. A much-anticipated state visit by President Xi Jinping to Japan, set for April 2020 amid hopes for improved China-Japan relations, had to be postponed because of the coronavirus pandemic. U.S. China policy, already hardening, seemed to be careening toward unrelenting confrontation on all fronts. Ezra, longtime architect of engagement, spoke with some sadness as he addressed Harvard's Chinese Students Association in September. But he ended on a hopeful note: "As one who is near the end of his career, I salute you as you are beginning your career. I pay my respects to those of you who will help maintain constructive relations between our two countries. I wish you a good and constructive time at Harvard and a long life as bridge builders between our two nations." May those of us so admiring of Ezra Vogel's lifetime contributions carry on our own bridge-building work in the years to come.

Chunli Li

Aichi University

Ezra was a master of napping. He could slip off into a nap on the stage of a conference or seminar, on the train, or anywhere, and then rouse himself later into immediate awareness.

I still remember clearly the first time I met Ezra in 1996. I was at an international symposium on the U.S., China, and Japan at the International House of Japan in Tokyo, and Ezra had left the room for a while after lunch. When he returned to the venue, he told us with a little embarrassment, "I was actually just taking a nap."

The memory still remains with me that the participants at the venue burst out laughing at his honesty. Later, by chance, I stayed at the Fairbank Center for Chinese Studies at Harvard University as a visiting scholar from 2004 to 2005 and at the Asia Center as a fellow from 2018 to 2019, with my exchanges with him deepening further over each of those one-year periods. They also afforded me more opportunities to witness Ezra napping.

I became interested in Japan after reading Ezra's famous book, *Japan as Number One*. After studying in Japan, I came to teach at Aichi University. During my stay at Harvard, I participated in various events organized by Ezra and was even invited to his home for lively discussions. He was very pleased when I told him that Professor John King Fairbank had once been invited to Aichi University to give a lecture.

In May 2009, I was invited to speak at a Fellows Seminar organized by the Asia Center at Harvard University on the topic of "The Social Cost of Automobiles and Environment Policies in Asia: A Comparative Study on China and Japan." Ezra served as the chair, and Professor Andrew Gordon, acting director of the Harvard-Yenching Institute, and Professor

Michael McElroy, chair of the Harvard-China Project, served as discussants. The professors' stimulating comments and lively discussions proved to be very useful for my research.

In November 2019, when Ezra visited Hong Kong and Japan to coincide with the publication of the Chinese and Japanese editions of his last book, *China and Japan: Facing History*, he gave a lecture at the "Open Lecture on China" organized by Aichi University in Nagoya. About 1,000 people attended this lecture, and since there were many more applicants, we had no choice but to draw lots to grant admission. At the end of the session, I asked Ezra what message he would like to give to the students of Aichi University. This is what he said:

> As one of my mentors in graduate school told me, and I tell my students, the most important part of studying sociology is making friends. It takes a lot of effort and work to understand your friend's point of view, but this is how we are able to learn so much. Friends can teach you essential things that will lead you to a deeper understanding of their society.

Oddly enough, this was Ezra's last lecture in Japan. In commemoration of this event and in order to preserve a record of it, we decided to publish a book on the presentation entitled *The Last Lecture: Ezra Vogel on China and Japan* (Ezra F. Vogel and Chunli Li; published by ARM Publishing House in Japan) in August 2021 as a special commemorative publication of the Aichi University International Center for Chinese Studies.

In his talk at Aichi University, after sharing his message to the young students, Ezra reflected on his own journey:

> I remain happy that I made so many Japanese friends when I was young. I still keep in touch with them; in fact, the friend that I will be meeting tomorrow is someone I have known since 1959. I think there is no better way to understand a country than through friends, because you can have fun while deepening your understanding.
>
> *The Last Lecture: Ezra Vogel on China and Japan*

Ezra cherished his friends throughout his ninety years of life. There is no doubt that, even in heaven, he is still surrounded by many friends, happily chatting.

Li Shengping

Beijing, China

My friendship with Ezra Vogel started in 2009, when he was writing *Deng Xiaoping and the Transformation of China* (2011). He interviewed me in Beijing to talk about Hu Yaobang during the Reform and Opening Period and later, in the Deng Xiaoping book, he quoted the two books that I had compiled: *Materials for a Chronological Record of Hu Yaobang's Life* (2005) and *Chronicle of Hu Yaobang's Thoughts* (2007).

In April 2013 I was invited to participate in a forum in China on *Deng Xiaoping and the Transformation of China*, with Professor Vogel also present. I said that Professor Vogel's book was a biography of a great Chinese man written by a very serious foreign scholar, and it was very meaningful. It was significant that Professor Vogel's book was published in China at a time of debates about important historical issues. I also said that as a Hu Yaobang scholar, I saw inadequacies in its presentation of some historical facts; and of course, I also had some different opinions with regard to specific historical facts and would like to communicate further with Professor Vogel in the future.

At the forum, Professor Vogel listened with sincerity and modesty to the scholars' discussions and took the criticisms from those who held sharp views without being offended in the slightest. After the meeting when I talked with him, he said that he would begin studying Hu from then on and would like to write a biography of Hu, because that was the wish of most Chinese scholars, officials, and economists he had met. We talked about how *Deng Xiaoping and the Transformation of China* was volume 1 of the historical scroll of China's reform and opening, and his biography of Hu would be its sequel. In other words, these would be volumes 1 and 2, respectively, of a monumental work. Thus began the inseparable bond between Professor Vogel and me.

In October 2016 I came to the Fairbank Center for several months as a visiting scholar. During that time, Professor Vogel and I met dozens of times to share information and ideas about Hu Yaobang's life and thought. At one academic salon, when I gave a talk on the ideological heritage of Hu, Professor Vogel acted as the commentator on my speech, which made the salon much more interesting.

In our many years of interactions, I could sense the deepening of Professor Vogel's understanding of Hu's life and thought. Professor Vogel spoke of the historical documents formulated under Hu with great familiarity. He commented that Hu Yaobang was the Secretary General of the Chinese Communist Party at the Third Plenum of the 11th Central Committee in 1978 and led the drafting of the famous Communique, which clearly stated a political course that would be "centered around economic development." The five annual rural "#1 policy documents" Hu pushed for were important documents guiding rural reforms in the 1980s, and Professor Vogel believed that these documents directed and promoted the historical transformation of China's vast countryside and were important thought resources for China's market reforms. The several documents on Special Economic Zones (SEZs) laid the foundation for the theories and policies for the implementation and development of SEZs, and Professor Vogel, based on knowledge gained from writing about the economic takeoff of Guangdong in earlier years, realized the role Hu played in supporting SEZs.

During my time at Harvard, Professor Vogel and I had many discussions about the relationship between Hu and China's economic reforms. We counted the unique and tremendous contributions Hu made in rural reforms, in the household production contract system, in making urban self-employment honorable, in supporting specialized rural production/trade households to develop into private businesses, and in the creation and development of SEZs. Previous books, such as Ronald Coase and Ning Wang's *How China Became Capitalist* (2012), had argued that China's reforms were much more successful than those carried out in Russia and Eastern Europe because China's reforms centered on freeing up market-based enterprises and entrepreneurship, not rapidly privatizing the state planned economy, but these works were missing the story of who was the leader behind this approach. And with all due credit to Deng Xiaoping as the overall architect of China's transformation, the leader in formulating these specific market-oriented policies was Hu Yaobang.

A clear description of Hu's pushing for, and contributions to, the creation and development of reforms such as the household production contract system in rural China, urban self-employment, township and village enterprises (TVEs), and SEZs would have been one important and refreshing part of Professor Vogel's biography of Hu Yaobang. In January 2020 Ezra Vogel visited Beijing again to attend a conference, and while there he outlined his plans to complete the research and writing for his biography of Hu Yaobang. He said he intended to return to China in July or August for further research. Who would have thought that the pandemic situations in both China and the United States would disrupt his plans? And then, just when I thought it was time for Prof. Vogel to start writing his book, came the terrible news of his death in December 2020!

A wise man has departed from us in the blink of an eye, and we are forever separated from him. But Professor Vogel's hearty laughter and bright smile, his letters in which he called himself "Old Vogel," and his words and signatures on the great books he gifted to me as their author, will remain in my heart forever and become long-cherished memories. Professor Vogel has left us, but his spiritual heritage, his kind friendship to the Chinese people, as well as his concerns for the progress of Chinese society live on. May his unfinished biography of Hu Yaobang continue to be completed.

Jundai Liu

University of Michigan

I got to know Professor Ezra Vogel when I was a graduate student in the Department of Sociology at Harvard, after he had retired from teaching. From November 2018 to August 2019, I worked as Ezra's research assistant on his latest project, the planned biography of Hu Yaobang. As I remember him now, it is as if I am again trekking up the quiet street in Cambridge: A thin layer of snow covers the ground, I ring the doorbell and Ezra appears, always with the warmest welcome.

We met from 5 to 6:30 on most Tuesdays and corresponded during the rest of the week. A winding staircase led into the basement, where books covered entire walls. Ezra worked in the basement, and we sat with heated blankets on our laps to keep warm—something Ezra said he picked up from his days in Japan. Later into the winter, when the cold became even more unforgiving under the misleadingly clear New England sky, Ezra's workstation got "upgraded" into the living room— and onto a foldable picnic table.

The table was almost bare, save for a calendar, a notebook, Ezra's yellow pencil, and whatever documents and books we were reading that week. Two folding chairs stood in front of it, and as I settled in, Ezra made us tea—a little water, an infuser packed with leaves, always strong. On occasion, we read a piece of a document together. But most often when we met, we reported to each other what we had read or found during the week. Afterward we posed questions to each other, asked for clarifications and elaborations, and usually found ourselves with more unresolved puzzles than when we sat down. These questions became the map that guided our individual research for the following week.

Ezra often said that his PhD was in Social Relations under Talcott Parsons, rather than in Sociology. To him, the Parsonian AGIL paradigm was important—politics, economy, cultural traditions, and social structure should be considered together. In our conversations, Ezra emphasized a holistic grasp of historical events and social structure as his approach. The questions he raised were frequently centered on people and relations, driven by an abiding and compassionate interest in the personhoods within the structure. Ezra used to say that for him, a path to understanding historical turning points and decisions was through disentangling the relations among individuals. He prized interviews and conversations alongside written records.

Deep into our discussions, language became a stream flowing over tiny round pebbles. Ezra reminisced, recalling episodes from his life or people he knew. His bellows of laughter filled the room. The air buzzed with energy as Ezra told me stories from his book writing—and how he wrote his books. "Why do you write your book so slowly?" he once asked me, with a twinkle in his eyes, when we took a break from poring over the documents. He encouragingly suggested always having a clear vision of the main arguments, the big idea, and each chapter in one paragraph—a view of the central purpose and the big story, before going into the details. "我没有教过你，这就是我教你啦。" (I have not taught you before, so this is me training you.) He smiled, with that broad and warm smile that was Ezra.

Ezra cared about big stories but also about something more and closer to home. He talked often about the small Ohio town that he grew up in and his high school drama teacher having an enduring impact on him. Over the years, Ezra kept in touch with his high school friends and wanted them to enjoy what he wrote.

I remember Ezra also in a constellation of details—his herringbone newsboy cap in winter, how much he loved chocolate, the way he twisted his ring while talking. Always at 6:30, with a long "hao la" (好啦 [alrighty]) that concluded our meeting, Ezra got ready for dinner with Charlotte.

For all my meetings with Ezra, it was Charlotte who opened her home. Sometimes Charlotte and I would exchange a few words—about her research and reading, Charlotte pointing me to a reference for my work. In Cantonese, Charlotte Ikels, an anthropologist of Guangdong, called out "sihk faahn la" (食饭啦 [time for dinner]).

For work, there was always a next day, and a next week.

In our last email from November 2020, Ezra said he had to finish up a few speeches, but he was eager to return to his latest project in a few weeks. These few weeks, perhaps, have become "the road not taken."

Ezra was a fan of the poet Robert Frost.

FIVE

In the Classroom

Victor Nee

Cornell University

I n the fall of 1967, I arrived in Cambridge from southern California
to study modern China, while continuing my opposition to Lyndon
Johnson's escalation of the Vietnam War. I met Ezra at the opening
meeting for new students and was immediately struck by his casual
style and approachable smile. Ezra was sympathetic with the anti-war
zeitgeist of the time and shared the concerns of graduate students and
young faculty who formed the Committee of Concerned Asian Scholars. Later, after my first year of graduate study, Ezra recruited me to the
Sociology doctoral program to be part of a small cohort of graduate
students who would join him in the sociological study of China. He
encouraged me to transfer to the field of sociology, emphasizing its openness to new ideas.

Serving as teaching assistant for Ezra's course on Contemporary
Chinese Society was an enjoyable training in the art and craft of
teaching. Ezra projected his personable self, leaning forward as he
lectured with ease. He dissected in detail, and seemingly without notes,
the social organization of the mainland, with an eye to the nature of
everyday life in a communist society where the party reached down
into the street-level social structures of ordinary Chinese. In college I
had read Franz Schurmann's *Ideology and Organization in Communist
China,* a pathbreaking book for its analysis of Mao's practical ideology
and how it guided and motivated Chinese Communist organizational
practices and forms. But Ezra's lectures opened up a different dimension,
one closer to the social anthropologist's concerns with the practical lives of
ordinary people and how they managed their social organizations. I
was duly impressed that Ezra acquired his knowledge of Chinese society without ever visiting the mainland, let alone doing field research

in China, by interviewing refugees from communist rule in Hong Kong. I imagined what it might be like to actually do street-level field research in China, whether in an urban neighborhood, factory, or village.

Ezra invited graduate students he was working with to his home in Cambridge. We arrived at his house after dinner. There would be a small dessert for us in his living room, easy conversation, and then we walked upstairs to his office on the third floor. We talked books. I remember well several of these evenings when we discussed William Hinton's *Fanshen*, a documentary of revolutionary land reform in a North China village. I was struck by how Ezra's reading was like my own. He found compelling Hinton's accounts of the social upheavals—redistributive and violent—that destroyed the lives of the landlords and rich peasants, and yet he underscored the norms of social justice that inspired the rebuilding of the social organizations of village life. His generosity in opening his home to us has had an enduring influence on me. I do the same with graduate students here at Cornell. Ezra was also generous with his teaching assistants, inviting us for occasional lunches at the Faculty Club on his tab.

Years later I invited Ezra to Cornell to give a lecture where I introduced him as my graduate school mentor to a capacity audience in an auditorium in Rockefeller Hall. In March 2016, Ez invited me to his house for breakfast when I was in Boston to attend the annual meeting of the Eastern Sociological Society. In late 2019, Ezra accepted my invitation to give three lectures for the Messenger Lecture Series at Cornell. I received an email from Ezra on January 26, 2020, just as the COVID-19 epidemic gained traction in America, and was amazed to learn that he was so vigorous in his late eighties, leading a delegation of the National Committee on a long visit in China. He wrote again that he was working on preparing his lectures for Cornell, but he wasn't sure he would be up to traveling to Cornell to give the lectures in person. However, he would work hard on them. At Cornell University Press there was interest in publishing a small book from his Messenger Lectures. Sadly, Ezra's death prevented us from benefiting one more time from his wise comments on East Asia.

Mike Smitka

Washington and Lee University

I first met Professor Vogel—I could never bring myself to call him otherwise—as a sophomore over a Wednesday sherry at Harvard. I didn't know what he taught, but the math department was urging me to look for another major. I had taken Harvard's famous "Rice Paddies" introduction to East Asia as a freshman, my first real exposure to a region other than the U.S. I followed that up with Reischauer's Japanese politics course and Donald Shively's history of Tokugawa Japan. Over those sherries, Professor Vogel—okay, Ezra—fed my interest, and helped guide me to the newly created undergraduate East Asian Studies (EAS) program. Since it looked unlikely that I could travel to the PRC, I chose Japanese as my language. I remember attending a number of EAS seminars, encountering the Talcott Parsons 2x2 framework, and gaining sensitivity to the challenges of data collection. Ezra was very much the sociologist.

I never took one of his classes. But then as a senior I was on my way to meet Edwin Reischauer to ask him to be my thesis adviser, only to find Ezra at the door with his bicycle, looking like death—he'd been in bed with pneumonia. Why was Ezra there? Reischauer had suffered a stroke in his office, and an ambulance had just taken him off to the hospital. Now Ezra didn't have to do that, but he didn't want to leave those with appointments that afternoon at loose ends. I think in the end he took over all of the Japan-side undergraduate advising for the new major, and I suspect he also looked after several graduate students. Anyway, I ended up in his office periodically, squeezed in between other appointments, and with the occasional phone call in Japanese or Chinese interrupting our discussions. Somehow he made time for all of us.

I've never been much for keeping in touch, but I saw Ezra periodically in Cambridge when I attended the (long-defunct) Japan Economic Seminar. In addition, while in Cambridge for meetings at MIT, I encountered him by chance while on his daily jog, not once, but twice. Of course, there were also the gatherings he organized in Tokyo, and we both ended up participating in a Center for Strategic and International Studies (CSIS) project on the U.S.-Japan security relationship. I even house-sat once for him in Tokyo, long enough ago that I towered over "Stevie," to whom I now look up, in more ways than one.

As with the other remembrances, what I saw was a man of gentle mien who took students at every level seriously, who applied his abundant energy to a broad array of research, teaching, and public service, all while making time for his kids. His talks were filled with good humor, and I was amazed that he was just as relaxed and funny when speaking in Japanese as he was in English. All my memories are fond. I am very sad that he's no longer with us.

C. Rose Cortese

Harvard University

Before LinkedIn and other social media existed, there was Ezra Vogel. A naturally gregarious person, Ezra easily connected with people from all walks of life. He was an early pioneer of networking—connecting students with each other and with Ezra's many friends and acquaintances. As staff members, we would joke that much like Kevin Bacon, every person on the planet was just six degrees away from knowing Ezra.

It happened to me repeatedly in the most unlikely situations. At a dinner party full of hard-core scientists, a story shared about a canceled flight from New York to Boston and a lively professor of Asian studies gathering a group of fellow passengers to rent a car and drive back to Boston together. It was Ezra. My elderly neighbor, a former scholar in the Department of Social Relations at Harvard—later known as the Department of Sociology—knew a young scholar who might still be at Harvard. Did I know him? Ezra something was his name. There perhaps were fewer degrees to Ezra than there are to Kevin Bacon.

The East Asian Studies (EAS) undergraduate concentration thrived under Ezra's leadership. Not situated in a department at that time, EAS was supported and enriched by the many faculty members throughout the Faculty of Arts and Sciences (FAS). Faculty members offered a diverse range of courses on East Asia to these forward-looking undergraduates and encouraged their study of languages and travel to Asia. Whether they continued in academia, or government, or the world of business, they remained part of Ezra's community.

Though more years have passed than I care to mention since I worked directly for Ezra, I clearly remember his enthusiasm for his students and that extra effort he made for them. In his ever-buoyant pace, he'd rush into the office and say, "There was a student interested in (some unique topic) in my class three years ago that is perfect for the job opportunity at XYZ company. Can you find out where they are now?" After some digging and my feeling a sense of accomplishment after having found the right student, Ezra would write a letter or make a phone call connecting the former student to the great opportunity.

Guiding students and former students in their academics, their research, their work endeavors, and even their advanced careers was part of Ezra's everyday activities. He was always willing to provide time for students from all walks of life, scholars, and even strangers.

Though I cannot say for certain, Ezra likely mentored thousands of students and scholars, not only in their academics, but also in life situations.

The Office Hours Rule was strict. After missing two appointments a student could not have another appointment. However, sometimes a particular student, having failed to show up for their appointment numerous times, would be given an exception. Ezra recognized the mental health struggles affecting students and would allow those students to make additional appointments in hopes that they would attend at least one. His insights into the stresses that affected our students gave those of us who worked with him a reminder to remain compassionate in our work with them.

Many years later, Ezra would—perhaps as a favor to me, or perhaps because he enjoyed students—agree to meet with students in the Regional Studies East Asia program for lunch and discussion. He gamely shared how he began to work in Japan. Afterward, I overheard him readily agree to speak with a student from China about her academic plans. I had to smile, knowing that Ezra hadn't changed.

Ezra never saw staff as mere employees assigned to complete the work of the university. Beyond the courtesy he afforded staff, he entreated us to join him in a common goal to aid students in the successful completion of their education, and after so very many years from the day he hired me, I am still willing to work toward that common goal. I hope that I live up to his expectations.

Timothy Cheek

University of British Columbia

I am one among scores, perhaps hundreds, of graduate students and Asia scholars whose professional life was touched by Professor Vogel. In time we came to know him as Ezra. As a graduate student in History and East Asian Languages at Harvard in the 1980s, I did my tour of duty as Junior and then Senior Tutor in the undergraduate program for East Asian Languages and Civilizations. At that time Professor Vogel was our mentor and, in a surprise to me, he held weekly sessions with all the tutors in the program at his house over pizza. Interested informality inflected his mentoring as he both trimmed our excesses and encouraged our engagement with our anxious undergraduates. Among his many pieces of sound advice is one I continue to use. To focus a student's writing in a paper, he asked: "So what? Why should someone want to read your paper? What have you got to offer here?" My students know this as the "so what?" requirement. In all, Professor Vogel trained us to care for our students, to avoid putting on airs, and to push for the best work possible.

After graduation, I mostly saw Ezra at Association for Asian Studies (AAS) annual meetings and at conferences. What struck me most was that he walked his talk. Over the years he was unfailingly warm (with an uncanny ability to remember our names from year to year), interested, informal, and encouraging. I came to know him as Ezra, who treated me and my cohort as his colleagues. That was both pleasant and encouraging, but what was inspiring was to find that as he aged his energy and grand projects continued unabated—the huge Deng Xiaoping biography, and interest in Hu Yaobang, a book on Japanese-Chinese relations. This engagement, I discovered, was not superficial, just good manners. I was contracted to review Ezra's *Deng Xiaoping* for a journal that allowed more than the usual 600 words. While absolutely impressed with the book, I had some differences of opinion (yes, the issue of Deng and Tiananmen 1989) but chose, instead, to explore the ways in which Ezra's interpretive thrust put one in mind of his famous opus, *Japan as Number One.* That is, he seemed to be drawing lessons for good governance from his material on Deng Xiaoping just as he extracted lessons for good economic management from the Ministry of International Trade and Industry (MITI) and the Japan of the 1970s. Next time I saw Ezra at a conference, he pulled me aside and wanted to respond in detail! I was amazed he had taken notice and was struck by his honest and comradely engagement with a younger scholar who didn't quite agree with him on all points. This is Ezra's model for me as I age. May we all be as energetic and fair-minded for as long as Ezra.

Susan Napier

Tufts University

Ezra Vogel was the first Harvard professor I encountered and the kindest, most aware, and most generous professor I would meet either as an undergrad or in graduate school. I met Ezra when he held a meeting for freshmen interested in concentrating in the brand-new East Asian Studies (EAS) major. The fact that he even held a meeting and was willing to guide it was in itself a welcome surprise—most of my subsequent professors never ventured out of their offices and showed no interest in talking with students.

Ezra began the meeting with his typical self-deprecating humor. He mentioned how the idea for East Asian Studies had come about because faculty had begun to feel that contemporary East Asia was an increasingly significant area of interest and that a major should be created that would reflect that. But who was to create the concentration and shepherd it through its early stages? "I was on leave," Ezra said. "And while I was away, my colleagues got together and decided that 'Well, Ezra's not here. Let's give *him* the job.'"

In fact, it was the best decision they could have made, at least for us lucky students. Although I was primarily in literature at that time, I chose East Asian Studies rather than the more literary concentration of East Asian Languages and Civilizations. I felt that literature did not exist in a vacuum and needed to be seen in relation to the cultural, political, and social forces that made up the world around us. I guessed, correctly, that EAS would offer that kind of intellectual structure.

But there was another reason why I joined East Asian Studies: Ezra treated me like a human being worthy of respect and consideration. That evening when we first met for the introductory session, Ezra asked us all to introduce ourselves. When it came to be my turn, Ezra said, "I remember you." Shocked, I just stared at him because I knew we had never met. "Yes," he continued, "I remember when you wanted to study Japanese in high school and your parents contacted me to ask for help in finding a graduate student who might tutor you. I'm so glad that you kept on with your Japanese. That's great." I was floored. The idea that an august member of the Harvard faculty would remember my name and even compliment me meant the world to me.

From then on I was Ezra's biggest fan. I never actually took a course from him, but I consider him my true mentor. He helped me with my undergraduate thesis—gently suggesting that an entire history of Meiji period intellectuals might be a bit big as a topic—and supported my decision to go on to graduate school. Above all, much later on in my career, when it came to the biggest professional decision of my life—to start working on Japanese animation (anime)—Ezra was the only one of my former Harvard advisers who encouraged me. Always intellectually voracious, he showed a genuine interest in anime and in the notion of the medium as a form of Japanese soft power. This was at a time when most academics regarded "Japanese cartoons" as a vulgar invader of traditional Japanese culture!

Ezra helped me substantively. A few years after I had decided to work on anime, the Japan Society of New York (JSNY) held one of the first American symposiums on anime. Ezra took a look at the promotional material for the symposium and couldn't find my name. "So," he told me, "I called up the head of the JSNY and asked him why you weren't on the program." Soon afterward I was invited to speak at the symposium.

I'm sure that Ezra gave that kind of help—a gesture that was direct, simple, and extremely fruitful—to many of the students he had encountered through EAS. And he probably didn't even think about how much it meant to them. It was just what he did.

I realize that in writing this remembrance, I'm talking about myself as much as about Ezra. But that's also the point. Ezra lives on in all of us who had the benefit of knowing him. Without him, I simply wouldn't be the person I am today. Thanks Ezra. For everything.

Sheila Miyoshi Jager
Oberlin College

Like many of his former students, my fondest memory of Ezra Vogel is of our weekly gatherings at his house in Cambridge where he entertained, fed, and nurtured us. I was not technically his student; I met him when I was finishing up my dissertation in anthropology at the University of Chicago. Before moving to Cambridge in 1989, I had written to him from Seoul asking whether I could become his teaching fellow. I did not want to return to Chicago and had heard from a friend how lively and fun his classes were. I never expected that he would become my mentor for life, a key supporting figure throughout my entire professional career.

The gatherings usually took place on a Friday afternoon with six to ten other teaching fellows. The course, Industrial East Asia, was so popular that Ezra held it in a large auditorium. We fellows would sit to one side of the room all huddled together. I remember thinking how theatrical it all was, with Ezra walking and talking onstage with his microphone in tow while we watched the performance, enthralled but also feeling rather special. We were *his* teaching fellows, after all. It was that sense of camaraderie, his ability to foster that unique feeling of belonging, a talent for leadership, a shepherd and his flock, that made Ezra so special. He loved connecting with people, but he also loved fostering connections between people. He once told me that many of his students have remained friends for life, and not a few among them found love and had gotten married. He was proud of that fact and it is part of his legacy.

Among Ezra's other gifts was his ability to listen. He had a talent for asking great questions because he was always interested in what other people had to say. Status and titles meant less to him than whether a person's observations were interesting and original. He was impatient with well-worn arguments. He also didn't much like narrow or theoretical topics and approaches, preferring "big ideas" that ordinary people could understand. I recall a meeting in Washington, D.C., soon after he became the National Intelligence Officer for East Asia on the National Intelligence Council. He had gone out of his way to meet me in a hotel lobby, and we talked for hours about Korea. I was just a newly minted PhD back then, jobless and unsure of my path forward. His gesture always stuck with me, not only because it was generous and kind, but because he had given me confidence that I had something worthwhile to say.

The last time I met Ezra was in 2018 at his home in Cambridge. He was full of energy and passion about his book project on Hu Yaobang, who was a close collaborator of Deng Xiaoping. I asked him whether he ever thought about retiring from his books and writing, perhaps travelling or doing something completely different, like taking up painting. He gave me a strange look, as if I had asked him whether he might want to move to the moon. "What?" he said. "Why would I want to take up painting when there are so many things I still have to learn?"

Ya-Wen Lei

Harvard University

Ezra Vogel pioneered the tradition of studying and teaching about China in Harvard's Department of Sociology. When Marty Whyte retired, I had the honor of being hired as a China sociologist. Being a part of this distinguished tradition is an extraordinary, albeit daunting, opportunity.

Ezra was an intellectual giant and an inspiring and dedicated educator. It was not uncommon for him to have two hundred undergraduates in his seminal China course. Many of his students and teaching assistants are now prominent figures in academia, business, and politics. It is impossible to overstate his contribution to how we think, research, and teach about China today. When I reflect on the generations of students and scholars that Ezra influenced, it is easy to question how I could possibly fill his shoes. Not surprisingly though, the person who convinces me every day to get up and try is Ezra himself.

When Marty moved to Maryland after his retirement, Ezra generously stepped in as a mentor and helped me to negotiate the transition from postdoctoral fellow to assistant professor. In September 2015, I bicycled to his house on Sumner Road to have a meeting with him about teaching. It was a beautiful day and the afternoon sun shone on his face as we sat in the living room and shared Chinese tea together. I still remember his amiable smile and joyful laughter.

At one point in the conversation, Ezra stood up and took down a folder from his shelf. In it was an original copy of his 1977 syllabus for "Sociology 101: Chinese Communist Society," the paper now yellowed and fragile with age. It was a yearlong course and Ezra, showing his Parsonian roots, had divided the course into four sections: political organization, economic organization, community, and values and their preservation. The syllabus was over thirty years old, but it was still relevant and insightful.

Ezra talked to me about the importance of connecting macro-contexts with people's lived experiences—helping students, in other words, to see both the forest and trees. He taught me the value of using stories to catch students' interest and then, once you've got it, the importance of teaching them how to analyze primary sources so they can engage with ideas themselves. He still remembered his students' names. By the end of our meeting, I was awestruck but also calmer, more confident, because that was Ezra's effect. He never used his expertise to intimidate; he shared his knowledge to generate new conversations and questions.

Since I began teaching in fall 2016, my Contemporary Chinese Society course has expanded from a small seminar to one of the largest courses in the department. Ezra and I continued to meet every year to discuss pedagogy. He always wanted to know how course registration was going and what sort of things my students were interested in. One year, I balked at the growing number of students who wanted to take the course; I worried how this might conflict with the pressure I was already under to publish. But Ezra urged me to accept everyone, reminding me that it was the interactions and relationships with students that would become the most meaningful aspects of my work. I've followed this advice ever since and can happily report that Ezra was right.

His wisdom has also guided me throughout the years as geopolitical tensions have grown between China and the U.S., alongside resurgent forms of nationalism and authoritarianism in many parts of the world—conditions that often make teaching sensitive topics extremely difficult. Seeing this, Ezra told me to hold on to the principles of respect and empathy. Such simple yet profound advice has helped me to keep the classroom an open space for students to talk about thorny issues and express different viewpoints.

My last interaction with Ezra exemplified his deep commitment to his students. In the fall of 2020, he asked me to help one of his former students apply for a fellowship. Sometime later, he emailed to ask about the status of the application, but made no mention of the fact he was already in Mount Auburn Hospital. His sentences were uncharacteristically fragmented and incomplete. Puzzled, I replied but heard nothing back until three days later, when I received the heartbreaking news of his passing. He was a caring and generous teacher, right to the end.

In the strange, socially distanced world, I did not know how to process his death at first. Eventually, I drove to his house on Sumner Road and thought about everything he had given me as a teacher, a mentor, and a friend. I can no longer join him for tea, but he continues to guide my scholarship and my teaching every day.

SIX

Mentoring Harvard Students
for Academic Careers

Patricia G. Steinhoff

University of Hawaii

E zra Vogel was a mentoring presence throughout most of my adult life. I first met him in 1962–63, when he came to the University of Michigan to give a talk on his research. I was finishing an undergraduate major in Japanese and turning to sociology, so he embodied the rare combination to which I aspired. After a year of advanced language study in Tokyo, I entered the sociology doctoral program in Harvard's Department of Social Relations to work with Robert Bellah, the department's senior Japan specialist. Ezra's PhD was from the same department, and he had just become a lecturer there after a short stint at Yale and a post-doc studying Chinese at Harvard. He remembered me and invited me to join a small group to help keep up our Japanese. Every week we each had to report on what we were reading in Japanese. My contributions were minuscule because I could only manage to read a few pages each week, but the sessions gave me a glimpse of Ezra's disciplined approach to continuous language learning and obliged me to keep reading Japanese.

Harvard's sociology doctoral program in the mid-1960s was very condensed: two years of coursework with some of the giants in the field plus some requirements in the broader Department of Social Relations, followed by comprehensive exams in sociology at the end of the two years. Students were admitted to the doctoral program directly from a BA, and if you failed the comps, they gave you an MA as a consolation prize. If you passed, you went off to do dissertation research. They did not actually teach the nuts and bolts of sociology as other graduate programs did, but instilled in us the confidence that we could achieve whatever we set out to do. The Harvard doctoral program was on such a fast track because American higher education was expanding rapidly, and there were jobs for assistant professors even before they completed their dissertations.

During the second year, while my cohort of eight male sociology students and I studied together amicably for comps, Bellah shaped my dissertation topic. He latched onto my initial interest in Japanese students who had experienced a *tenkō* (change of ideological direction) after the 1960 Ampo protests, saying *tenkō* was a great topic, but I needed to study the *real tenkō* problem in the 1930s. So without any background in history, my topic became a socio-historical study of the suppression of the prewar Japanese communist movement through the process of *tenkō*. I obtained funding to do the fieldwork, and Bellah arranged for his friend Takeshi Ishida to sponsor me at the Institute of Social Science at Tokyo University.

By the time I came back from Tokyo in early 1968, Bellah had moved to Berkeley and Ezra, now a full professor, took me under his wing. His open, friendly manner was a sharp contrast with the austere and intellectual Bellah. So although I had gone to Harvard to study with Bellah and was completing a Bellah-inspired dissertation, I became Ezra Vogel's first doctoral student. He was unfailingly supportive. In that final semester at Harvard he read early dissertation chapters and helped me find my voice, while guiding me through a simple job search process that was totally different from what graduate students today endure. He became my role model for how to work with graduate students. He taught me the value of regular group meetings to keep students on track and the importance of providing positive, personalized support.

Over lunch just before I left to take up a position in Hawaii, Ezra suddenly asked me: "What is your social psychology of Japan?" The question stayed with me and profoundly shaped my thinking about Japanese society. In those days Talcott Parsons's grand theoretical framework dominated the Harvard sociology program. It permeated the atmosphere, so we basically learned by osmosis to think in terms of its categories. Both Vogel and Bellah had been students of Parsons, and Ezra's undergraduate course on Japan was organized around the four-box framework of Parsons's theory. At the height of the Vietnam War, my cohort of doctoral students was more interested in social conflict than in social order. Ezra's simple question shaped my undergraduate course on Japanese society: half the course was on social interaction at the micro-level (social psychology) and the other half at the macro-level (major social institutions), with a focus on how they were interrelated and how conflict worked in Japan.

Although I never took a course with Ezra, I learned from his publications how to combine close observations of social interaction with the rich detail of open-ended interviews to describe common patterns of Japanese life. I wanted to turn my dissertation into the expected book, but was increasingly uncomfortable with its functionalist argument that the process of *tenkō* contributed to social order. So it languished. Twenty years later, Ezra invited me to participate in a Garland book series based on unpublished Harvard dissertations, which allowed me to publish the dissertation as I had originally written it, as a historical relic.

In the meantime, I had embarked on a comparative study of resistance to *tenkō* pressures in the radical New Left student movement of the late 1960s and early 1970s. The research began in 1972, when I did a prison interview in Israel with the sole surviving participant in a Japanese terrorist attack on Israel's Lod Airport. Ezra was very excited about it and decades later would still introduce me as having done that interview.

Despite the distance between Boston and Honolulu, I continued to see Ezra in Cambridge, at International House in Tokyo, and at Association for Asian Studies (AAS) meetings. In later years he often attended the Japan Sociologists Network meetings that I organized at the AAS. I view him as the inspiration for those sessions, through his early weekly sessions to keep up our Japanese skills and his lifelong desire to connect people with similar interests.

Vivienne Shue

Oxford University

I came to Harvard in the fall of 1969 to do a PhD in Government on some aspect of Chinese politics—which aspect exactly, still very much a matter of conjecture. The incomparable Benjamin Schwartz, whose faculty appointment was in Government and History, and whose spellbinding, two-semester lecture course on the Intellectual History of China swept from the Dao to Mao, would eventually agree to be my dissertation supervisor. But it was Ezra, whose course on Japanese Society I also took my first year, and in whose undergraduate course on China I would later serve as a teaching assistant, who was to become for me a genuine mentor. In one memorable graduate seminar Ezra taught on the Cultural Revolution during spring 1970—in which both Deborah Davis and Jay Mathews were also keenly enthusiastic students—he set us neophytes to work reading translations of Chinese newspaper articles and whatever else we could get our hands on in those still data-starved days. We were to select a city or province and help fill in the blanks on how the Cultural Revolution unfolded in localities around the country much less studied than Beijing. Wrestling hard, then, even to get our minds around the incendiary rhetoric and the risky street politics of that volatile era, I was astonished when Ezra said he'd learned a lot from our papers and insisted on publishing them together, as a volume in the Harvard East Asian Monographs series. Really? I wondered. But it turned out, he wasn't kidding! Ezra, it seemed, had seen us from the beginning not as students, but as younger colleagues.

I had spent the two years before coming to Harvard doing a first graduate degree in Politics at Oxford. Almost everyone I'd known there, students and teachers alike, had already long concluded that the U.S. war in Vietnam was not only doomed to failure, but every day a mounting disgrace to America's reputation around the world. I was surprised when I got back home to discover just how many Americans, including academics and students (and their brothers, cousins, and friends who might any day be drafted), still believed the war in Vietnam could come to a beneficial end for Vietnam's people.

Harvard campus discussions of politics were heatedly divided in those days—especially after the 1969 occupation of University Hall and President Pusey's decision to call in city and state police for help in ejecting the protesters; and after the expansion of U.S. bombing into Cambodia, the resulting Kent State shootings in 1970, and student strikes on campuses all across the country. The Committee of Concerned Asian Scholars (CCAS) then became a focal point of anti-war theory and action. CCAS members, along with other students and younger faculty at Harvard, convened many sessions to which more senior Harvard Asianists—many of whom supported Pentagon strategies and Nixon administration decisions—were also invited to speak and explain. In those tense days of teach-ins and demonstrations, I had several opportunities to watch as Ezra struggled with where he would stand vis-à-vis his students, and CCAS, and Washington too. I observed him and the dilemmas he tried to cope with quite closely in those fraught times and perceived the depth of his own personal pain.

Ezra just couldn't bring himself to agree that the virtue of peace should be put before all *other* human moral principles; but he also, so plainly, sympathized with victims (on all sides) and hated war. More than twenty years later, as a professor and department chair at Cornell, I would be called upon myself to speak at highly emotional campus rallies and vigils, this time in reaction to the bloody crackdown on protestors in Tiananmen Square who refused, when ordered, to disperse. By that time, having read much more of Ezra's work on politics and society in China and having learned much more about all that for myself, I thought back on the model mix of reason with humanity that Ezra had set when he'd been speaking to highly intelligent, but also incensed and frustrated, young people who cared passionately about their country and the world. I reflected then that, despite his family's Jewish faith and his later education at Ohio Wesleyan, Ezra's own personal moral compass must have been forged neither in the teachings of the Old Testament, nor of the New, but instead, firmly in the teachings of Aristotle and the ideal of a golden mean. At the midpoint between what is reckless and what is cowardly, Aristotle teaches—that is where to locate *true virtue*, which is courage. This was the rule by which Ezra had always thought it right to live, I concluded, as I then tried summoning my own composure to address the angry, weeping crowd of students massed in front of Uris Library.

I would shamelessly continue sending drafts of my own work to Ezra, time and time again over the years; just to ask for his honest assessment— which was always delivered promptly, and always as encouraging as ever. The last new work I ever sent him for his thoughts, in fact, went out on September 30, 2020, as America's election day fast approached. He responded, with helpful comments and caveats as always, on November 1; attaching a draft copy of *his* own thoughts about what the next administration should do with respect to China. This I read and replied to—in a chatty message of thanks, with still further thoughts on U.S. and Chinese politics—on election day, November 3, 2020.

At age ninety, Ezra died before his time.

Tom Gold

University of California, Berkeley

Certainly, one of my main takeaways from my relationship with Ezra Vogel was the importance of *guanxi*, usually translated as personal connections. I don't recall the details, but soon after arriving at Harvard in 1973 for the master's program in Regional Studies East Asia, he invited me to join a group of sociology graduate students who would be meeting with him on a regular basis to discuss contemporary Chinese society. That became the tight-knit group whose other members are also contributing to this volume.

An example of using his *guanxi:* sometime in the spring of 1974 he called me in the dorm and the conversation went something like this:

EFV: You studied martial arts in Taiwan, didn't you?
TG: Yes, but. . . .
EFV: And your Chinese is really good, isn't it?
TG: Better than some I guess.
EFV: Would you be interested in interpreting for a *wushu* (martial arts) group coming from China this summer?

My knees buckled. I had been in Taiwan during the exchange visits of the U.S. ping-pong team and Shenyang acrobat group, but since my Chinese wasn't up to the level of the American interpreters, I had no chance of being recruited. So now I had a real chance! Ezra said that a woman named Jan Berris, from the National Committee on U.S.-China Relations, would be coming to Cambridge and would interview me. The interview went well enough and I got what turned out to be the first of many interpreting gigs for the National Committee.

Ezra also used his *guanxi* to introduce me to the other organization handling delegations from and to China at that time, the Committee on Scholarly Communication with the People's Republic of China, and I stayed in Washington to arrange the visit of an agronomy delegation that I then escorted on its American tour that summer.

When it came time to develop a dissertation prospectus, I had planned to look into the role of delegations in Chinese foreign policy, but at that time, in 1976, U.S.-China relations took a sudden turn for the worse, and

Ezra cooled on China research after his enthusiasm had been stoked by his first trip to the mainland in 1973. He said, more or less, "You're interested in dependency theory and no one has used it to look at Taiwan. You know Taiwan well and have lots of contacts there, so why don't you do a project on Taiwan?" That made perfect sense, and I followed his advice and also made use of his *guanxi* for interviews in Taiwan as well as in South Korea and Japan. Ezra came through Taipei in the spring of 1978 for a conference, and we spent time together in his room at the Grand Hotel, discussing my research.

After I returned from fieldwork in the summer of 1978 and escorted two more Chinese student delegations, Ezra informed me that the U.S. and China were signing an educational exchange agreement and suggested I apply. I said I had planned to write my dissertation, teach for him in the East Asian Studies program, go on the job market, and get married. Plus, at thirty I was probably too old. He countered that this was a great opportunity to be in the first group, they wanted older students, he could find someone else to teach, the dissertation and job could wait and, well, he couldn't do anything about the marriage bit! Of course, I followed his advice and went to Fudan University in Shanghai.

At the end of December 1979, Ezra and Charlotte, newly married, came through Shanghai with two of his children and a Harvard alumni group. On December 31, I went to meet them at the Jingan Hotel. Ezra was encouraging as usual, telling me that I was one of two or three people who'd get a good job. I gave him a manuscript I'd written on the situation of youth in Shanghai and, without reading it, he suggested sending it to *China Quarterly*. With much revision, it became my first publication. I had thought of writing a guidebook, but he nixed that idea, saying I should do my thesis and a scholarly article to establish myself as *the* authority on some topic. He also advised me not to take any speaking engagement for less than $250 plus carfare.

He asked a lot of questions, mostly about elite politics, and I realized how far away from that I was, both by being outside Beijing and living day to day with Chinese students. He was planning to spend the next summer in Guangzhou to get a feel of daily life in a neighborhood, as he had done in Tokyo.

That evening I deployed my own *guanxi* and took Ezra and Charlotte to the home of Chinese friends of mine who were hosting a New

Year's Eve party. As usual, Ezra was engaging and also managed to "interview" our hosts about pricing policy and who made their new furniture. They left before the dancing started, but it was one of the most memorable New Year's Eves of my life.

Richard Madsen

University of California, San Diego

My first encounter with Ezra was by mail. In 1970, I was living in a dorm and studying sociology at National Taiwan University, and I was thinking of getting a PhD in sociology and China studies in the U.S. The problem was that my entire education up to that point had been in the insular communities of Catholic seminaries, and I knew very little about secular American universities. I had asked some American graduate students whom I met in Taipei about how to go about applying to graduate school. Someone suggested writing to Ezra Vogel at Harvard—one of the professors there who was most open and generous with his students. So I wrote a letter explaining my background and aspirations to apply for an MA in the program for Regional Studies East Asia, with a hope to go into sociology eventually and do a comparative study of Chinese "value systems" and be a bridge between China and the West. But I recognized that I didn't have the academic background to apply directly because my education had been in philosophy and theology. Ezra wrote back a gracious letter encouraging me to apply and promising to look out for my application. It was more warm and encouraging than any of the other letters I had received in response to my queries at other universities.

I got accepted to Harvard (after being rejected at most of the other places that I had applied to) and arrived in the fall of 1971, nervous but fascinated by a place so far removed from any institution I had been in before. I first saw Ezra at an orientation meeting presided over by the eminent and to me quite intimidating figures of John Fairbank and Ed Reischauer. Ezra was sitting on the floor in the crowded room. Here was someone I thought I could relate to.

At our first meeting, I told him that I was planning to take a course on statistics. He answered that if I wanted to study Chinese society it would be much better to take more courses on Chinese language, history, and culture. So I studied sociology without learning statistics—something unthinkable today, but characteristic of Ezra's approach to the sociology of China. He wanted to see the society not as statistical aggregates, but as real people interacting with one another in specific cultural and historical contexts.

He carried this approach into the way he treated his students. He was keen on bringing us together into a community. He saw each of us as a whole person, with our own strengths and weaknesses—focusing especially on the strengths. He invited us to his house for late afternoon sherry and occasionally for informal dinners. Sometimes he invited us to large gatherings with a wide array of scholars and journalists and other China hands. I can't stress strongly enough how important this was for me, completely out of my social element in an intimidating new environment. It took a long time, but I finally came to feel that I belonged at Harvard.

He encouraged those in my cohort to form a reading group in which we discussed popular fiction coming out of China to get a feel for how people there were talking and acting. We shared not only conversation but good food, not only academic knowledge but life experiences, and we became lifelong friends. Thanks to Ezra.

He not only helped us navigate the labyrinth of Harvard but the fog of Chinese sociology. There were no guidelines for how to study what was then a very closed society. We were making it up as we went along, a confusing, unsettling process, but sometimes a very exciting one.

When I was preparing for my own fieldwork, he invited me (as well as all of his other graduate students) to look through the file cabinet stuffed with his own interviewing summaries. The thing that impressed me was how he had asked about the details of ordinary life—what people ate, what their daily work was like, where they lived—not about their views on the grand political questions we were so interested in. When I was writing my dissertation, he told me to portray my subjects in a way that conveyed their basic dignity. This is how he did his own work.

And he wanted to help us build connections not only with our peers, but with wider networks of professional colleagues. He spent an enormous amount of time on this. Long after graduate school, I would be happily surprised by a phone call or email from him saying he had read some article or book I had published and was passing it on to other colleagues and encouraging me to do more of the same. In the late 1990s when I returned to give a talk on my current research to the Harvard Department of Sociology, he introduced me by quoting from the application letter I had written almost thirty years before—I hadn't even remembered what I had said.

He also gave life lessons. When I had a measure of success, he encouraged me in his down-to-earth, low-key way not to get arrogant. I have tried to follow his lessons and example and teach my students as he taught us—and to portray Chinese society as he did: not as faceless abstractions organized by abstractly conceived social structures, but as networks of individual persons each striving, though sometimes failing, to find dignity in the challenging contexts of their time.

Robert T. Snow

Boston, Massachusetts

In the fall of 1974, when I was getting ready to head off to Asia to begin my dissertation research, Ezra invited me to meet with him at his home on Parker Street on a Saturday morning. He asked me to come at 8:30 a.m. I have never been a morning person and was even less so during my graduate school years. But I arrived a little early and found Ezra in his driveway, unloading bags of groceries from the car. I helped him carry the bags in, realizing that I had never pictured a professor at Harvard hauling in the family groceries. That down-to-earth, practical image of Ezra has always stuck with me.

The dissertation prospectus that we discussed that morning was skeletal. I was thinking big, and very unrealistically. Ezra listened patiently, and in a very low-key, kindly way, essentially said that I should get out to the field, observe, listen, and then revise and focus the plan. It was, of course, the best advice.

I had first met Ezra in the early fall of 1968 during my senior year of college. We did not get off to the best start. I was checking out a range of graduate schools and trying to decide where to apply. I knew I wanted to combine sociology with the study of Asia, especially China. In 1968 there were not many graduate schools that offered that combination, and, of course, Ezra's name kept coming up as the best person in the U.S. to study with. My interest in China at that point was, alas, largely inspired by a romantic misreading of the Cultural Revolution. It was 1968: my hair and beard were long. I was very sure of my pro-China, anti-Establishment, political positions.

Ezra made time during what was obviously a busy day to talk with me. He explained the program in sociology and how Asia, especially China, could fit in. But then, not unkindly, he asked—given my political views—whether graduate school was really the right path for me. I was taken aback, but I assured him that I did, indeed, want to pursue study of the changes occurring in Chinese society.

Despite that initial interview, I was admitted to the sociology program and would have begun my grad school career in the fall of 1969, but the Vietnam War and the draft intervened. I was lucky enough to be granted conscientious objector status and was able to secure a position with an alternative service-approved program that sent me to Hong Kong. My job there gave me the chance to live in a working men's hostel and to study Cantonese.

Not really expecting a reply—after all he barely knew me—I wrote a letter to Ezra soon after I arrived in Hong Kong to describe what I was doing and what I was learning from the factory workers among whom I was living. To my surprise, he wrote a detailed letter back, suggesting questions I might pursue. He mentioned scholars based in Hong Kong that I could meet, and he encouraged me to keep a journal. Other letters followed. All of his suggestions proved invaluable.

I finally began graduate school in the fall of 1972. Ezra introduced me to other grad students with similar interests. As others have written, Ezra gave his graduate students—at least the batch that he mentored in the 1970s—permission to balance on the borderlands between anthropology and sociology. It was a time when sociology was importing techniques that seemed to some of us to be more suited to the world of physics or chemistry. Ezra preserved and encouraged a more humane approach to the study of human society.

For Ezra, it was all right to settle into a community, look closely at the lives of a set of individuals, and see where their story lines led. Those story lines took me to places that I could not have imagined when, back in Cambridge, I had drafted the grandiose dissertation prospectus that Ezra and I discussed that morning after he'd unloaded the groceries: real people's lives so rarely fit the ideal types of the theorists.

Along with fostering a commitment to curiosity and stories, Ezra managed to inspire a sense of cooperation and mutual support among his graduate students. As others of the 1970s grad student cohort have described, Ezra encouraged us to form a study group to read newspapers and fiction from China to get a sense of how official sources portrayed the changes happening in Chinese society after 1949. Unlike the competition fostered in many formal grad school seminars, under Ezra's guidance the reading group became a mutually supportive gathering. We often cooked and ate together. Largely because of the model and mentorship that Ezra provided, the bonds that he fostered in the band of sociologists of China and Japan that he assembled at Harvard in the 1970s have continued for decades.

Despite his many accolades, the image of Ezra that always comes back to me is the sight of him carrying in the family groceries early on an autumn Saturday morning: Ezra was indeed a great scholar and a mentor, but he also hauled in the groceries.

Corky White

Boston University

What makes your data sing? Ezra would ask, as I was mired in transcribed interviews, reading notes, Japanese ministry documents, and my fieldwork journals. It wasn't a call to theory—Ezra wouldn't have done that, at least not with me—and it wasn't a demand for a large sample size and a quantitative analysis—he wouldn't have done that either.

I thought myself a singer, some kind of scholar-warbler, humming random snatches. But what Ezra knew I had and I was to learn, is a song to sing. And the song was already there in my notes, in the voices of others. I had heard the voices but, as they say, I hadn't listened. Ezra was a seeker of voices and a listener: he said, "There's no one I can't learn from," and though we often teased him about his relentless stalking of people in airports, in supermarket queues, and so forth, he was truly interested in people—especially Chinese and Japanese people. To communicate, Ezra doggedly and effectively studied the Chinese and Japanese languages, never satisfied with his progress. He was never satisfied with my ability in Japanese either. It was his own drive that compelled him to drive me until finally (I think I was in my early sixties at the time) he said, "I think your Japanese has improved greatly." Knowing how hard he always was on himself, I felt the praise deeply.

When I was living in Tokyo doing my dissertation research, I muddled through myriads of interviews, finding my way through the data to something that allowed for sensemaking. That year or so, 1975–76, was setting up the path for the rest of my career. No hypothesis took me to Japan, only what might politely be called a "research question." I kept testing things out on Ezra. He was something of a captive, having taken the same year off from Harvard to conduct research in Japan. He and his family lived close to me (my daughter was actually in Eve Vogel's class at the same Tokyo school), so I had more access to an adviser during fieldwork than most young researchers do. And I was blessed with the richness of Ezra's network of people; in every field he seemed to know key people who generously offered to help me. Midway through that time I got very stuck: the interviews weren't grabbing my consciousness, even without a clothesline hypothesis to pin them on, and I despaired. Ezra reminded me that the stories just hadn't emerged yet, and also, that negative data are data too. I forced myself to be patient, against the grain, and story lines eventually emerged that were more potent than the wispy ones I'd imagined.

Later on, my dissertation book appeared. But this was after another book—one that gave me a bit of a not-very-academic splash due to the timing and turn of events. Japan was in the news for a different reason. This was in the late 1970s and early 1980s, well after the "economic miracle" of the late 1960s had drawn such attention. Americans in particular began to be wary of Japan's success in automobiles and wary in general of Japanese superior quality and efficiency. As several Japan-focused social scientists had noticed, Japanese education was getting some attention too, seen as key to productivity and social cohesion. Ezra's book *Japan as Number One* had come out with considerable fanfare and was a bestseller. As he noted, some essential aspects of contemporary Japanese society might contribute to the "number-one-ness" of Japan. My own work on Japanese education was an offshoot of my dissertation research, and I dove into schools, parental expectations, teachers' strategies, and children's lives. One of my advisers, Nathan Glazer, thought I should write an article for *The Public Interest* on schooling, and a publisher contacted me, asking for a book on this topic. Riding the wave, my publisher decided that the title of my ethnographic study should be *The Japanese Educational Challenge* in order to thrust the book into the heated controversy that had become the U.S.-Japan "trade war." Reviewing my book in the *New York Review of Books,* a writer thought he was dismissing me from consideration by saying that all one had to do was read the blurb on the back cover, written by Ezra Vogel, and one would know the book was from another "apologist" for Japan from "the Harvard School of Japan As Number One." Ezra and I had a good laugh over that. Japanese children, doing well in school, were seen as a subversive tool of Japanese economic aggression, and my description of classrooms was far too sunny for the critics: if they were doing so well, they must be dreadfully oppressed and inhumanly disciplined. We certainly wouldn't want that for *our* children!

Like Ezra, I got some heavy jabs in the public arena. On one Detroit radio show, a caller told me that if I loved Japan, I hated America: "Love it or leave it, lady!" And bad for book sales and for the Japanese economy, the Asian recession of the early 1990s took Japan out of the challenge, it seemed to many. At that time many publishers went for books on Japan's "soft power" (the term Joseph Nye had coined to epitomize Japan's cultural selling points). Politicians and economists, and most especially journalists, were less interested in Japan, but my university students were sold on anime, manga, and sushi. While Ezra turned more toward China, I turned more toward food anthropology.

Recently I have heard new songs. They come from another Ezra lesson: paying attention to where you already are. Finding myself as ever sitting in one or another Japanese *kissaten*, I thought: oh, I am HERE in an urban social space, as I've been off and on in Japan since 1963, and it is after all the most interesting place to be. This ordinary space sang to me, arriving without fanfare, humming under its breath.

Jeff Broadbent

University of Minnesota

I came to study with Ezra at Harvard in 1974 after doing undergraduate studies with Bob Bellah at UC Berkeley. Since Bob and Ezra were both students of Talcott Parsons, I expected Ezra, like Bob, to orient his sociological work around questions posed by grand theory. To my surprise, I discovered profound differences. After my fieldwork in Japan on environmental protest and regional industrial policymaking (1978–81), I submitted many drafts of my thesis to Ezra for comments. I was trying to write an analytical thesis based on Parsons's AGIL theoretical categories.[1] But Ezra was not interested in formal testing of theory and hypotheses. He was an ethnographer at heart. In writing up his research, his concern was to get the specific descriptive concepts right, so as to increase the non-specialist's understanding of Japanese or Chinese society.

Ezra had a profoundly humanistic relation to his subjects and fields of study. Through his scholarship, he wanted to enlighten a wide audience and help bring mutual understanding and cooperation among nations, especially Japan, China, and the U.S. He extended that warmth to many people, developing a wide and deep circle of friends and colleagues. To Ezra, all people, high and low, were equal participants in the human drama. In line with this style and purpose, while I was writing my thesis, Ezra kept urging me to drop the theory and just tell the story in ways that added to the non-specialist's understanding of the real world. I worked out a compromise that passed muster as a PhD thesis, graduating in 1982, but it took me another fifteen years before I could publish the book that began to approach his high standards. At that time, Ezra wrote me a note quoting the Chinese proverb, *dachi wancheng* "a big vessel is slow on the making," and congratulated me on making a big vessel. The book did receive two academic prizes, in response to which on September 3, 2000, Ezra wrote me, "Congratulations on getting an Outstanding Publication Award from the ASA [American Sociological Association]. You and I know how much work you did to get this and how richly deserving you are."

---

1. For a brief explanation of Parsons's AGIL theoretical categories, see the essay by Jundai Liu.

In his talk at his 2000 retirement party, Ezra said something to the effect that "sociology has mostly ignored us, and we have mostly ignored sociology." In other words, he recognized that his narrative research approach did not work within the typical hypothesis-testing framework of normal sociology, nor was he concerned that it do so.

Two years later, Ezra invited me to accompany him on his speaking tour in Kyushu, including Oita Prefecture where I had done my field research. This was shortly after the 9/11 terrorist attack on the World Trade Center and the Pentagon. Our first stop was Fukuoka, the largest city in Kyushu, where, sponsored by the local newspaper, he and I gave lectures in Japanese on U.S. expectations of Japanese support in the upcoming response to the 9/11 attacks. Then we attended a party with local business and cultural leaders, whose adulation of Ezra was very evident. After that, we took the train to Oita Prefecture, where we stayed at a hot springs hotel in the resort town of Beppu. That evening, Ezra invited me to enter the hot springs pool with him. Both naked in the hot water, towels folded atop our heads in Japanese fashion, we chatted. Slightly embarrassed by such egalitarian and friendly intimacy from the teacher to whom I owed so much (*onshi*), reserve nonetheless broke down. I blurted out to him the painful story of my broken childhood upbringing. Ezra, with his training in, and sensitivity to, psychiatry and family sociology, listened with sympathy.

In one of his last emails to me (September 3, 2019), Ezra commented, "I remember that you learned a lot from Bob Bellah. Although I know it is not popular any more, I still find AGIL a very useful way to think about issues, and when I attack some new problem, I still think through the problem in relation to AGIL, at lower levels or big national or even international levels. . . . Am proud of what you have achieved, especially after you told me about your youthful years, and hope our paths cross before long. Warm regards, Ezra." These snippets of my experiences with Ezra serve to illustrate how he kept up close, warm, and personally intimate relations with so many people. They also show that undergirding Ezra's narrative-oriented writing style lay a rich and integrative sociological understanding and imagination.

James V. Jesudason

Boulder, Colorado

As a young graduate student in sociology at Harvard in the late 1970s, I could not anticipate how fond and appreciative of Ezra I would become. When I thought of professors to work with, I had in mind Orlando Patterson, who taught the sociology of development, among other courses. My dilemma was to find supervisors in addition to Orlando to guide me. With some uneasiness, I gave my thesis proposal to Ezra to see if the scope of the East Asian region could be stretched a bit. To my pleasant surprise, he was quite happy to be my adviser, and sure enough, his fascination with the peoples and cultures of East Asia turned out to be quite elastic.

I established my perch in Singapore for my research and writing. Perhaps it was the isolation from the department, but my anguish over the dissertation began to grow. Working on a single case and thinking that writing was all about being theoretically bold, I had a hard time making the pieces fit. And I doubted I could ever answer Orlando's important question, "What is the thesis in your thesis?" as I was not sure I had one. I entertained the thought of giving up.

Ezra then became the savior to whom I will always be grateful. When I visited Harvard for the semester, Ezra suggested that I join the thesis workshop he held at his house. It turned out to be the supportive environment I needed. Ezra said there was no reason to be overly fixated on theory and mentioned that earlier he himself had moved away from doing high theory under Parsons to being more interested in capturing important and interesting processes in society. What made my fate serendipitously irreversible was Ezra's reading two chapters of my thesis before his yearlong sabbatical in Japan and stating that he fully trusted my efforts. Gosh, how could I possibly quit? I wrote the remaining chapters with more confidence and soon after completing the dissertation, it was accepted by Oxford University Press. It turned out that Ezra's nurturing hand would lead me to a career in academics.

Ezra's involvement with his students did not end with the dissertation. He was the quintessential Confucian father figure, nurturing and engaging his wards even as their hair turned gray. We met several times over the years in Singapore, where I had taken up a job at the National

University of Singapore, and in the U.S., primarily at the annual Association of Asian Studies (AAS) conference, a forum Ezra much preferred to the strictly sociological ones. It was always fun to meet with him in these conference settings and see him surrounded by scholars and former students. During my stint in Singapore, Ezra stopped by a few times to brief the Singapore cabinet at the invitation of Lee Kuan Yew, the country's foremost founding father and strongman. Wanting to have my take on the nation's situation, Ezra would invite me for lunch before his sessions with the Singapore leadership. I will always remember Ezra telling me how intriguing it was to see Lee Kuan Yew in action, running the sessions like a professor conducting a tutorial. Lee would pose questions to Ezra and pontificate on Ezra's responses, with the rest of the cabinet listening or nodding in agreement. Being with Ezra allowed one to enter a world to which the typical scholar generally has no access. But what struck me most about Ezra was his endearing humility, a humility that never went away even with fame and his association with so many elites and leaders. His interest was never to hobnob with them or boast about his connections, but rather to gain insight into the leadership's thinking. For Ezra, the key variable in charting societal development and progress was the nature and quality of the elite. He once asked me what I thought was the key problem facing East Asian societies. As I stumbled for an answer, mentally searching my menu of favorite ideas and concepts, he interjected with "political succession." Ezra put great stock in leaders who improved the lives of their citizens, provided basic stability, educated the population, and cultivated national pride and strength. He never took for granted the quality of government, which for him needed continual nurturing. This reinforced to me that he was a Confucian at heart.

One question that I dreaded from Ezra, especially after I returned to the U.S. to take a job at the Colorado School of Mines, was "What are you working on now?" I don't think the reply that my university was a narrow engineering school not conducive to my scholarship was convincing to him. He mentioned that Alvin Goulder had written an excellent book, *Patterns of Industrial Organization*, using the gypsum industry as case material. Ezra thought there could be interesting sociological questions to be asked of the mining sector. This recommendation to seek new possibilities was typical of Ezra's scholarly dynamism. Perhaps to goad me on, he would always introduce me to his circle of friends at the

AAS conference. But alas, not all of us have Ezra's persistent curiosity and passion.

What ultimately made me feel close to Ezra was that our conversations inevitably touched on family matters. He knew my wife Judy and was especially thrilled to learn that one of his favorite undergraduate students at Harvard, Frank Packer, whom he subsequently met often in Japan and Hong Kong, was Judy's brother. Even as a famous scholar, Ezra enjoyed the human connection with his students. On more than one occasion, he invited me to stay in his Cambridge house. I will always regret not doing so. Ezra seemed so fit, and I would tell myself that I would visit him sometime in the future.

I will always treasure my relationship with Ezra. Through quite accidental circumstances, I was fortunate to come to know a great scholar, a kind and cheery soul, and an optimist for the human condition, who truly made a difference in my academic and personal life.

Satohiro Akimoto

Sasakawa Peace Foundation USA

One of the luckiest, if not *the* luckiest, things that has ever happened to me was to meet the late Professor Ezra Vogel. I came to Harvard in 1987 not knowing what kind of life I was stepping into in Cambridge. Ezra generously gave me guidance, support, and encouragement from the very first day I met him. His warm mentorship continued for three decades until his untimely passing last December. I am forever grateful to him.

Ezra's scholarship on Japan and China made him a true giant in East Asian studies. There have been many great scholars of East Asia, but none displayed a scholarly understanding of both Japan and China to the extent Ezra did. He was simply in his own league in terms of his mastery of the history, politics, economy, society, and languages of the two respective nations. Ezra was also unmatched in his extensive network of well-learned and well-connected friends in both Japan and China.

No single methodology defined Ezra's scholarly approach. However, he always emphasized the importance of getting the big picture right before focusing on smaller details. Ezra said his approach was influenced by the structural-functionalism methodology of Professor Talcott Parsons, who was his teacher. Of course, he understood the usual criticism of structural functionalism. Still, he thought it was useful for understanding the big picture, particularly when it was combined with other approaches.

Ezra thought acquiring language skills was very important in conducting scholarly research in East Asia. He was fluent in both Japanese and Chinese and continuously made efforts to retain his language skills. When he found out I was teaching Japanese as a drill instructor under the late Professor Tazuko Ajiro Monane, he even asked to converse with me in Japanese so as to retain his Japanese language skills. His son Steven Vogel is correct in saying that his father took pride in his ability to conduct research and give public lectures in both languages.

While Ezra's scholarly work covered a wide range of issues, such as family life, social welfare, industrial development, and foreign relations, his main contribution was to help the West understand the historic rise of East Asia, particularly Japan and China. He saw Japan, which was the first non-Western state to successfully modernize and industrialize, as a developmental model for countries in the region.

Ezra wrote many widely read books on the rise of East Asia to educate scholars, students, policymakers, politicians, business leaders, and the general public. *Japan's New Middle Class: The Salary Man and His Family in a Tokyo Suburb* (1963), *Japan as Number One: Lessons for America* (1979), *One Step Ahead in China: Guangdong under Reform* (1990), *The Four Little Dragons: The Spread of Industrialization in East Asia* (1993), *Deng Xiaoping and the Transformation of China* (2011), *The Park Chung Hee Era: The Transformation of South Korea* (2011), and *China and Japan: Facing History* (2019) are among his most important works.

I was fortunate enough to be Ezra's student at Harvard from 1987 to 1995 when I was pursuing an MA in East Asian Studies and a PhD in sociology. Until Ezra became the National Intelligence Officer for East Asia at the National Intelligence Council, I was his head teaching fellow, with ten to twelve other teaching fellows under me in his signature course, Industrial East Asia. The class was a large survey course looking into how modernization in East Asia was achieved first by Japan and then by other countries that followed the Japanese development model in a "flying geese formation." Ezra demonstrated truly amazing wisdom and depth of knowledge of Japan, South Korea, Southeast Asia, and China, stimulating his students' interest in non-Western civilization. Needless to say, this course provided a conceptual foundation for the professional careers of many future scholars, policymakers, politicians, and business leaders.

Ezra told me that it was not easy to continue his course, Industrial East Asia, after he came back from Washington in 1996. It was mainly because Japan had entered the beginning of "the lost decades" following the bust of the economic bubble. In short, Ezra noticed that students were skeptical about the Japanese model and were more interested in China. Japan seemed to be muddling along after the 1990s, but Ezra never lost faith in the Japanese people's ability and willingness to meet new challenges.

Several months before he passed away, Ezra said that Japan still has many things to offer a world where numerous countries struggle with problems arising from rapid globalization, such as economic disparity, violence and riots, political instability, and extreme political views. He said he would encourage others to take up Japan in its new global context.

Even though Ezra was an internationally respected scholar, he retained the humbleness and kindness he inherited from his Jewish immigrant parents in Delaware, Ohio. I have never met a professor so devoted to and supportive of his students.

Some of my fondest memories of Ezra were when I was tasked with going to his house an hour and a half before the Industrial East Asia morning class to get lecture notes from him so I could make copies to distribute to around 150 or so students to help them study. He would often greet me wearing a gown over his pajamas. We would chat on his porch about various subjects in a mixture of English and Japanese. These were precious moments for me. His parting word was always *"Ganbare!"* accompanied by a warm smile. Ezra, I miss you.

Ezra was deeply troubled by heightened tensions with China in the latter part of his life. His concern about how to live with China, a country that has become more confident and assertive, was reflected in the final chapter of his last book, *China and Japan: Facing History* (2019). Although Ezra is gone, the issue of how to deal effectively with China will remain an urgent global issue for this century. I am confident that Ezra's numerous students in the U.S., China, Japan, and elsewhere will do their best to navigate this challenging situation while reflecting upon what Ezra would say.

Barbara Molony

Santa Clara University

Kathleen Molony

Concord, Massachusetts

BARBARA AND KATHLEEN

Ezra's role as a mentor to so many cannot be overstated. We were both Fulbrighters in 1975–76, a year when Ezra was also in Japan conducting research and brushing up on his Japanese. Already quite fluent, he met occasionally with a language teacher in the Stanford Program offices, where we saw him from time to time. That was typical Ezra, wanting to improve in an area where he already excelled. We were part of a group of graduate students who met regularly that year to share our ideas and experiences of living and researching in Japan. We knew we could count on Ezra to comment and offer an important perspective, should we seek him out. He was, in many ways, a "father figure" to our group.

KATHLEEN

I was fortunate to encounter Ezra Vogel at pivotal moments in my career after the Fulbright year in Japan and after I earned my PhD in modern Japanese history. I taught briefly as a lecturer at Princeton, but then decided to leave academia and move to the Boston area, where I began work as an economic analyst. It was a heady time to work on Japan, then the world's second-largest economy and growing faster than other industrialized economies, even with the setbacks of two oil shocks. *Japan as Number One* had just been published, an important book as I started out in my new consulting job. I had the pleasure of seeing Ezra many times, and on these occasions, he often lent encouraging words about my work. I recall a conference where we both spoke; the joint briefing that we gave then-Governor William Weld as he prepared to lead a trade mission to Japan; meetings of the Japan Society of Boston when we both served on the board; and the time that I spoke at a seminar of the Program on U.S.-Japan Relations (before participating in the program myself as an advanced research fellow in 1993–94). He offered public support, as when he spoke to the *Boston Globe* following my appointment as executive director of the Massachusetts Office of International Trade and Investment (MOITI), and he agreed to write a recommendation letter for me to an important organization. I ran into him many times with my sister, often at Association for Asian Studies (AAS) conferences, and he took the time, though busy catching up with everyone there—*and Ezra knew absolutely everyone!*—to ask after our family. He had a talent that few people of his status and stature possess: the ability to care about individuals and to take a genuine interest in helping them achieve their potential, both in and out of academia. As an administrator at Harvard over the past twenty years, I never missed the chance to hear Ezra speak. He was a teacher, a mentor, and a friend. He will be missed.

BARBARA

Back in Cambridge after my Fulbright year in Japan, I was swept right into teaching as a tutor in East Asian Studies (EAS)—all the while trying to finish writing my dissertation. EAS was Ezra's baby, and he ran a wonderful program. He encouraged the gang of tutors to collaborate with one another and to have close collegial relationships with our undergraduate students. A number of people reading this will recall that EAS crossed disciplinary boundaries, enriching everyone's perspectives. Corky White, Sociology; Maryruth Coleman, Government; Howard Spendelow, History; Tom Gold, Sociology; Kent Guy, History; and I were all tutors at the same time—and we all went into academia, with Maryruth later entering the State Department and rising to a senior embassy position. A lot of our students in the late 1970s went into academia and related fields too (Susan Napier, academic and leading scholar on *anime*; the late Nancy Abelmann, anthropologist of Korea; Tom Levenson, academic and prolific author and documentary filmmaker; Renée Tajima Peña, academic and multiple award-winning documentary filmmaker; Tom Keirstead, academic and leading scholar on medieval Japan; Charlie Kupchan, academic, diplomat, and presidential adviser; and Susan Chira, a multiple award-winning journalist at the *New York Times*) and the list goes on. That was just a small percentage of EAS students in a three-year period; there have been hundreds more over the years. The EAS climate of collegiality and multidisciplinary cooperation is what inspired so many of us, and Ezra was the one who created that.

Ezra continued to play a role in my life after those wonderful years on the third floor of the old Coolidge Hall at 1737 Cambridge Street. As Kathy wrote above, Ezra was always there, both professionally (conferences) and personally (at my wedding, for example). When I had just started teaching in California, he flew out to give a lecture that elevated my status. My colleagues told me later that it was his supportive letter that was the most persuasive in putting me at the head of the list of candidates for my job. I literally owe Ezra my career, and I know I'm not the only one to say this. Ezra was one of a kind—a true mensch.

Sook Jong Lee

Seoul, Korea

Ezra's passing came as a shock to me. The last time I met Ezra in person was in October 2016, when I organized a seminar with the Belfer Center at the Harvard Kennedy School. In my opening remarks, I proudly paid tribute to Ezra, seated in front of me, as my "lifetime teacher."

My fond memories of Ezra go back to my graduate years at Harvard University in the 1980s. When I arrived at Harvard, Ezra was widely known as a Japan expert, largely due to his bestseller *Japan as Number One* and also his earlier book, *Japan's New Middle Class*. I soon found out that he had also written *Canton under Communism*. I was very impressed by his fieldwork abilities, not to mention his fluency in both Japanese and Chinese. Ezra's presence in the Sociology Department influenced me to pursue Japanese political economy as my area of concentration.

My personal ties with Ezra were strengthened when I served as his teaching and research assistant. Ezra had started a large undergraduate course titled Industrial East Asia, a course in which more than one hundred students were usually enrolled. I became one of the six or seven teaching fellows for the course. He used to invite us to his house near William James Hall, where he fed us barbecue he cooked himself on the porch. Ezra naturally became my thesis adviser and introduced me to several important people to interview during my fieldwork year in Tokyo.

Ezra attracted many Asian students and scholars. Through his support of them, Ezra contributed to Asian solidarity in the department and on the larger Harvard campus. I think he was able to do so not only because of his expertise and great connections, but also due to his character. He appreciated the virtues of humility and respect, as Asians do, and became an interlocutor of Asian intellectuals.

All Korean students remember Ezra as a warm and friendly teacher. In the doctoral sociology program during the 1980s, there were more students from Korea than from any other Asian country. Ezra empathized with Korean students and intellectuals, understanding the country's ongoing struggles for democratization against an authoritarian regime. He was an ardent supporter of Korea's democratization and welcomed dissidents and former activist students on campus. At the same time, Ezra recognized Korea's economic achievements during the Park Chung-hee era and the merits of conglomerates, both of which Korean leftists criticized. His principled approach and fair assessment marked him as a scholar respected by many Koreans of both conservative and progressive leanings.

Ezra's ability to transcend mutual conflicts for the common interest was equally applied to the tricky relations between Korea and Japan. Through his books and a vast array of writings, Ezra emphasized reconciliation and cooperation between Korea and Japan as well as between China and Japan. He used to discuss how the three Northeast Asian countries had influenced one another historically. His most recent book, *China and Japan: Facing History*, is a manifestation of the consistent position he has held since I was in graduate school. In a nutshell, Ezra was a true unifier for Asia and he anticipated its rise as one region.

As I prepare to retire from a university professorship myself, Ezra's relentless pursuit of study and research has set a good example for me to follow. With respect and a warm heart, I wish for my teacher Ezra Vogel to rest in peace, and hope that his family knows how much he is loved and missed.

Mary-Jo DelVecchio Good

Harvard University

In 1968 Professor Ezra Vogel changed my life. Ezra took me into his Social Relations PhD program in Comparative Sociology to study for a joint
degree in Sociology and Middle Eastern Studies. I was in my final semester of a two-year MA program at Harvard's Center for Middle Eastern Studies when I first met Ezra, and I was thrilled. He embraced those
of us in his new, fully funded program. He taught us the core theory
course and thus became our scholarly model, a gentle, generous mentor
as well as our professor. Ezra's kind of sociology instantly became what
I aspired to do. More than any other faculty member at Harvard, he shaped
my intellectual frame and my research endeavors. Throughout research
and scholarly adventures in Turkey and Iran (1969–76), and since 1996 in
Indonesia, Ezra has always been on my mind. Whenever we met, recently as well as in the distant past, he always asked engaging questions
about the societies where I worked.

Serendipitously, my professorship at the Department of Global Health
and Social Medicine, Harvard Medical School (1983–2019, emerita
July 2019) led me to become Co-Principal Investigator of a Fogarty Training Program for Chinese psychiatrists. The Fogarty grants my husband
Byron Good (Principal Investigator) and I wrote and directed, with input
from our colleagues in Beijing and Shanghai, were renewed with robust
funding for seventeen years (2000–2017). Our many brief yet intense
visits to China to recruit new fellows, hold conferences, and work with
former fellows and colleagues at the Peking University Institute for Mental
Health and the Shanghai Mental Health Center increasingly made us
wish we had formally studied Chinese, especially as we traveled to the
provinces with senior psychiatrists to meet clinicians and patients and
their families and to assess mental health needs and new programs' effectiveness and deficiencies. Early on we turned to Ezra's (and Charlotte's)
China studies to ground and guide our efforts to understand the rapid
transformations in Chinese society and to make sense of policies and
practices driving our fellows, their colleagues, and their esteemed institutions, which were responsible for leading a revolution in psychiatry, psychiatric practices, and mental healthcare for the entire country. Ezra and

Charlotte attended many of the Fogarty conferences at Harvard, in a show of interest and support that was highly valued. Many fellows greatly appreciated that Professor Ezra Vogel was my PhD adviser, even though my dissertation research was on Iran, not China. Our Fogarty Fellows, now leaders of the Shanghai Mental Health Center, nominated me for the Magnolia Silver Award from the Shanghai Municipal Government, in appreciation for support for Shanghai's development. When I received the award in 2012, Ezra was on my mind.

Ezra continued to influence Byron's and my life. In 2011, we were selected by the Asia Center to give the Harvard Ezra F. Vogel Malaysia/Singapore Initiative Public Lecture Series at Nanyang Technical University in Singapore and the Malaysia National University in Kuala Lumpur.

Fifty-one years after first meeting Ezra, we had our final email exchange. I excerpt some of that here:

May 15, 2019
Dear Ezra,

When I received word of my upcoming Silen Mentoring Award [a Harvard Medical School award for lifetime achievement in mentoring], I thought of you. You were truly my Mentor-in-Chief at Harvard during my years as a graduate student in Sociology. From selecting me to join the first comparative class, to teaching us the core course on sociological classics where we read Bellah, Weber, Durkheim, and Marx, to your wonderfully ethnographic, historical, and exceptionally detailed lectures on Japan and China, you were an inspiration and taught me how to learn about another society. In your Japan lecture course you told us in detail about the variety of kitchen equipment in Japanese Salarymen's homes. You invited us to your house and showed us your kitchen with the variety of wonderfully colorful gadgets. It struck me how to pay attention, what small things reveal about economic and cultural transformations. I took that lesson to the field in Iran and to my dissertation research. I recall you wrote a comment about my thesis, calling it impressive but noting I could have included more on the economy of the Iranian town I studied. And your amazing work on China has been my key source for understanding the astonishing changes in Chinese society over these many decades. I am so very grateful too for your ongoing kind and respectful support through my odd faculty career here at Harvard. When asked "who did you study with at Harvard?" I always tell people "with Professor Ezra Vogel." I shan't forget the many bumps or major hills you gave me a lift over.

May 16, 2019

Mary-Jo,

Wow. You are kind to send me this and wonderfully generous in your statements. And again I can be proud of you for what you have achieved. Now that our country is so nasty to Iran I always wonder what you think. . . . If you have more time when we visit you, I would like to hear in a little more detail. See you soon.
All the best
Ezra

Professor Ezra F. Vogel was an extraordinary mentor to so many. I was fortunate to have him as my PhD adviser and extraordinary mentor-in-chief. He celebrated his students' achievements with such warmth and joy. On the day before Ezra died, I was composing an email with details on Iran and Indonesia. *Selamat jalan, old friend.*

Nana Oishi

University of Melbourne

It is with both sadness and gratitude that I share my thoughts and memories of the great Ezra Vogel on his passing. I had the privilege of getting to know Ezra personally and professionally as one of his last PhD students at Harvard. The renowned scholar took me under his wing, calling himself my "*Amerika no otōsan* (American father)" and offering his unwavering support. My appreciation and respect for him were such that I later asked him to be the *nakōdo*, or intermediary, for my Japanese nuptials. He kindly accepted and gave an inspiring speech at our wedding reception on the top floor of William James Hall in the summer of 2001.

I have many precious memories of Ezra, but the highlights are from my final years at Harvard in 1998–2001, which coincided with the final years of his teaching tenure there. As a teaching fellow for his very last course, Industrial East Asia, I was fortunate to witness his incredible passion for teaching. Despite his godlike status as an eminent scholar and his busy schedule as the founding Director of the Harvard Asia Center, Ezra truly cared about his students—not just about their academic and intellectual development, but also their confidence-building and reflective transformation. This particular class was large, with over two hundred students, but he still tried to ensure that everyone felt included. To assist the introverts and international students to speak up, he suggested that all students bring a short paragraph (three to four lines) to the section each week, which established a rather stress-free equilibrium. Students were provided with constructive feedback from us throughout the semester; they honed their skills, developed confidence, and became active learners. Ezra even organized lunches for all students who took his graduate course and provided us with valuable advice. He truly enjoyed empowering his students, helping them with networking, and inspiring them to contribute to U.S.-Asia relations in their own capacities. I admired Ezra for his dedication and holistic approach to teaching, which I have been trying to emulate throughout my own academic career.

I got to know Ezra even more closely when he invited me to be his personal language tutor. Although his Japanese was almost impeccable, he never stopped making efforts to sustain and improve it, an incredible feat for someone of his age and eminence. I was invited to his Cambridge home every fortnight, where we spent forty-five minutes discussing my dissertation and forty-five minutes poring over Japanese newspapers. It was a precious opportunity for me to assist him as well as discuss Japanese politics and social issues, not least given that he was the world's best scholar in Japanese studies. Ezra also shared intriguing life stories with me from time to time, such as his long-term friendship with prominent Japanese politicians and economic giants, which I thoroughly enjoyed. I still close my eyes and fondly remember those days when we were sitting on the sofa in his living room, happily sipping the special herbal drink that he made and talking about the future of Japan.

Ezra was an exceptional role model, not only as a scholar, but also as a changemaker. He often told me that scholars should make more effort to make a positive impact on society by actively sharing our knowledge and expertise with the government and the public. His commitment to both academia *and* the broader society resonated with me. Ezra inspired me to get involved in Japanese government and UN projects even after resigning from the UN in Geneva and commencing my academic career in Japan, for which I'll remain forever grateful. For nearly ten years, until I moved to Australia, Ezra and I continued to meet when he visited Tokyo annually, and he was gracious enough to express appreciation that I was following his path.

Ezra's scholarly quest to build constructive international relations and better mutual understanding in the Asia-Pacific will continue to inspire his former students and future scholars. Indeed, Ezra's last book, *China and Japan: Facing History*, is an essential resource for academics and students alike. I am convinced that my future students and next-generation scholars will continue to learn from all of his scholarly work. Some of my former students are already pursuing their careers in fields where they can utilize their expertise in Asia. Ezra's legacy will continue to influence and inspire future generations of students and scholars.

Ezra will be remembered in Asia and the world not only as an "academic giant," but for his far-reaching intellectual horizons and commitment to being a "conscientious peacemaker." Ezra's research has greatly contributed to a better understanding of the Asia-Pacific. All those fortunate enough to know Ezra personally will remember him as an extraordinary human being, graced with tremendous kindness, a humble attitude, a deep dedication to society, and a contagious smile. He will remain in our hearts and memories forever.

Yoshikazu Kato

Trans-Pacific Group

It was always a nerve-racking process to face Vogel-*sensei*, even though he was such a humble and kind person. Emailing him, scheduling appointments with him, visiting him at his home next to the Harvard campus, discussing with him, I would get nervous and sweat. Was it because he was a famous and influential white scholar, or was it because I, a yellow man from a small Eastern island, felt inferior in front of so-called Westerners?

I am sure that it was not his problem but mine. My feelings and situation also seem to be a collective problem that "we" Asians have to seriously think about and try to solve sooner or later. I have always wondered what Vogel-*sensei* was trying to convey and teach us through his words and actions and what historical lessons and intellectual nourishment we should have drawn from them.

Vogel-*sensei* is my mentor. I went to Harvard in the summer of 2012, started my study and research, spent two years in Cambridge, and then moved to Washington, D.C., to continue my study and research at the Johns Hopkins University School of Advanced International Studies. All the contacts and recommendations needed for these studies were arranged by Vogel-*sensei*. Without him, I would not even have come to the United States.

During my stay at Harvard, I often met and exchanged thoughts with my *sensei*. When he was not traveling, we had individual meetings about every two weeks. Appointments were made by email. We never missed an appointment we had made, and we always met at his home. No exceptions, ever.

I usually arrived about ten minutes early after wandering around for a while, organizing my thoughts in a nervous state, and ringing his doorbell when it was almost the appointed time. He always greeted me with a modest, kind smile and said, "Hi Kato-san, come in!"

Shortly after I arrived at Harvard, the so-called nationalization incident between Japan and China occurred. As Japan's ally and China's strategic competitor, the United States was bound to get involved. *Sensei* was very concerned and worried about the change in and escalation of the "status quo" in the region. We particularly focused on how Japan and China could overcome communication barriers and on the lack of channels to bring the crisis to a soft landing and put Japan-China relations back on a healthy track.

The second half of 2012 was also a "political season" in China. The 18th Party Congress was held in autumn. During that time, we mainly discussed Chinese politics, including domestic power struggles and their implications for external relations. In retrospect, Japan-China relations and Chinese politics were the topics of most common interest between *sensei* and me. Of course, we also discussed many other issues: Taiwan, the nuclear issue, the Japan-U.S. alliance, the South China Sea, the East

China Sea, the American Dream, the issue of foreign students from China and Japan at Harvard, and the future development of Japan and China. There were never any Japanese-style pleasantries or Chinese-style politenesses between us; we just went straight to the issues, finished our conversation, then went our separate ways.

I vividly remember that before *sensei* went on a business trip to China (Japan), he would ask me, "Kato-san, would you please discuss things in Chinese (Japanese) today? I am going to give a speech in Chinese (Japanese), so I want to practice." With extraordinary humility and sincerity, he never stopped working on improving his Japanese and Chinese.

Whenever I needed *sensei*'s advice or help, he listened to my ideas and helped me find solutions. In fact, as far as I know, this approach was not only directed to me; he always cared for and assisted young people. The "Vogel *juku*" (study group) was certainly one of his platforms. *Sensei* worked to nurture the future talents of Japan and China, not by one-way teaching, but by reciprocal exchanges.

In December 2017, when I had the opportunity to return to Harvard, we engaged in a three-hour discussion one afternoon. When I left, I told him that I would like to conduct a long interview with him and make it into a book. I hoped to record his work, experiences, beliefs, and messages, which all of us could absorb as lessons. *Sensei* readily agreed. I remember that he said in Japanese, "If it's with Kato-san, I'm willing to do it. Don't say anything about an interview, let's just have a conversation." At that moment, I was so moved that I almost shed tears on the spot. When I left his house and walked along Cambridge Street, I calmed down and thought from the bottom of my heart, "I wish I could be an 'old man' like him" (*sensei* always described himself as an "old man"—*rōjin*—in Japanese).

At the end of August 2018, on the eve of my new appointment in Hong Kong, I stayed at *sensei*'s house for three nights and had a four-day conversation with him. The content of the conversation was actually a continuation of our previous discussions: Chinese politics, Japan-China relations, Sino-U.S. relations, and geopolitical circumstances in the Asia-Pacific region. But this time he also shared with me many personal stories about his family and scholarly life.

I was honored to be able to publish *Rebalance: China, Japan, and the United States in a New Era* (Diamond Press, 2019) in Japan and *A Sinologist*

Speaks: Ezra Vogel on Relations between China, Japan, and the United States (City University of Hong Kong Press, 2021) in Hong Kong. I tried to figure out how Vogel-*sensei* conducted research over the course of his life after encountering Japan and China, and what kinds of experiences and field research led to the formation of his thinking and writing. In conclusion, working with *sensei* was simply fun.

Hu Xiaojiang

Beijing Normal University

The death of a ninety-year-old man should not come as a surprise to anyone: time is relentless, and the end comes to us all. And yet, I still remember the shock I felt on December 21, 2020, when I learned that my former PhD adviser, Ezra Vogel, had passed away. Talking to some of my fellow former advisees, it seems that everyone was similarly caught off guard, because in our heart of hearts, we truly believed Ezra would live forever.

The Chinese students in the Department of Sociology at Harvard never called him "Professor Vogel," as Chinese culture would require. Those Chinese who called him "Professor Vogel" were mostly visiting scholars, government officials, and media people. Their eyes focused on "Professor Vogel's" grand career. We, his students, saw him differently. He was Ezra, our mentor, always jovial, generous, and fair.

What is the legacy of a scholar? There is of course their written work, which others in this volume will undoubtedly address. There is a legacy of impact in the real world in the form of policies shaped and ideas implanted in public discourse. There is the continuing intellectual legacy of their students and mentees. And there is a much more diffuse legacy of simple wisdom that gets passed around to those around them, unspoken lessons not so much of "what" but of "how" to approach the world and our work. In the twenty years I knew Ezra, he left me with so many memories and fragments of this kind of wisdom.

Ezra did not care about the various theoretical paradigms popular in mainstream American sociology, even those theories derived from research on China or Japan. He focused on the concrete and the empirical.

His speeches were of a similar style, citing mountains of material from his rich experience and impressive memory, but he would not make theoretical abstractions. This fact caused some American sociologists to dismiss him, thinking that he had made no "true" theoretical contributions. But Ezra didn't care about those grumblings. He rejoiced in his concreteness.

Ezra started to learn Chinese only in early middle age and still insisted on improving his Chinese skills into his seventies and eighties. I served as his Chinese tutor for quite some time. Often I felt that the vast amount of time and energy he spent on improving his Chinese language skills might not be well spent. He could have used that time on something more useful, something that could not be replaced simply by using a good interpreter. But many years later I understood the value of his actions. By using Chinese or Japanese language in his interviews, he showed to his interviewees his earnest and genuine effort to learn from them. This gesture of respect made a huge difference and opened a lot of doors for Ezra.

Ezra's home is right next to the Harvard campus, and student clubs often invited him to give lectures. He almost always said yes. Such lectures are mostly off-the-cuff, informal affairs, but they still take a good deal of time and energy, so some clubs have funds for honoraria for guest speakers. Ezra always refused, and he took it for granted that everyone else was just like him. Once he was surprised and puzzled and angrily said to me: "I heard that some professors accept money from student organizations? What money can student clubs have?" Charging for off-campus activities was one thing, but serving the students was to him an intrinsic part of a professor's job. He always retained this devotion to the purity of campus life, despite being so aware of the messy reality outside of it.

After retirement, Ezra did not "retire." At parties everyone praised him with the usual "You look great!" He responded jokingly, "If people are telling you 'You look great!' it means you are very old." Even though he said that, he really didn't think he was old. He didn't plan for a leisurely retired life. He still got up early every day and went for a run or bike ride on the Charles River, unimpeded in winter and summer. The monthly gatherings of Chinese sociology students and scholars at his home continued for another twenty years. His books came out one by one, with several projects "in progress." Whenever major international events happened, the Chinese media would come and interview him. A few years ago, he told the media that China needed to take Japan as a lesson for the dangers of the encroachment of ultra-nationalism. As a Japan expert, Ezra knew all too well how uncontrolled nationalism could lead a country into unspeakable disaster. These were the heartfelt words of an old man who had a deep understanding of, and great goodwill toward, China. His last interview was about the coronavirus pandemic.

The last time I went to Harvard was ten years ago. One night in heavy snow, I passed by Ezra's house and wanted to turn in just to say hello. I hadn't informed him in advance. His house was dark. Where did this eighty-year-old go on such a snowy night? Most likely invited to give a lecture by another student club. I stood outside the door and saw that his bicycle was still parked in the familiar spot under the eaves. It was still the same old road bicycle, the thin wheels and the tall frame stained with mud. But there was no dust on the handlebars and seat. It was obviously a bicycle that was often on the road. So, I knew everything was fine with Ezra. I turned away with peace of mind, taking it for granted that he would continue like this forever.

Yun Zhou

University of Michigan

As I remember Professor Ezra Vogel, I think of light-filled rooms. We—the China sociology group—gathered at Ezra and Charlotte's home almost every month for dinner followed by a research presentation. These monthly gatherings, organized by Professor Ezra Vogel and Professor Martin Whyte, were where sociologists working on China—a lot of us graduate students at Harvard—connected and workshopped our ongoing research.

Dinner was always Chinese food from a local restaurant. A wooden table stood in the middle of the dining room. We sat, elbow to elbow, with colorful, mismatched mugs filled with steaming tea: Ezra, Marty, and Charlotte telling stories about their decades of doing research in China—interviewing refugees in Hong Kong during the 1960s and 1970s; Ezra's newest work on Deng Xiaoping; Ezra and Marty bantering and recounting old lore from when Social Relations was still a department;

Ezra pouring tea and nudging us to get another helping of the food; Marty warmly joking about Ezra's busy schedule and boundless energy.

Throughout the ups and downs of my graduate school years, these gatherings were a source of much-cherished constancy. After a summer away, I always looked forward to the first meeting of the new school year: Cambridge was at its most beautiful in those early autumnal days, with a slight chill in the air and leaves ablaze. A quick walk from the Department of Sociology, turning onto the quiet street, I could already see light streaming out of Ezra's living room windows. In that moment, no matter what else was happening, I would know exactly what to expect—conversations with mentors and friends in light-filled rooms.

I learned a great deal from attending and later presenting at the China sociology dinner meetings. Our speakers rotated every month, with priority given to presentations by graduate students. It was at those meetings that I got to know my colleagues and their diverse interests and work—from religion to technology. Having a space, with comfortable chairs nonetheless, dedicated to a wide range of sociological research on China fulfilled an intellectual lacuna.

After dinner, as we gradually settled into the living room, Ezra would always sit next to the presenter. The format of the presentations varied, from our dissertation chapters and third-year qualifying papers, to less-polished research proposals and occasionally, the inkling of an idea. It was *the* place to receive practical advice on how to get certain people to sit down for an interview; how to make a plan A, but also plans B and C when doing fieldwork. The comments Ezra gave were encouraging, but also had a sharpness that cut through the triviality that sometimes bogged down the researcher. When I presented one of my dissertation chapters, Ezra urged me to "tell a story" rather than running through a list of models, numbers, and robustness checks.

On occasion, Ezra and Marty would present their work too. The first China sociology dinner meeting I ever went to, as a first-year student, was Ezra's book talk on Deng Xiaoping. Throughout the talk I was frantically taking notes, feeling greatly unnerved by the vast ocean of knowledge that was unfamiliar to me. A few years later, I heard Marty's talk on "challenging the myths of the one-child policy," and in the process found some of my own previously held myths challenged. Both times were meaningful experiences—to learn and to discover, to rethink the "familiar," and to keep sharpening my analytical lens.

It was at those China sociology dinner meetings that I gradually began to grasp what it means to be a sociologist studying China—a process that I am still discovering. But through Ezra's example, I know what a joyful lifelong discovery it can be.

After each meeting ended and after Ezra and Charlotte had urged us to take some leftover food, standing under the porch light, Ezra would shake hands with each one of us and thank us for attending. An inky night stretched before us—we walked on, thinking, until the next time.

SEVEN

Mentoring Non-Harvard Students
for Academic Careers

Thomas P. Bernstein

Columbia University

I first met Ezra in Hong Kong in 1964, when I was starting research for my dissertation. Ezra was then morphing into his second persona as a China specialist, the first having been as a Japan specialist. I had not known who he was since I knew only a few Japan experts, mainly at Columbia. I found out that he had done fieldwork in a suburban village in the late 1950s, which eventually resulted in a book, *Japan's New Middle Class.*

Almost immediately afterward he plunged into the study of Chinese communist society, a country very different from Japan, and became an eminent scholar of both. I had been studying Soviet politics, but also added China in 1960 with the intent of comparing the two, focusing on the collectivization of agriculture. It wasn't a case of emulating Ezra's example, since I didn't know of him at that time, but his success in writing on China and Japan inspired me, though I must add that he was far more successful in pursuing his dual interests than I was in mine. In 1964 he encouraged my work. He was eager to learn more about Chinese communism from anyone he encountered, and so he asked me many questions, some of which I couldn't answer. His intellectual curiosity, boundless energy, and devotion to his work were truly amazing.

Our contact in 1964 was limited since I was working at the newly established Universities Service Centre for foreign students and scholars studying China, whereas Ezra chose not to use this facility, though he occasionally visited the Centre. Once, he presented some research findings there which became his famous article, "From Friendship to Comradeship." In due course he became one of my mentors, along with Doak Barnett and John Hazard.

In 1968 Ezra invited me to do research at the East Asian Research Center, where I visited in the spring semester and also in the summer of

1969. Of course I was deeply grateful for his support. My time there was extremely valuable. I got to know Ezra quite well, even though he was extremely busy with his duties as deputy director of the Center and with his scholarly work and teaching. In 1978–79 I taught Chinese politics at Harvard, so this was another opportunity for me to engage with him, which I greatly enjoyed. I very much appreciate what must have been his favorable recommendations for my positions at Yale and later at Columbia.

In 2016 I wrote a lengthy review of a book by Alexander Pantsov, with Steven Levine, *Deng Xiaoping: A Revolutionary Life*, for the online journal, H-Diplo-Roundtable Review. In it I compared their book with Ezra's *Deng Xiaoping and the Transformation of China*. I thought that the two authors had slighted the importance of Ezra's book, which I found to be more enlightening than the Pantsov-Levine volume. Not surprisingly, Professor Pantsov wrote a critical rejoinder.

I mourn Ezra's death.

Bernie Frolic

York University

Ezra Vogel recruited me into the China field fifty years ago, and he remained a special friend afterward. Although we lived and worked in two separate countries, he always kept in touch with "his Canadian cousins." Just a year ago, when he was almost ninety years old, he traveled to Toronto from Cambridge to help my university inaugurate a new China research program and to talk about his latest book.

In 1970, I was invited to give a talk at the Harvard Russian Research Center. I had returned from the Soviet Union, where I was doing doctoral research, and I had also spent time in China. My paper ("Optimists and Pessimists in the Study of Communism") compared the two countries. It seemed that China was on the rise, whereas a year spent in Moscow had convinced me that the sun was starting to set on the Soviet revolution. After the talk, Ezra said, "You've studied the USSR for almost a decade, why not do the same with China? I began with Japan, and now

I've moved to China." He invited me to Harvard, gave me a key to the East Asian Research Center library, arranged for full-time Chinese language lessons, and introduced me to new colleagues in sinology. He generously let me and my family stay in his house in Cambridge. When I went to Hong Kong to do field research on the Cultural Revolution, Ezra arranged for me to be the director of the Universities Service Centre (USC). The USC was the only place at the time where Western scholars could do field research on China. Later in the 1970s, when I had finished my book on the Cultural Revolution (*Mao's People*) and was looking for a publisher, he personally took my manuscript to Harvard University Press to recommend its publication.

Last year I was finishing another book, this time on the political history of Canada's fifty-year relationship with the People's Republic of China. Given the growing rift between China and Canada, it was difficult to find the right conclusion. Ezra asked to take a look at the manuscript, "to see if Canada had done any better with China." He said that I shouldn't get caught up in an anti-China moment. "Always try to take a long-term view. Highlight the positive links with China over the past fifty years and find the best way to write about the current situation." His suggestions made all the difference.

It wasn't just that he recruited me into the China field, or that he helped me to publish two books. It was his academic foresight and his generosity that made him so special. He served as a scholar's model. What I will remember is his vision, his willingness to take a chance on new scholarship, his quiet brilliance, and his lasting friendship.

Deborah Davis

Yale University

When asked to reflect on experiences with Ezra, the memory that first surfaces is of gatherings. Reaching back to 1969, I recall the very first: a gathering in his living room where Ezra shared his pleasure in having recently discovered how many types of cheese one could buy in Cambridge supermarkets. Soon barriers between overwhelmed newcomers and visiting luminaries broke down, animated conversations flowed, telephone numbers were exchanged, and often lifelong friendships began. There are also memories of more formal gatherings, but even in those settings one recalls disparate people commencing a shared journey. One vivid image is of Vivienne Shue and Jay Mathews poring over newly declassified documents in an unrenovated Coolidge Hall seminar room because Ezra had befriended the visiting diplomat who sat at the head of the table. Then there are less formal but equally memorable gatherings, such as one in an attic office on Parker Street where he gave me permission to use the first-person pronoun even when writing to an authority. And most recently I remember one of his monthly dinners for all "China sociologists" in the Boston area, a gathering around take-out Chinese food that created intellectual synergies across academic affiliations, nationality, and generations.

And reverberating behind those many gatherings was his earliest advice when I was about to leave for my first fieldwork: don't forget you can always learn something from everyone. The clear implication was that every interview, no matter how awkward or even unpleasant, would yield insight and lead to better questions and more complete explanations. Later I discovered that his advice completely aligned with the Confucian proverb 三人行 必有我师, that "when three walk together, I am sure to find teachers among them." And over the decades, both when teaching and in the field, I repeatedly found myself quoting the phrase and remembering Ezra's wise guidance. But recently when I shared this memory with Charlotte, she confirmed that while indeed this openness to learning from every encounter did shape Ezra's interactions during fieldwork, it also explained his behavior when standing in a line at the Department of Motor Vehicles.

Charlotte also offered a more accurate wording as well as a fuller story of the origins of this pithy wisdom. It did not emerge from immersion in Chinese or Japanese sources or from decades of fieldwork in East Asia. Rather, the quote, which Charlotte felt might more accurately be translated as "he's so smart he can learn from anyone," was passed on to Ezra by Rollie Walker, his Bible Study professor at Ohio Wesleyan, whom Ezra frequently invoked as "the sage of Delaware."

Over his long scholarly career, Ezra not only fondly acknowledged his debts to the "sage of Delaware," he also worked with ferocious intensity and cared deeply about crafting a text to express his own point of view. Ezra always listened in order to learn from whomever he encountered, but when he wrote, he was the author.

Susan L. Shirk

University of California, San Diego

Ezra was my mentor and dear friend for more than fifty years. I was an MIT PhD student in political science (entered 1968), with Lucian Pye as my main adviser, but I never was persuaded by Lucian's cultural explanations of Chinese behavior—I thought they were an intellectual dead end. I came over to Harvard to take Ezra's graduate course on Chinese society and found his view of how people adapted to the Mao-era political structure much more compelling and amenable to empirical analysis. His brilliant 1965 *China Quarterly* article, "From Friendship to Comradeship: The Change in Personal Relations in Communist China," was the inspiration for my own dissertation research on middle school students. (If you read it today, you'll be depressed to see how much of the Mao-era climate of political anxiety that Ezra described has returned to make people wary of one another.) Ezra was one of my dissertation advisers and devoted hours of attention and encouragement to me. He also taught us the new art of refugee interviewing in Hong Kong and put his own interview notes in a file cabinet for all his students to read. He was a wonderful interviewer because of his warmth, empathy, and objectivity, all qualities that I sought to emulate in my own interviewing.

We were always in close touch, including during his time and then mine in the Clinton administration. His policy judgments were judicious and wise. And of course his extraordinary energy and productivity in his later years put everyone else to shame. Remarkably, he never slowed down at all. To keep up that pace, that sense of purpose, until you suddenly fall off a cliff—that's a life truly well lived.

Ezra's death leaves a big hole in my life and in the lives of his many other former students who became his lifelong friends. We'll also miss his wisdom as we struggle to understand China under Xi Jinping and how the U.S. should respond to it.

Anne F. Thurston

Johns Hopkins University

On the occasion of Ezra's ninetieth birthday, invited to share with him some special memory, I was delighted to record my memory of our first meeting. It was at the Universities Service Centre in Hong Kong in March of 1972. Arriving in Hong Kong via freighter after nearly three weeks at sea was an exhilarating experience, all the more so because sometime during my journey President Richard Nixon and Chairman Mao had met in Beijing and changed the course of history. The Universities Service Centre was the place to get the real story about what was happening inside China and was abuzz with excitement over both the changing U.S.-China relationship and the deepening American war in Vietnam. Many of the American China researchers in Hong Kong at the time (myself included) joined an all-night anti-war vigil outside the American consulate on Garden Road in Hong Kong Central. Within the Centre, tensions between the left-leaning activist members of the Committee of Concerned Asian Scholars (CCAS) and more mainstream moderate researchers were just below the surface. Hong Kong was becoming the jumping-off point for Americans to visit China, and with only rare exceptions, such visits were made by groups rather than individuals. Some members of the CCAS believed that their organization should serve as the clearinghouse for who would be allowed to visit China, and indeed a CCAS delegation was one of the first groups to be granted visas. John King Fairbank was the rare exception who traveled alone. I also met him for the first time at the Universities Service Centre, when he delivered a talk just after his first visit to China in more than twenty years.

That Ezra and I were at the Universities Service Centre at the same time was fortuitous for me. We were both on the more moderate side of the political spectrum and hence more naturally compatible. More importantly, Ezra's *Canton under Communism* was already one of the most important China books of its time and the inspiration for my PhD dissertation, "Authority and Legitimacy in Post-Revolution Rural Kwangtung: The Case of the People's Communes." The central question was how the Communist Party, after the disasters of the Great Leap Forward, had been able to retain its legitimacy in rural areas. Ezra was generous with his thoughts and advice but worried about the still-limited research access to the facts. On the ground research in Guangdong was still out of the question. He thought I was asking the right questions but was not sure I would find the answers. He was right, of course.

I was flattered when Ezra invited me join him for lunch with Sydney Liu, the veteran Hong Kong bureau chief of *Newsweek* who was almost universally admired as the most thorough and reliable reporter on both China and Hong Kong. In the presence of both Sydney and Ezra, I was awestruck and humbled. Their facility with all things Chinese was leap years ahead of my own. Sydney lived in near luxury, but he was as thoroughly acquainted with Hong Kong's rampant poverty as he was with high-level politics. He had covered the 1967 Hong Kong riots firsthand and was a frequent visitor to the squatter huts that dotted the hillsides of Hong Kong Island and the so-called resettlement estates in Kowloon where refugees from China lived in squalor, crammed and crowded in tiny rooms the size of large cages. He and Ezra encouraged me to visit such places for a better understanding of both Hong Kong and China. Taking their advice to heart, I spent the rest of that afternoon exploring the "other" Hong Kong. Over the months to come, I continued to visit as many huts and hovels and boat people as I could. Much of my writing at the time carried the subtitle: "A Study in Contrasts." My long-standing interest in grassroots China, the "other," "invisible" China surely began with those early contrasts in Hong Kong, encouraged and made possible, in part, by Ezra and his measured, generous advice.

But memory is fallible. When I shared this story with Ezra on his ninetieth birthday, he said we had met much earlier than Hong Kong. He remembered, albeit hazily, that I had visited him at Harvard while still an undergraduate at Tufts, seeking advice about the possibility of going into China studies after graduation. He must have encouraged me to continue my studies, and it seems I took his advice to heart.

Stanley Rosen

University of Southern California

I was never a student of Ezra's, but he was always incredibly supportive of my work. Of the many examples I could give, I will focus on just one, his gracious invitation at the beginning of the 1980s for me to visit him at Zhongshan University, where he was doing research for a project that became *One Step Ahead in China: Guangdong under Reform* (1989). I was then doing research at the Universities Service Centre in Hong Kong, where Ezra had been one of the founders. Ezra knew of my interest in Guangzhou because in 1979 he had asked if he could read my just-completed dissertation on Red Guard factionalism in the Chinese Cultural Revolution, which focused primarily on Guangzhou. He offered to pay for photocopying and postage, after which he sent me a six-page letter of comments and suggestions for revisions. In other words, the invitation to visit was not primarily going to be a social call, but was of a more scholarly nature, since we were both working in the area of politics and society in Guangzhou.

Once I arrived, and knowing my interest in education, he invited me along to an interview he was doing with the head of the Guangdong Provincial Higher Education Office. It was a great opportunity for a very junior academic who had done all his interviewing with former Red Guards and other refugees who had fled to Hong Kong in the 1970s. In watching and listening to Ezra's probing, but polite, method of interviewing a senior Chinese official in Mandarin, I learned a great deal, which I was able to put to good use in my own interviews with Chinese officials in subsequent years. Moreover, Ezra was gracious enough to allow me to ask my own questions and, by introducing me to "Guangzhou/Guangdong officialdom," he put me on the path to developing my own *guanxi* relationships, which were very helpful on my subsequent visits to Guangzhou to conduct research.

By the way, his son Steven, who was nineteen at the time if I'm not mistaken, was dispatched to various offices on the Zhongshan campus to help Ezra gather data and, not coincidentally, to learn about doing research. At least that's my memory from forty years ago. I believe this example reveals a number of reasons why Ezra was so important for the field of Chinese studies and why he was held in such high esteem by so many. He was able to marry his own unending quest for knowledge and strong work ethic with his support for junior scholars, always imparting knowledge while learning from others, all in the service of producing the best research possible.

Mike Mochizuki

George Washington University

Although I never took a class from Ezra or served as a teaching assistant in one of his legendary courses, he was my *sensei*, a lifelong friend and mentor. Among my early memories of Ezra are the lunch discussions about Japan that were held periodically at Harvard during the mid-1970s. The dominant theme then was about the United States pressuring Japan to change and be more like America. During one presentation, I saw Ezra energetically doodling in Chinese characters while appearing to listen patiently. When the session opened up for comments, Ezra unleashed his unconventional view that it was the United States that needed to learn from Japan. Although I was skeptical of his glowing portrayal of Japan, I was impressed by his verve to challenge popular thinking at the time.

This analysis became Ezra's *Japan as Number One*. The book came out while I was doing my dissertation fieldwork in Tokyo, and I was amazed by the constant television commercials promoting the Japanese translation and by the book's rapid climb to the top of Japan's bestseller lists. When I went to see Ezra talk about his book at the Foreign Correspondents' Club of Japan, he was welcomed like a rock star. Ironically, rather than convincing Americans to learn from Japan, I believe the main effect of this bestseller was to revive Japan's confidence after the malaise that had set in after the oil crises and political scandals of the 1970s. But *Japan as Number One* did have the intended effect on my father. I gave the book to him as a gift, and my father made photocopies of chapters of the work and distributed them to his team at the Federal Aviation Administration at Los Angeles International Airport. Dad felt that Ezra was right: Americans had much to learn from Japan about quality control, management styles, and teamwork.

Ezra made a major impact on my career when he offered me a postdoctoral fellowship to stay at Harvard to retool in international security studies. While much of the Japan field was focused on political economy, Ezra believed that Japan's security role was destined to increase. I was initially reluctant to accept this offer because, as I told Ezra, I was a pacifist and had been a vigorous anti–Vietnam War protester as an undergraduate

at Brown University. My hesitation evaporated when Ezra stated that security policy specialists should not be limited to those fascinated with the
military, and it was important to have security experts who have a critical
perspective. Ezra connected me with Michael Nacht, a scholar of nuclear
strategy, and I became the first postdoctoral fellow in Harvard's U.S.-
Japan Relations Program, which Ezra directed at the time.

This career turn led me to work at RAND and the Brookings Institution. When I moved to Washington, D.C., in January 1995, Ezra picked
me up on an icy evening and took me to one of his favorite restaurants in
Friendship Heights. He was then serving as the National Intelligence Officer for East Asia. He spent three hours briefing me about the Washington policy community. He told me how he had convened a group of young
American Japan experts and Japanese officials to discuss strengthening
the U.S.-Japan alliance.

Throughout his time in Washington, Ezra participated in policy seminars and workshops that I organized regarding North Korea and other
regional security issues. But we also had our disagreements. Ezra criticized my calls for a drastic reduction of the U.S. Marine Corps presence
in Okinawa after the September 1995 gang rape of an Okinawan school
girl by three U.S. servicemen. While he agreed that the crime was especially heinous, he believed that the Marines' departure would weaken the
U.S.-Japan alliance and deterrence. I countered that the concentration
of U.S. forces on Okinawa was excessive. Eventually, Ezra came around
to my view. He later gave me valuable advice for my efforts to reduce the
U.S. military presence on Okinawa.

Ezra introduced me to China. In summer 1991, I joined a small group
of American Japan specialists, led by Ezra, to visit China and interact with
Chinese experts on Japan. Sponsored by the National Committee on
U.S.-China Relations, this trip enabled me to visit Changchun as well as
Beijing and Shanghai and to pursue a new area of research and policy
analysis. Since I had known him primarily as a Japan scholar, it was great
to see Ezra in action in China. My conversations with him during that
trip inspired me to work on Japan-China relations, especially the process
of historical reconciliation.

Over a decade later, when Sino-Japanese relations became tense
because of Prime Minister Koizumi's visits to the Yasukuni Shrine, a project that I had helped to organize on "Memory and Reconciliation in the

Asia-Pacific" was unjustly attacked by a right-wing Japanese newspaper and influential Japanese conservative politicians because the endeavor had been funded by the Japan Foundation. This episode led to the darkest period in my professional career. Ezra became a source of moral strength for me, and he worked hard to defend academic freedom. I later learned that he had also helped to protect my George Washington University colleague, Celeste Arrington, from similar attacks because of an essay she had written on the comfort women issue.

During the last years of his life, Ezra and I frequently exchanged emails about Japanese politics and the interaction between Japan, China, and the United States. We shared concerns about the negative dynamic in U.S.-China relations and the hope that Japan might exercise more leadership as a middle power to moderate U.S.-China strategic competition. When he came to George Washington University in October 2019 to discuss his book, *China and Japan: Facing History*, he reminded the audience about how much the Chinese and Japanese had learned from each other. This was unfortunately the last time I saw Ezra. As I recall seeing him kindly talking with my students, I am inspired anew by his life and legacy and by the value he placed on human relationships, especially the bonds of friendship.

Kellee S. Tsai

Hong Kong University of Science and Technology

Ezra deserves credit for whatever warmth and compassion I have shown to my students, staff, and colleagues over the years. Here's why.

I did not know anyone when I first arrived in Cambridge in the summer of 1997 as a pre-doctoral fellow at the Harvard Academy for International and Area Studies. After eighteen months of field research in China, writing up my dissertation would be the final, daunting stage of graduate student training. While the Harvard Academy had a regular schedule of catered events at the elegant Harvard Faculty Club and Loeb House, feeling "fresh off the boat" from fieldwork, I gravitated toward seminars at the Fairbank Center and the Asia Center, then directed by the legendary Professor Ezra Vogel. I had admired his books since I was an undergraduate, starting with *Japan's New Middle Class* in Carol Gluck's class on Japanese intellectual history, to *Four Little Dragons* and *One Step Ahead in China: Guangdong Under Reform* in courses on the political economy of East Asia. When I was admitted to the Academy Scholars Program, my Columbia adviser Andy Nathan mentioned that he and Ezra had studied Chinese together and encouraged me to get to know him. As it turns out, I never had to invoke academic *guanxi* to justify my relevance to Professor Vogel.

Ezra had a truly rare ability to make anyone he was speaking to feel like they mattered. He invited me and other new Harvard arrivals to dinner at his home. He put me on the distribution list of the China Business Project that he was organizing. During my Academy Scholars interview, a faculty panelist had asked, "Why should political scientists care about informal finance in China?" It was a reasonable question to pose from a disciplinary perspective. But Ezra naturally appreciated that whatever students were working on held intrinsic interest, and he asked thoughtful questions rather than challenging my judgment in pursuing an apparently esoteric topic. His acceptance of my preoccupation with informal finance and *getihu* provided much-needed confidence to persist through uncertain days and nights of dissertation writing. I often think of Ezra when graduate students from other universities contact me, and I have joined defense committees as an external examiner with his kindness in mind.

After the publication of my first book, *Back-Alley Banking: Private Entrepreneurs in China* (2002), Merle Goldman invited me to return to Harvard to give a talk. Ezra's sparkling eyes and wry smile in the audience assuaged anxiety that the product of so many years of work might have been a disappointment. Shortly thereafter, Saadia Pekkanen—a political scientist specializing in Japan from my Academy Scholar cohort— and I decided to edit a volume on *Japan and China in the World Political Economy* (2005). Because the contributing authors were untenured junior scholars focusing on either China or Japan, we invited Ezra to write a foreword to the volume to bridge the gap in area expertise and lend our relatively unknown names more credibility. We also asked, sheepishly, if he would be willing to have his name on the cover alongside ours. "I would be honored to do so," he responded. Such humility and generosity. Saadia and I were assistant professors without experience in organizing and publishing an edited volume. Yet Ezra readily agreed to share his reputational fame and made it seem as if he were fortunate to collaborate with us. By way of karmic thanks, a decade later I agreed to co-edit a volume with chapters written by junior social scientists based in Taiwan— *Evolutionary Governance in China: State-Society Relations under Authoritarianism* (2021).

During the mid-2000s, Ezra became a dedicated Senior Scholar escort on various delegations of the National Committee on U.S.-China Relations' Public Intellectuals Program (PIP), which was established to nurture the next generation of China specialists. I was admitted to the first PIP cohort in 2005 and know that Ezra's commitment to the program was a signature attraction. Ezra exuded more energy and spirit than many of us significantly younger PIP-ers. He became an academic grandfather to all of us in PIP.

In May 2012, Ezra's Deng Xiaoping book talk to a fully packed lecture hall at Hong Kong University of Science and Technology (HKUST) coincided with my recruitment visit. I confided that I might be leaving Johns Hopkins. Ezra was reflexively supportive, saying that HKUST would be lucky to have me lead their Division of Social Science. In that capacity, once again, I followed Ezra's example in bringing people together to build a sense of intellectual community.

My most recent and poignant interactions with Ezra were during his visits to Hong Kong in November 2019 and January 2020. At meals with other Hong Kong–based PIP-ers, Ezra empathized with our situation, understanding it was a challenging time to be in academic administration, mediating tensions among faculty and students during so many months of social unrest. Ezra cheered us on in person and through emails. Following the introduction of Hong Kong's National Security Law (NSL), on July 1, 2020, I shared a message addressed to our humanities and social science faculty with PIP. Ezra wrote, "Kellee, Wonderful to see how you have grown as a leader as the situation needs it. With great respect." That same month I expressed gratitude for his long-standing support in a recorded ninetieth birthday Virtual Hug greeting. What turned out to be our final exchange was on Thanksgiving Day. I shared an announcement about a webinar on academic freedom and the NSL that we were hosting. His response was characteristically encouraging, authentic, and gracious: "Kellee, Bravo. Today I give thanks that we are getting rid of Trump. And I give thanks for what you and other able courageous young people are doing to preserve good values in a troubled world. best, ezra vogel." He always discerned promise in us and made us feel worthy of his time. Trying to be more like Ezra is the best way to honor his legacy as a prolific scholar and generous mentor.

Ashley Esarey

University of Alberta

Ezra Vogel was an inspiring scholar and generous mentor. We met in Atlanta at the 2008 Association for Asian Studies annual conference. I had been a fan of his work since I read *Japan as Number* One in college. After encountering "Ezra" (as I would eventually call him) in a book stall, I nervously explained that I had just received an offer to go to Harvard as a postdoctoral fellow in China studies. A brief conversation ensued about my background and research interests before Ezra mentioned that he had a vacancy for an apartment on the second floor of his house for the upcoming academic year. "Maybe you would like to live there?" he asked. Our exchange lasted minutes, but it illustrated one of Ezra's remarkable characteristics: even in advancing age he bravely opened the door to new friendships.

As I would learn soon after moving in, the home that Ezra shared with his wife Charlotte Ikels was buzzing with activity. I encountered Ezra giving interviews to Chinese or Japanese journalists (in their native languages), having long conversations in Mandarin with his live-in research assistant, formal conversations with visitors from East Asia, or a chat with Elizabeth Kaske, a German postdoctoral fellow who rented the third-floor apartment. If Ezra was speaking with someone whom he thought I should meet, he would casually hail me to join a conversation that resulted in the exchange of business cards and a new contact. The postbox at the house overflowed with what seemed to be mountains of mail from all around the world. All of this was taking place nearly a decade after Ezra's official retirement.

While I lived at Ezra and Charlotte's for roughly fifteen months in 2008–10, Ezra labored on his book about Deng Xiaoping, writing from home. Although he was in his late seventies, Ezra worked harder than anyone I knew. He transported research materials into one room of the house for a few days, cleaning up, then moving into another room. Sometimes I encountered Ezra poring over books in the Fung Library. He painstakingly drafted chapters, circulated them to trusted scholars for input, and rewrote. Judging by the hours at which Ezra returned emails, he worked late. "I have trouble sleeping," he confessed, a condition that he mentioned treating with a glass of wine before bed. When I left the house to run along the Charles River in the mornings—something Ezra loved to do, before his aging knees forced him to ride a bicycle—the absence of the *Asahi Shimbun* newspaper from the front porch meant that he was up, and I assumed, preparing to put in another long day.

Curious about the work habits of one of the most prolific scholars of East Asia, I asked Ezra why he didn't use his state-of-the-art office at Harvard's Fairbank Center. He explained that he got more done at home, wearing comfortable trousers, knit caps, and house slippers. Soon thereafter the Center contacted me to suggest that I was welcome to make use of Ezra's campus office (along with postdoctoral fellow Todd Hall).

Most of my early conversations with Ezra were brief. He guarded his time carefully. We spoke Chinese. I assumed this was because Ezra took every opportunity to keep up his language and perhaps because my Japanese wasn't great. Emails were the preferred medium for conversations that he seemed to design to be ongoing and open-ended. Ezra replied to my queries swiftly with wisdom, advice, or suggestions for someone else I might contact.

In longer chats over Chinese food in Cambridge, or on walks back from events at Harvard, or dinners at historian Merle Goldman's place, Ezra would offer novel perspectives on China based on personal experiences, a trip to East Asia, or a trusted source, whether a close friend or a good book. Our non-academic conversations ranged widely: romantic relationships ("all you need is one good partner"); couture ("always overdress a little—it will make the people to whom you are speaking feel respected"); parenting ("I wish that I hadn't worked so hard when my children were small"); brain-tanning deer skins (he was surprised that a mammal's brain could be used to tan its own hide); and running as a scab in the Boston Marathon (Ezra dreamed of doing this and encouraged me to do so).

After my fellowship at Harvard, I took a job at Whitman College in Walla Walla, Washington. Ezra included the college as a stop on his

whirlwind book tour for *Deng Xiaoping and the Transformation of China.*
The college president delighted Ezra by giving him a black cowboy hat to
celebrate what was jokingly referred to as his "Journey to the West" 西游记.
Whenever I returned to Harvard, Ezra invited me to stay in his home.
Regardless of the length of my visit—whether for two nights or for one
week—we'd have a long conversation in which we caught up on each other's projects and personal lives.

As recently as July 2020, Ezra joined a webinar on the "Xi Jinping
Effect" that I co-organized through the University of Alberta's China Institute. He expressed pleasure at the opportunities that online video
technology provides for connecting with old friends and global audiences.
His own contribution was the keynote, "Leadership in China: A Dengist
Perspective," in which Ezra compared Xi Jinping's leadership to that of
Deng Xiaoping.[1] From our email exchanges in the last months of his
life, it was clear that Ezra felt fortunate to have been so hale for so long
and that, despite diminishing energy, he had plans to do much more.
News of Ezra's loss saddens me greatly. Yet I remain deeply grateful for
the gifts he gave me as an invaluable mentor and the model he provided the
world as diligent scholar, bridge builder, and friend maker.

Lawrence C. Reardon

University of New Hampshire

After reading *Canton under Communism* in my first Chinese politics class in
1976, I became fascinated by Guangdong Province's economic transformation and political turmoil. I pursued this interest while conducting my dissertation research in Guangzhou, Shenzhen, and Hong Kong in the 1980s.
At the 2008 Harvard conference on adaptive authoritarianism, I told Ezra
about the importance of his book to my research, which among other things
prepared me to talk with a Guangzhou entrepreneur who claimed to have
stormed Zhao Ziyang's office during the Cultural Revolution.

---

1. Ezra Vogel, "The Leadership of Xi Jinping: A Dengist Perspective," *Journal of
Contemporary China.* Published online March 16, 2021.

Several weeks after the conference, Ezra invited me to lunch. While I had some trepidation, Ezra immediately put me at ease with his warm smile and genuine interest in my research. We casually talked about the changes in Guangdong during the 1980s, and he talked about his progress on the Deng biography. I was honored when he asked me to comment on his chapter concerning Guangdong, Fujian, and the Special Economic Zones (SEZs). He also encouraged me to complete my second book on China's 1980s economic development and offered to help me gain access to restricted Harvard library materials. Despite his deadline to complete his book on China and Japan, Ezra took time to comment on several chapters of my first draft in 2017. As this draft primarily emphasized Zhao Ziyang's role as the architect of China's opening, Ezra subtly urged me to strengthen my emphasis on Deng's ability to implement the reforms without incurring elite divisions.

Finally, I will forever be indebted to Ezra for his invaluable help in publishing *A Third Way: The Origins of China's Current Economic Strategy*. In early 2019, Ezra sent my completed manuscript to Harvard's Asia Center with a recommendation that it be considered for their East Asian Series. Ezra asked me to keep him informed about the decision process and whether I encountered any roadblocks. When I told Ezra the faculty publications board had accepted the project, Ezra stated that "it is nice to be in a position where I can be helpful to a deserving person for a deserving project." On 29 October 2020, I asked for his mailing address to send him a copy of the newly published book. He stated that he "hoped some day after COVID-19 is no longer a problem that we will have a chance to meet again." This was our last correspondence. Yet, Ezra will continue to be my model of a true scholar who has an open, inquisitive mind and does their best to help others.

FIGURE 1a. Edith Nachman Vogel, Ezra's mother, emigrated from Russia as a child, n.d. Courtesy of the family.

FIGURE 1b. Joseph Herschel Vogel, Ezra's father, emigrated from Poland as a young man, n.d. Courtesy of the family.

FIGURE 2a. Interior of The People's Store in Delaware, Ohio. Proprietor Joseph (Joe) Vogel, Ezra's father, is on the right, 1930s. Courtesy of Fay Vogel Bussgang.

FIGURE 2b. Fay Vogel Bussgang and Ezra as children in a park in Shelby, Ohio, late 1930s. Courtesy of Fay Vogel Bussgang.

FIGURE 3a. Ezra as a college student, late 1940s. Courtesy of the family.

FIGURE 3b. Ezra in his army uniform. He served at Valley Forge Army Hospital in Pennsylvania as a social work technician during the Korean War, 1952. Courtesy of the family.

FIGURE 4a. Ezra and Suzanne Hall Vogel (on Ezra's right) conducting research in Japan in 1959–60. This research was the basis for Ezra's first book, *Japan's New Middle Class: The Salaryman and His Family in a Tokyo Suburb.* Courtesy of the family.

FIGURE 4b. One of the first U.S. science delegations to China included social scientist Ezra, 1973. Official photograph. Courtesy of the family.

FIGURE 5a. At the end of the semester, East Asian Studies students and faculty play baseball—China vs. Japan. Is Ezra batting for China or Japan? 1977. Photo by Corky White.

FIGURE 5b. The founding of Harvard's Program on U.S.-Japan Relations with Ezra in the second row center and Edwin Reischauer on his left, 1980. Courtesy of the Program on U.S.-Japan Relations.

FIGURE 6. Wedding reception of Ezra and Charlotte Ikels. The groom is feeding the bride. The bride is playing defense. November 3, 1979.

FIGURE 7a. Ezra, who was escorting a Harvard alumni tour of China, amazed the locals with his Chinese language ability, winter of 1979–80. Courtesy of the family.

FIGURE 7b. Steven Vogel, Charlotte, and Ezra in front of their Zhongshan University residence dressed for the summer weather of Guangzhou, 1980. Courtesy of the family.

FIGURE 8a. Ezra and Prime Minister Yasuhiro Nakasone, n.d. Official Photograph Office of the Prime Minister. Courtesy of the family.

FIGURE 8b. Vogel family vacation in Bermuda. Ezra's children Eve, David, and Steven are on the left, followed by Susan Sherrerd, Ezra, Charlotte, and Nava Niv-Vogel. David's two sons, Caleb and Nathaniel, stand in the front, winter 1991–92. Courtesy of the family.

FIGURE 9a. Ezra delivering an emotive speech at the University of Wisconsin at River Falls, 1991. Courtesy of the family.

FIGURE 9b. Ezra and Charlotte being received by the Emperor and Empress of Japan at a White House state dinner during the Clinton administration, 1994. Official White House Photo. Courtesy of the family.

FIGURE 10a. Ezra with Ban-ki Moon, who had been an associate with the Program on U.S.-Japan Relations in 1984–85, long before heading the UN, n.d. Courtesy of the family.

FIGURE 10b. Ezra with Premier Zhu Rongji, ca. 1998. Courtesy of the family.

FIGURE 11a. Former student Mary Lord arranged the production of this spoof *U.S. News and World Report* cover announcing Ezra's departure from his Washington posting as National Intelligence Officer for East Asia, 1995. Courtesy of the family.

FIGURE 11b. Ezra and the students in his Sociology 265 course, New Institutionalism in Asia, on his final teaching day at Harvard, May 4, 2000. Courtesy of the family.

FIGURE 12a. Ezra at the lectern delivering a speech, ca. 2005.

FIGURE 12b. Ezra in his basement home office, still in his athletic clothes following a bike ride, 2005. Photo by Charlotte Ikels.

FIGURE 13a. Three Asia Center directors flank Victor Fung, a major benefactor of the Center and its programs. From left to right: Tony Saich, Ezra, Victor Fung, and William Kirby at the tenth anniversary of the Asia Center, 2007. Courtesy of Lisa Cohen.

FIGURE 13b. Ezra surrounded by audience members following his talk at the Stanford Center at Peking University, 2015. Photo by Charlotte Ikels.

FIGURE 14a. The Vogel extended family on a visit to Deng Xiaoping's home village in Sichuan, 2015. Courtesy of the family.

FIGURE 14b. Michael Szonyi (left), Ezra, and Rod MacFarquhar (right) speaking at the Fairbank Center Sixtieth Anniversary Symposium, October 2017. Photo by Lisa Abitbol. Courtesy of the Harvard University Fairbank Center.

FIGURE 15. Ezra enjoying a vacation breakfast on the private balcony of a modest Venetian hotel, 2015. Photo by Charlotte Ikels.

FIGURE 16a. At a "Vogel *juku*" reunion in Tokyo. Ezra's longevity was celebrated with the gift of special purple clothing (quilted vest and hat) associated with the ninetieth year of life (when one is eighty-nine by Western reckoning), November 2019. Courtesy of the family.

FIGURE 16b. Ezra with Susan Pharr (left) and Christina Davis (right), his two successors as Director of the Harvard Program on U.S.-Japan Relations, for which he served as Honorary Chair, 1987–2020. Taken at the program's holiday party, December 2019. Photo by Shinju Fujihara. Courtesy of the Program on U.S.-Japan Relations.

FIGURE 17a. On a fall morning, Ezra, son Steven, and daughter Eve prepare to launch on a bike ride from Sumner Road in Cambridge, 2019. Photo by Charlotte Ikels.

FIGURE 17b. The Vogel extended family arrayed on and about the living room couch at a holiday party—a continuous tradition since 1995, December 2019. Photo by Ben Rosser. Courtesy of the family.

FIGURE 18a. Ezra signing a copy of his latest book, *China and Japan: Facing History*, for a holiday party guest, December 2019. Photo by Ben Rosser. Courtesy of the family.

FIGURE 18b. Home memorial shrine erected by Charlotte for Ezra. His unexpected death occurred on the day originally scheduled for the 2020 extended family party, December 2020. Photo by Charlotte Ikels.

EIGHT

Mentoring Future Journalists, Business Executives, Diplomats, and Others

Jay Mathews

The Washington Post

I was a weird duck among the young people who hung around 2 Divinity and the East Asian Research Center in the 1960s and 1970s. By the end of my sophomore year at age twenty, I knew I wanted to be the China correspondent for the *Washington Post*. I planned to get an MA in the program for Regional Studies East Asia, but I made clear I was going no further than that in academia.

Ezra was then a young professor who was amazing people, including me, with his command of both Chinese and Japanese and of what was going on in those two countries. He immediately understood what I wanted to do and why.

In graduate school he signed me up for a seminar on the Cultural Revolution that my over-inflated ego assumed was created just for me. My first paper was on the Cultural Revolution and what available documents disclosed about what happened during those years in Sichuan Province. The second was on how the American press covered the Cultural Revolution. He managed to get both of my papers published, and he distributed the second one at a journalism conference on happenings in Asia.

Since authoring those two somewhat clumsy attempts at academic writing, I have now been writing for publication for fifty years, but I have rarely enjoyed anything as much as skewering the dumb and celebrating the brilliant among journalists who covered the Cultural Revolution. Ezra knew that and made sure the word got out that I was ready for that job at the *Post* that nobody had offered me yet.

Ezra's books have been a boon and an inspiration to journalists like me for a long time. He has always been clear and provocative and always on top of the facts. He was a wonderful source as well as a good friend. I miss him.

Richard Bernstein

The New York Times

"Let a hundred flowers blossom," Ezra said. It was 1997. I was long gone from graduate school, working at the *New York Times*, and had co-written a book, *The Coming Conflict with China*, whose main argument, I was pretty sure, Ezra didn't agree with. He had recently done his two-year stint as an adviser on China at the National Intelligence Council and, as I understood from his public remarks, he believed in the necessity and likelihood that the U.S. and China could work out their differences. While I didn't feel that way, I was open to the possibility that he was right and I was wrong. Because of the book, I was invited to be on a panel at the Bilderberg Conference, an annual trans-Atlantic gathering of rich and influential people, and when I arrived there (the conference was on a private island in a lake not far from Atlanta), I discovered that Ezra was there too and that he would be on the panel with me.

I was very pleased by this and also nervous, for two reasons. One, I didn't relish the idea of having a disagreement with an intellect as powerful as Ezra's, and before the likes of Henry Kissinger, David Rockefeller, and Gianni Agnelli. And two, given who Ezra was and my respect for him, I didn't want a mere disagreement over China policy to lead him to think less of me. The morning of our panel, Ezra, friendly as always, told me he'd not slept well, nervous about what he would say to the august assembly. Needless to say, I hadn't slept well either for the same reason. But for a mere ink-stained wretch as myself to have spent an uneasy night seemed normal; that a renowned professor, director of the East Asian Research Center at Harvard, etc., would also feel the tremors of insecurity surprised me. But it also reflected on Ezra, his modesty, his extraordinary likability, his lack of pretension, his ability to put other people at ease, his genuineness.

It was around this time that I expressed my misgivings about disagreeing with him before an audience focused on China. That's when he patted me on the back and said, "Let a hundred flowers blossom," and I knew all would be well. The panel, by the way, went off as the model of civil discourse that one would expect from a man like Ezra, who really did want a hundred flowers to blossom. Would that there were more like him today.

Douglas Spelman

Reston, Virginia

I met Ezra when I enrolled in his Chinese Communist Society course at Harvard in 1966, and last saw him in the fall of 2016, with Charlotte and my wife Nancy, at his home in Cambridge. During those fifty years I always looked forward to the chance to get together, to enjoy his remarkably engaging personality—always upbeat, congenial, and considerate—and of course to learn from his vast store of knowledge and insight.

Since the focus of my Foreign Service career was East Asia, many of our meetings took place there. My job was to understand what was happening in those various posts, but Ezra was always able to deepen my appreciation of local people, events, and trends. In Shanghai he drew on his intimate knowledge of Guangzhou to compare and contrast these two leading cities and their relations with both the provinces surrounding them as well as with the central authorities in Beijing. In Hong Kong in the early 1980s, I remember his trenchant analysis of the ongoing negotiations which led to the Sino-British Joint Declaration of 1984, based on his personal ties with several leading officials on both sides. He knew Singapore well and refined my understanding of the complex interplay among its relations with China, the giant to the north, and its non-Chinese neighbors in Southeast Asia. In Beijing, he made a point of contacting and encouraging our daughter Brooke during her early Foreign Service tour there.

I also remember with great appreciation how he continually opened doors for me to expand my own professional experience, both before and after my Foreign Service career. Two examples: In the late 1960s he arranged for me to interpret for Edward Chan, his research assistant on *Canton under Communism,* who was living in Cambridge, when Chan spoke to interested local groups about his life as a Communist cadre. In 2008, after I retired, Ezra invited me to present the Neuhauser Lecture at the Fairbank Center. He asked me to focus my talk on contemporary China from the perspective of an academic turned diplomat. I welcomed this opportunity to reflect more systematically on and integrate these two strands of my China experience. In doing so, I drew on the intellectual skills so evident in his impressive body of scholarly work, skills which inspired me throughout our long acquaintance.

Ezra's life was indeed well lived. I and my family, along with many, many others, will miss him greatly.

John Zwaanstra

Penta Investment Advisers

I am sure Ezra will have already received much written praise for his research/scholarship and for his leadership of the East Asian Studies program over the years. All such accolades are well deserved.

For me, however, the most impressive thing about Ezra was the degree to which he really cared about all the students. He had a great knack for making even the lowliest undergraduate feel special and worthwhile. A visit to Ezra's office during office hours was always uplifting, and one invariably left academically re-purposed and re-energized after spending time with him.

I spent my junior year studying at Keio University in Tokyo. Ezra wrote me several letters—keep in mind this was before the internet—inquiring as to how things were going and asking if I needed any assistance. He kindly arranged for me to meet several scholars in my field and also got me access to the library at the International House in Roppongi.

Ezra was also the adviser for my thesis in my undergraduate senior year. He helped me to hone my ideas and to whittle down my turgid prose into something close to readable. My "honors" should really have been given to Ezra thanks to his editing skill!

After graduation in summer 1988 I subsequently met Ezra in Asia on perhaps ten or eleven occasions, including two completely unscripted meetings at Narita airport. On each occasion he was so warm, introducing me to all of his colleagues/traveling companions. With absolutely no prompting, he kindly recalled my thesis topic, my recent work history, and after a while even my marital status and the correct number of children. Seeing him on those occasions always left me with the same feeling as in my undergraduate days—uplifted and re-energized.

Professor Ezra Vogel, I will miss our interactions. Goodbye . . . and thank you for everything.

Melinda Liu

Newsweek

Ezra was a towering, unique, humanistic force in the world. Today, you can barely find someone with such deep expertise and yet genuine modesty, someone who ventures out far beyond the halls of power and the ivory towers of academia.

That was Ezra's all-of-society approach to life. His roots were in sociology and in ethnography. His optimism, his enthusiasm, his deep respect for original research also meant he wanted to know everything: the good, the bad, and the ugly. That's probably one of the reasons he enjoyed talking with journalists. He respected the media's need to dig deep and dig hard for nuggets of information.

In Beijing, Chinese journalists saw him as a professorial "rock star." He was constantly being interviewed by the *China Daily*, CCTV, CGTN, and so on. This past Christmas, after his death, I happened to be watching a Chinese-language program on Phoenix TV that specialized in interviewing foreign VIPs. I heard a familiar voice—there was Ezra, holding forth with the anchor in fast-paced Mandarin for more than an hour.

Ezra was an equally huge draw for foreign journalists. For years, visiting delegations organized by the National Committee on U.S.-China Relations would visit Beijing a couple of times annually. Usually organizers would ask for an evening meeting with foreign correspondents in Beijing. On a number of such occasions I invited everyone to gather at my apartment. The reporters flocked to attend when Ezra was part of the group.

He had a knack for making people feel comfortable, enabling them to open up to him—and him to open up to them. In June 2020 I asked him to talk online about his most recent book on China and Japan. Attendees were members—including diplomats and artists, teachers and entrepreneurs—of the Royal Asiatic Society Beijing, which my husband Alan founded here. Ezra agreed without hesitation. During the Zoom talk, he discussed with candor and humanity the challenges of writing about two countries which had been at each other's throats for so long— and precisely why this makes it so important for them to reconcile, or at least keep talking. His presentation was articulate and thoughtful, packed with facts and dates and incisive analysis. At the top of his game, Ezra kept the audience enthralled.

Afterward he said it felt good to talk with the group. The deep appreciation and enthusiasm of the audience "brought out the best in me," he claimed. Long story short, he thanked us at least as much as we thanked him. That degree of thoughtful empathy was very Ezra. He also asked me to make sure that some of his Chinese acquaintances in Beijing received a digital copy of the recorded talk, since some of them didn't have easy access to Zoom.

Ezra treasured friendships and relationships. He was a ninja of *guanxi*—I mean that in a good way. He carefully nurtured acquaintances, whether they were VIPs or just ordinary folks. I was definitely part of the latter category. He was my undergraduate thesis adviser at Harvard, and we met regularly in 1972–73. I was in awe of him—Ezra had energy, spoke Asian languages, and conducted research among southern Chinese refugees.

The big mystery is why Ezra agreed to advise me. I spoke no Asian languages well and had barely traveled outside the U.S. My thesis project was a documentary film focused on second-generation Chinese in Boston's Chinatown. He was incredibly patient with my inchoate attempts to tell that Chinatown's story in an amateur film. But one key takeaway from that experience stayed with me all my life. Ezra opened my eyes to the fact that traveling overseas and diving deep into unfamiliar societies and cultures could not only be fascinating but also fodder for a career.

After graduating from Harvard, I traveled to Taiwan under the auspices of a Michael C. Rockefeller Memorial Fellowship. (I'd hoped to spend the year in mainland China, but Beijing wasn't issuing individual visas for that sort of thing in 1973.) I studied Peking Opera and the Chinese language in Taipei. Learning Mandarin and being in Asia just as Deng Xiaoping unleashed his modernization drive helped launch my journalistic career.

Now I've spent nearly four decades living and reporting in Greater China. And until Ezra passed away, he made a point of keeping in touch. In more recent years his work on the Deng biography allowed me to spend chunks of time with him. While visiting Beijing to interview sources, he stayed at my apartment a number of times. When we had meals together he'd pull out notes handwritten on a yellow legal pad and discuss events of the 1980s. It was truly an honor to be asked for my recollections by Ezra—and, after the book's publication, to read what he wrote on the title page when he gave me a copy: "To Melinda, for all her help in making this possible."

Ezra was supremely modest and deeply committed to family and friends. To him, each relationship was something to treasure. Half a decade ago, Alan and I happened to be in Boston at the same time as Perry Link, a protégé of Ezra's. Ezra and Charlotte invited all of us to breakfast at their home. When we arrived, Ezra was preparing to do us the honor of making pancakes. But not just any ordinary slapdash pancakes. These were lavished with the same care, discipline, and attention to detail that Ezra showed in his professional life. Charlotte and the rest of us had been yakking for a while, and I wandered over to the stove to observe Ezra's work. He apologized for having to pay attention to the stove: "I've got to take care to get the shape just right."

He made the most beautiful, golden, delicious pancakes ever—and they were perfectly round. As with so much in life, Ezra got it just right.

John Kamm

Dui Hua Foundation

Professor Ezra Vogel wrote two books on political and economic developments in Guangdong Province. His first book, *Canton under Communism* (1969), drew heavily on refugee interviews at Hong Kong's Universities Service Centre. His second book was *One Step Ahead in China: Guangdong under Reform* (1989). I got to know Professor Vogel when he was based at Zhongshan University doing research for this book.

I had opened the first foreign office in Guangzhou in 1979 and worked out of a suite of rooms in the Dongfang Hotel. In my work selling products in Guangdong, I was aided by my knowledge of Cantonese. Ezra's Mandarin was excellent, not so his Cantonese.

I had managed to secure an air conditioner, one of the only ones in Guangzhou at the time. It didn't take long for Ezra to hear about my air-conditioned suite, and he became a frequent visitor. In the sweltering

heat of the summer months, we would drink beer in the office and sometimes go out for walks to local restaurants and parks. We spent many
hours in long conversations about how Guangdong had changed since
I first visited the city in January 1976, just as the Cultural Revolution
was beginning to wind down.

Guangzhou underwent great changes in the aftermath of the reforms
initiated in late 1978, changes that Ezra chronicled in *One Step Ahead in
China*. I had been involved in early joint-venture discussions and made
some of the first sales to county foreign trade organizations and willingly
became a resource for Ezra. Eventually he asked me to write a chapter for
the book, which I gladly did.

By 1989 the manuscript for *One Step Ahead* was ready for footnoting
and editing. Unexpectedly, political unrest broke out in Beijing and other
Chinese cities, including Guangzhou. Many people were killed or
wounded, and thousands were detained. To people like Ezra Vogel and me
these events were shocking. My views of China changed, and I began to
work on human rights.

As the publication date of *One Step Ahead* neared, Ezra wondered
whether to address the killings and arrests of the 1989 protest movement.
I encouraged him to do so. Finally, he penned a preface to the book that
was released in December 1989. The opening sentences reveal the strength
of Ezra's condemnation:

> In June 1989 the massacre of students in Beijing's Tiananmen Square
> stunned China and the rest of the world. It was not the first time that Chi-
> na's rulers had ordered soldiers to slaughter unarmed civilians. . . . The
> 1989 massacre was the first such atrocity played out under the vigilant eye
> of modern telecommunications, and it was thereby instantly and dramati-
> cally accessible to people everywhere. It marked the definitive end to an
> era in which the Chinese state could monopolize the flow of information
> in and out of China.

In his many years in academia and government service, Ezra Vogel
was seen as a mild-mannered, cautious man little interested in the struggles of the Chinese people for human rights and rule of law. That was
not the Ezra Vogel I got to know. He used his connections in Guangdong to advocate for political prisoners, sometimes with my help. He

worked behind the scenes on important causes, like helping scholars disliked by Beijing secure visas. He was a longtime supporter of my Dui Hua Foundation and the source of much sage advice. He helped organize some of my speeches at Harvard. Ezra tried to bring America and China together, an increasingly difficult task in recent years. He will be deeply missed.

Rick Dyck

Tokyo, Japan

Ezra, newly appointed professor in the Harvard Department of Social Relations, was moving into his office in Coolidge Hall when I first met him in the summer of 1967. Although he was entitled to an office in the newly built William James Hall, he preferred Coolidge Hall, a recycled hotel where the East Asian Research Center had turned a block of former guest rooms into offices. Ezra took delight in showing me his 1920s-style tiled bathroom with an old-fashioned footed tub, which served as his file cabinet.

Ezra was the first friendly person I met in Cambridge, where even store clerks and bus drivers seem confrontational to a rural Californian. He turned our conversation into a kind of field interview, asking mainly about me and my experiences in Japan. Around noon, he asked if I would like to join him for lunch at his home on Parker Street, where he fixed BLT sandwiches—a specialty we enjoyed many more times over the decades.

Ezra was in the final stages of finishing *Canton under Communism*, and it was time for him to re-connect with Japan in preparation for a course on Japanese society scheduled for the spring semester. Out of the blue, Ezra asked if I would be his teaching assistant. His plans for the course were well underway, with half of his bathtub filled with research articles and essays and the other half filled with notes for *Canton*. I was given free access to the Japan side of the bathtub and began making copies of the essays. I also began attending a weekly discussion group of graduate students at his house—an example of the mutual support networks he established in his academic ecosystem.

Ezra arranged for me to take a course taught by George Homans, the quintessential Boston Brahmin who chaired the Department of Sociology. The course consisted of weekly presentations by a stellar array of scholars, including David Riesman, Seymour Lipset, Nathan Glazer, Talcott Parsons, Alex Inkeles, and Ezra. To Homans, there was a natural link between the Department of Sociology and Harvard's two regional research centers, the Russian Research Center (founded in 1948) and the more recent East Asian Research Center (founded in 1955). Ezra gave two sessions on Canton, which Homans called "inductive sociology," similar to the studies from the 1950s by Alex Inkeles, Merle Fainsod, and Clyde Kluckhohn on the Soviet Union. The data for the Russian studies were a combination of primary materials and interviews of émigrés, many in the Boston area, much the same as Ezra's interviews of refugees in Hong Kong. Ezra's methodology evolved over time, but his use of intensive interviews in all of his projects shows a DNA stemming from the work of Fainsod and Kluckhohn.

Canton received strong reviews both among sociologists and China scholars, and it won the Harvard University Press faculty book of the year award. But in the politically charged atmosphere of 1969, it sparked student protests. Students did not want to hear Ezra's dispassionate description of the revolution, particularly his claim that the Guomindang could have carried out successful reforms in Canton comparable to what the Chinese Communist Party had done if they had been able to maintain public order.

Homans mounted an energetic defense, noting that theories such as those of Marx or Weber are guideposts in research, but that the conclusions must come from the scholar's analysis of the data.

Ezra was thirty-nine when he published *Canton under Communism.* In the context of a long and prolific academic career, it now seems like an early work. In every subsequent decade he continued producing major books that seemed to take his lifetime achievement to a new height.

From about 1980 on, my relationship with Ezra had been rooted in the perspective of my base in Japan. With Ezra, physical distance was never an impediment. In fact, I think it made our relationship even closer through frequent travel, constant correspondence, and Ezra's continuing keen interest in Japan.

In Japan, Ezra's level of celebrity is beyond remarkable. Among Japanese over sixty-five (a large portion of the current population), Ezra will forever be remembered as the author of *Japan as Number One.* The book sold over 500,000 copies in Japan and placed Ezra among the five most recognized foreign scholars of all time, along with Albert Einstein and Arnold Toynbee.

Although he did not write major books focused solely on Japan after publishing *Number One*, he continued coming to Japan several times a year. His reputation gave him a voice, which he did not hesitate to use for causes he cared about. For example, in the days of trade disputes, he spoke out about market access. When many U.S. scholars were concerned about censorship by Japanese funding agencies, Ezra called on the Foreign Minister. When he was concerned about the Prime Minister's official pilgrimages to Yasukuni, he paid a visit to the Prime Minister's office.

He also kept up his personal networks in Japan. Every year, he visited the original six families of *Japan's New Middle Class* and organized reunions with former students and colleagues. He was active in funding and organizing conferences on Asian issues where Japanese scholars were well represented. Ezra's book on Deng was masterfully translated into Japanese by Masuo Chisako, a prominent trilingual China scholar who had studied with him at Harvard.

Ezra's final book, *China and Japan: Facing History*, was, like *Japan as Number One*, written more from his concern about a crisis than for a scholarly purpose. To strike a balanced perspective, he did extensive interviews with Japanese scholars, diplomats, and China experts. In his final trip to Japan in November 2019, he took his case directly to the Japanese public. He filled major auditoriums in Fukuoka, Osaka, Nagoya, and Tokyo, giving lectures in Japanese about his concern about Japan's relationship with China.

The trips to Japan were a mirror of the man—the caring teacher, the eager student, the Jewish boy from Ohio—somewhat embarrassed by his celebrity, but using it to make the world a better place.

Mario Filippo Pini

Italian Ministry of Foreign Affairs

The year was 1967, the exact month and day long forgotten. I only remember that I was standing outside Coolidge Hall on Cambridge Street with Geoffrey Perret, a friend of mine who later became a well-known biographer of American presidents. All of a sudden, we saw our teacher Ezra Vogel on his bicycle coming toward us. The sight did not surprise us; we had often seen him pedaling around campus. What surprised us on that particular day was the fact that Ezra stopped and announced that he had just become a tenured professor. To Geoffrey and me, graduate students trying to cope with life at Harvard, a tenured professorship there seemed like the holiest position a human being could possibly attain. And yet the man who had achieved such an incredible honor was just next to us, sitting on the saddle of his bike, balancing himself with one foot on the curb, speaking in the same casual, friendly voice that he always used, in the classroom and everywhere else. Ezra is gone; Geoffrey is gone. Coolidge Hall is gone, too, demolished and replaced by the Knafel Building. But that encounter of fifty-four years ago is still vivid in my mind. Perhaps because, when it happened, I was still used to old-fashioned Italian professors who did not go around on bikes, who did not speak to lowly students unless it was necessary; I expected them to be formal and aloof. Many years later, Ezra told me that he was the first professor at Harvard to spread the habit of addressing everyone by first name. That offhand remark explained everything. Ezra was an erudite scholar, but he never became a pretentious one, a trait in keeping with his tendency to deliver thoughts truthfully, without useless frills. In fact, whenever during our conversations I began mumbling pleasantries to avoid controversial subjects, he invariably exclaimed: "You are the perfect diplomat!" I am not sure he meant that as a compliment.

Without a doubt it was Ezra's lack of affectation, so different from academics I had known, that has preserved the encounter I described above. Then again, Ezra's bicycle never completely disappeared from my visual field. When I spent a year at Harvard as a visiting scholar, Ezra was almost eighty and still in the saddle of his beloved bike, no longer as a means of moving quickly around campus, but for exercise along the less crowded streets of Cambridge. I once asked him what he thought about while he was dutifully cycling to keep in shape, and he replied that he was going over the list of people who had done him wrong. There was a twinkle in his eye, but given his candid way of speaking, the joke might well have contained a grain of truth. A harmonious workplace devoid of all conflict is a utopian daydream; in practice, the competitive world of academia has more than its fair share.

After getting my MA from Harvard, I joined the Italian diplomatic service, and in spring 1971 was posted to our newly opened embassy in Beijing. Exactly two years later Deng Xiaoping was rehabilitated. He was back, but he knew that the radicals hated him, and he needed to tread softly. One day at the airport, when a foreign dignitary arrived for an official visit, I had a chance to witness his cautiousness firsthand. The Chinese Foreign Ministry used to line up diplomats on the tarmac, divided in lines according to our rank. To our right stood the Chinese leaders, also arranged hierarchically. While awaiting the arrival of the airplane carrying the important guest, I looked around, bored, and noticed that Deng Xiaoping was a short distance away, ranked as I was, in the third line of his group. Small and impassive, always with white socks and pants too short, he stood there quietly, a man who had been the General Secretary of the Party up until the Cultural Revolution, while in the first line Mao's wife Jiang Qing, the most prominent radical personality of the regime, chatted happily with Foreign Minister Qiao Guanhua. The latter turned, saw Deng, went to say hello, took him by the arm and with a broad smile dragged him to the front line. Deng let himself be led forward, but after a few seconds he turned and went back to the third line. It is not surprising that a man of such patience and tenacity later become the most important Chinese leader, the real successor to Mao Zedong.

I told this anecdote to Ezra while eating lunch together a few years ago. He said nothing, but took a piece of paper from his pocket and jotted down a few notes in his small, precise handwriting. I was surprised. He had by then already published his biography of Deng Xiaoping. My little story, although suggestive, was certainly not important. What could he possibly gain by recording my words? When the Fairbank Center announced his passing, it pointed out that Ezra Vogel had described himself as a student first and as a teacher second. Ezra had recorded my words because he was always ready to learn something new, no matter how trivial, with unaffected interest. And, as all people who knew him understood well, he was always pushing himself to the limit.

On December 3, 2020, seventeen days before he passed away, I wrote to Ezra, asking for help with a project of mine. He answered the same day, surprising me. Somehow, I had never gotten used to the fact that he always answered his messages immediately, in spite of his eternal busyness. He explained that before he could help, he had certain commitments to see to, but he "should be in better shape in a couple of months." I wrote back that I was stubborn and therefore willing to wait as long as necessary for his much-needed help. Within a few minutes he shot back another message:

Dear Mario,
Thank you for your understanding.
I call it perseverance, which is a good thing. Not stubbornness.
Ezra

I do not think that anyone could receive a warmer farewell from an old teacher and friend.

Susan Chira

The Marshall Project

My head kept drooping, and my pen dropping, as I struggled to stay awake in a class Ezra was teaching. It was not from lack of interest—as ever, his insights were engaging, and his class stimulating—but because I spent most nights until 3 a.m. working at the *Crimson*, then attending classes in East Asian Studies and History during the day.

Embarrassed, I struggled to hide my fatigue; my notebook (in those pre-computer days) was a mix of dutiful notes when I was awake and incomprehensible squiggles when I nodded off. Many years later, I heard that Ezra had noticed but never said a word to me.

It is typical of Ezra's kindness that he never called me out; he knew I was a serious student of Asia and an aspiring journalist. Indeed, it was his desire to cultivate both of those passions that launched my career. I was deep into my thesis on Japanese land reform—and simultaneously leading the *Crimson* as president—when Ezra first suggested to me that I could combine these two parts of my life. Because the newspaper ate up so many hours, I was unable to take Japanese as an undergraduate, so I chose History as my major field of concentration with East Asian Studies as a minor. Ezra somehow conjured money for a grant allowing me to live in Japan with a family and study Japanese after I graduated.

At the same time, he reached out to one of his many acquaintances, Joe Lelyveld, then the deputy foreign editor of the *New York Times* (and later its executive editor). He urged Joe to interview me, arguing that journalism needed more people with deep knowledge of Asia and Asian languages. So Joe decided to take me on as an intern in the *Times's* Tokyo bureau, where I contributed freelance articles while studying Japanese.

This was 1980, the year after *Japan as Number One* catapulted Ezra to stardom in Japan and helped ignite recognition that Japan, seen condescendingly as a junior partner to the U.S., was lapping its former occupier. It was an important early lesson in the perils of American hubris. Living in Japan as a young college graduate, with a Japanese family who took in Japanese college students as boarders and imposed a curfew on us all, I had an unusual opportunity to experience Japan without some of the layers of privilege or distance that other expatriates had.

I absorbed a central lesson from Ezra and other East Asian Studies professors, that a society must be viewed on its own terms, with appropriate humility and openness to alternatives to the American way. This lesson was a touchstone throughout my career, as a foreign correspondent in Japan and an editor supervising international coverage for the *Times*, first as deputy foreign editor and then as foreign editor, culminating in the extraordinary year of 2011, with the Arab Spring and the fallout from Fukushima defining one of the most tumultuous periods in international affairs in generations.

It's easy for foreign correspondents to compare their country condescendingly to the U.S., as lesser than, or less advanced than, their home society. But many of us learned early that using the U.S. as a model had grave pitfalls, even as we cherished the freedoms and institutions that had shaped us as Americans. The Trump era and the events of January 6, revealing the fragility of American democracy and the folly of triumphalism, was just the latest evidence of something I learned under Ezra's and his colleagues' guidance in my student days. And indeed, the Japan I left in the late 1980s experienced its own check on hubris, as it entered a period of economic stagnation and watched China challenge its economic prowess.

Ezra, as ever, was kind enough to follow my career and reach out to make sure we stayed in touch. I had the pleasure of dropping by when I could to see him in Cambridge, where his intellectual curiosity was never sated and his zest to better explain Asia undimmed. It's hard to believe I won't find him there now, listening eagerly and asking incisive questions. But his generosity of spirit and intellect, the legions of people he mentored and helped, remain as an enduring legacy.

Dorinda (Dinda) Elliott

China Institute

It is no exaggeration to say that Ezra Vogel changed the course of my life. When I was a sophomore at Harvard studying Chinese, he said, "You can't truly learn Chinese here. You have to go!" He was so right. Off I went for more than a year of study in Taiwan, where I worked on my characters and—as Ezra knew I would—learned so much more about Chinese culture, family structure, and traditions. After that year, there was no turning back.

Professor Vogel was one of those brilliant thinkers who of course did serious academic research but also understood the value of personal experience, and, yes, on-the-ground reporting. He encouraged my desire to return to Asia for my thesis research, based on interviewing "refugees" from China (at the wonderful Universities Service Centre in Hong Kong, which he helped found) about their families and drama-filled lives. Throughout the rest of my life, Ezra encouraged me as a journalist, covering China and East Asia. Though I was far from one of his best students, he was always so welcoming—and intellectually curious, asking tons of questions—whenever I visited him over the years. I will always be tremendously grateful to Ezra and take great inspiration from his boundless drive to ask questions and learn—as Deng Xiaoping said, to seek truth from facts: 实事求是.

Frank Packer

Hong Kong Special Administrative Region

Others must feel, as I do, how difficult it is to do justice to their memories of Ezra in a few pages, but I will give it a shot. Here are a handful of remembrances under a few overarching themes.

Sociology 270: It's who you know. I first met Ezra in the fall of 1980 when I was a senior at Harvard and was taking Sociology 270, Japanese Business and Society. It was a legendary seminar whose students were mostly graduate-level and more high-powered than I was, though each class attendee gave presentations. But Ezra always had the last word: I remember him telling the class that the key to Japanese society was understanding that it was about "who you know." If someone else were to have said this, it would have sounded terribly simplistic, arrogant, or both. But in his case, it was simply informative, given his own observations and experience. And of course, he was a living example of the more general point. To know him was quite likely to change your own life. He helped me in many ways, not the least of which was to get started in my early career in Washington, D.C.

The value of sharing the journey. During the second semester of my senior year I met with Ezra a few times for career advice, though he was incredibly busy and in demand. Once, while I was waiting for an appointment with him, he came out of his office early to tell me that he needed to go elsewhere for another event that had come up, and would I like to chat with him and share notes on the five-to-ten-minute walk? Over the course of the walk, his answers to my queries were thoughtful and the conversation rich. I remember his advice to this day. This was a pattern we often followed over subsequent decades, though with a twist, for he would often also invite me to sit in on the meetings or lectures that were the next destination. There I got to observe Ezra's influence close-up and meet some of his friends.

Tokyo meetings of "acolytes." My subsequent graduate studies (at the University of Chicago and Columbia University) as well as work opportunities frequently brought me to Japan for both short and multi-year stints. When in Japan, it was my great fortune to attend the International House annual meetings of Ezra's "acolytes," as the organizer Rick Dyck put it. Everybody would introduce themselves or provide updates and listen attentively to Ezra as he shared his opinions on developments in the U.S., Japan, China, or elsewhere. Ezra was always extremely interested to hear not just others' opinions, but the personal stories underlying their views. None of my other mentors over the years had quite that same combination of accomplishment and down-to-earth curiosity about the personal and detailed affairs of others.

The power of Harvard. It wasn't until many years after my graduation that I came to the realization that Ezra epitomized in some sense "the power of Harvard." Harvard was both a global network and a focal point. The community had the power to move resources and inspire, and Ezra internalized this keenly. In this light, I recall the relish with which Ezra would tell stories of Harvard undergraduates he knew who were visiting their international classmates all over the globe after graduation. And over the decades that followed, I saw how Ezra brought Harvard grads together in Tokyo, Hong Kong, and Beijing.

The value of language training. I am sure many readers of this volume will be aware of Ezra's fluency in both Mandarin and Japanese. It was clear how keeping up his language skills had contributed to his network, influence, scholarship, and worldview. I frequently joined him in gatherings in which he gave lectures in Japanese in Tokyo; often I also heard him speak in Mandarin. He invited me to join him at breakfasts in which the conversation proceeded in Japanese. I was impressed to hear that he did not rest on his laurels but regularly employed tutors to brush up on his language skills. More than once he noted for my benefit the difficulties of gaining knowledge of a region or being an area specialist without having a grasp of the language. Even if I were never to achieve his level of fluency in either language, the lesson I took is that studying the language and maintaining skills at whatever level one could allowed one to dig more deeply into the society and gain an extra layer of wisdom that could complement scholarship and research.

Ezra's scholarship on Japan was greatly appreciated in China. I moved to Hong Kong in 2009, and my subsequent work frequently took me to the mainland on business trips, where I interacted with Chinese scholars and bureaucrats. A few years later, Ezra's book on Deng Xiaoping came out. Though I knew that Ezra already had a reputation as a China scholar, what I didn't know when I moved to Hong Kong was how significant a reputation it was. But not only was Fu Gaoyi, as he was known in China, highly respected for his knowledge of China among the many Chinese whom I met, I found that many were quite knowledgeable about his work on Japan, starting with *Japan's New Middle Class* published fifty years earlier. As for *Japan as Number One*, sometimes referred to with a smile among academics in Japan or the U.S. who remember that it was a bestseller, trained observers in China rather saw it as an integral part of the body of Ezra's work analyzing Japanese society in comparative context, containing many lessons for other countries' development.

Glen S. Fukushima

Center for American Progress

I first met Ezra in September 1974, when I arrived in Cambridge to enroll in Harvard's MA program for Regional Studies East Asia. Although I had committed to an academic career, I had not yet decided whether to pursue a PhD in sociology, political science, or history. Ezra knew that I had declined Yale's offer of a generous Sumitomo Fellowship, and he also knew that Hugh Patrick, then a professor at Yale, wanted me to attend Yale for my PhD. Instead, Ezra encouraged me to apply to the PhD program in Harvard's Department of Sociology during my first year in the MA program.

I followed his sage advice and ended up spending eight years at Harvard: one year in the Regional Studies MA program, three years in the Sociology PhD program, and four years in the JD/MBA program at the Law School and Business School. I also had the privilege of serving as a teaching fellow for three academic titans: Ezra (Sociology 114: Postwar Japanese Society), Edwin Reischauer (Government 118: The Government and Politics of Contemporary Japan), and David Riesman (Social Sciences 136: Character and Social Structure in America). Those eight years provided me with the intellectual foundation for my subsequent career in law, government, business, and think tanks.

Although I left Harvard in 1982 to be a Fulbright Fellow at the University of Tokyo, I kept in close touch with Ezra over the ensuing forty years. After serving in Washington, D.C., in the 1980s as Deputy Assistant United States Trade Representative for Japan and China, I moved to Tokyo in 1990 as Vice President of AT&T Japan. Over the next thirty years, I served as an informal "control officer" for Ezra when he visited Tokyo. I would set up and host breakfasts, lunches, and dinners for him to meet with his extraordinary range of contacts in Japan. These meetings revealed those qualities of Ezra's that contributed to his success as a teacher, scholar, mentor, and public intellectual.

First, Ezra truly appreciated the value of human relationships in Asia—*ningen kankei* in Japan, *ingan kwangye* in Korea, and *guanxi* in China. He asked me to arrange meetings for him in Tokyo with Japanese leaders in politics, the government bureaucracy, business, journalism, and academia. Among the most interesting were lunches with former Japanese diplomats who had spent time as visiting fellows at Harvard, some from as far back as the 1960s. Insights and anecdotes from these discussions found their way into Ezra's research and writing, especially his last two books—*Deng Xiaoping and the Transformation of China* and *China and Japan: Facing History.*

Second, Ezra almost always spoke in Japanese with his Japanese contacts, probably because he wanted to show respect and allow his friends to express themselves fully. His approach of meeting Japanese on their own terms was laudable, and a reason so many Japanese respected him. His commitment to language study was such that in the mid-1970s he hired my wife, Sakie, who was then teaching Japanese at Harvard, to tutor him in Japanese five days a week from 7 to 8 a.m.

Third, Ezra was insatiably curious. Despite being one of the world's premier scholars of Asia, he was always eager to ask questions and to learn. In July 1993, he visited Tokyo just before joining the Clinton administration as the National Intelligence Officer (NIO) for East Asia. I hosted a dinner for him, inviting a dozen American business executives with extensive experience in Japan. Ezra stayed until past 10 p.m., taking detailed notes on what the executives complained were barriers American companies faced in the Japanese market.

Fourth, Ezra's curiosity about Japan extended well beyond the bilateral relationship. Some of his most interesting discussions in Tokyo were breakfast meetings I hosted, inviting ambassadors to Japan from the Five Eyes countries—the United States, Britain, Canada, Australia, and New Zealand. Another memorable meeting was a lunch I hosted in 2010, which Chinese Ambassador to Japan Cheng Yonghua attended.

Fifth, Ezra was always generous in sharing his knowledge and contacts. For instance, when I visited Russia, Australia, and New Zealand in 2019, he introduced me to colleagues in all three countries so that I could have productive discussions with them about their country's relations with the United States, Japan, and China.

Finally, Ezra was always modest and humble, never pontificating, in his interactions with others. Japanese often commented that, unlike many prominent American scholars, he always stayed at the International House of Japan in Roppongi. This symbolized Ezra's humility and identification with the Japanese academic and intellectual community, despite the easy access he enjoyed to Japan's political and corporate elite.

I learned much from Ezra during my eight years at Harvard as his student, teaching fellow, and dissertation advisee. But it was during the subsequent forty years that I came to appreciate his human qualities—the value he placed on long-term human relationships and on language expertise, his curiosity, his holistic view of Japan, and his generosity and humility. These are reflected in this passage from his memoirs, which he began writing in 2019:

> [A]t Harvard I had the good fortune to have many able graduate students interested in studying Asia. . . . They mostly took an initial course with me on Japanese Society or Chinese Communist Society, but after that they became my friends. Many of them became my teaching assistants. . . . Some Japanese students respectfully called me "Vogel Sensei" but almost no one called me Professor Vogel. I was "Ezra," a friend a little older than they were. I learned a great deal from them, from the questions they posed, from their perspectives, from their research and sometimes their advice about the research I was trying to do. In most cases, the personal friendship continued after they received their PhD. Many have become lifelong friends.

I am proud to be Ezra's former student and lifelong friend. He provided a model not only of a nonpareil teacher, mentor, scholar, and public intellectual but also of a human being of exemplary decency, humility, and integrity.

Fred Hiatt†

The Washington Post

When the *Washington Post* Foreign Desk chose my wife, Pooh Shapiro, and me to head the East Asia bureau in Tokyo (and, incidentally, to become the first job-sharing couple to do such a job), we turned to Ezra for advice on how to prepare. He made us an offer we couldn't refuse.

As one of his many initiatives to improve cross-border understanding, Ezra had launched the U.S.-Japan Program, which was intended to bring mid-career civil servants, military officers, and business executives from both countries to Harvard for a year to study bilateral issues—but even more, to get to know each other in an intensive but informal setting. He was finding it easier to recruit Japanese than Americans, so he urged us to sign up for an academic year and told us we could also study Japanese language with Harvard's marvelous teachers.

In early-morning language class, we struggled to keep up with Harvard undergraduates. But in the program, we connected with people who would remain some of our closest Japanese friends when we moved to Tokyo. Even better, we joined the multitudes for whom Ezra would remain forever a wise and trusted mentor. From then on he took great pride in our careers; and when he felt we were falling short (he sometimes judged that, in my later career as an opinion writer, I lacked balance in my approach to China and human rights), he would let us know in the gentlest manner imaginable.

How fortunate we were to forge such a connection.

Susan Lawrence
Takoma Park, Maryland

I first met Ezra in my first year as an undergraduate at Harvard, in 1984, when I enrolled in his Industrial East Asia core curriculum course. I had no prior exposure to the Four Little Dragons—Taiwan, South Korea, Hong Kong, and Singapore—but Ezra's enthusiasm for the subject was infectious. Ezra encouraged me to apply to the concentration in East Asian Studies (EAS), for which he served as chairman, and invited me to come to see him in his office. When I arrived for my appointment, Ezra was finishing up a meeting with Ben Makihara, who would a few years later become President and CEO of Japan's Mitsubishi Corporation. With his trademark democracy, Ezra introduced me to Ben Makihara and Ben Makihara to me, giving the sincere impression that he expected a senior Japanese business executive and a seventeen-year-old Harvard undergraduate to henceforth become great friends. That was my first introduction to Ezra's indefatigable bridge building and his complete disregard for hierarchy, both of which were among his many endearing traits.

I enrolled in EAS and instead of studying European history, as I had planned, became a China person, with Ezra serving as a lifelong inspiration and mentor. I remember with great fondness the regular departmental gatherings Ezra hosted at his home at 14 Sumner Road. We undergraduates crowded into the living room for discussions with visiting titans of Japan and China studies over mugs of hot apple cider and cookies, building bonds with leading scholars and with each other.

After college, I became a journalist, based for many years in Beijing. Ezra had already seeded the ranks of China journalism with his students, giving me an immediate network of more senior journalists to tap into, including Melinda Liu and Dinda Elliott. As journalist Susan Chira noted on Twitter, "He loved journalists—many academics disdain them." Ezra saw us all as having roles to play in helping very different cultures understand each other.

My first stint in Beijing as a journalist was from 1990 to 1996. Access to officials was difficult. Ezra helped me understand official thinking by occasionally taking me along to meetings with his contacts as his notetaker. I feared that my presence would jeopardize Ezra's relationships with his sources. That none of them objected was testament to the high regard Chinese interlocutors all had for Ezra. All his life, Ezra was reflexively generous with his extraordinary contacts.

I spent two wonderful years at the Fairbank Center, from 1996 to 1998, while Ezra was its director, and got a chance to see up close some of the myriad ways Ezra was working to try to bridge the gaps between the United States and China. He had me accompany a Kennedy School of Government faculty member to meetings in Beijing to establish an executive training program for senior Chinese military officers and then persuaded me to serve as program chair for the first two iterations of the annual program. The program's funder, Nina Kung (also known as Nina Wang), was Asia's richest woman, but in China Ezra was more famous, and it was he the Chinese officers were most excited to meet.

Ezra also talked me into a minor role in Chinese Communist Party General Secretary and State President Jiang Zemin's visit to Harvard on November 1, 1997. Ezra had advocated for the visit, despite deep skepticism from some of his colleagues and many students, and he oversaw the myriad details of the visit. He assigned me the job of interpreting for Harvard's president, Neil Rudenstine, in his private meeting with Jiang. Ezra then presided over the high-stakes public event immediately afterward.

Jiang's representatives had initially wanted assurances that Jiang would not have to face protesters, and they resisted exposing him to questions. Many Harvard faculty and students felt strongly that no visiting leader should be shielded from tough questioning. Ultimately, Jiang's representatives agreed to two questions submitted in advance, to be chosen by Ezra and three Harvard colleagues. Ezra and his colleagues defused some of the criticism they faced for that arrangement by selecting two pointed questions for Jiang. (The first was, "Why did the Chinese government order tanks in Tiananmen Square on June 4, 1989, and confront the Chinese people?") After the second question, Ezra unexpectedly announced that Jiang was "willing to take a question from the audience." Asked what he had learned about democracy from the protests that greeted him in each city during his U.S. visit, Jiang answered, to laughter, that he had gained a "more specific understanding" of American democracy. He added that at seventy-one, "my ears still work very well," so he could hear the protesters outside the hall, and "I believe the only approach for me is to speak even louder."

Before the visit, Ezra had told *The Harvard Crimson*, "We hope that [Jiang] and his group go home with an impression that democracy works, that discussion is possible without creating chaos." The visit Ezra orchestrated made the point powerfully. Jiang's answer to the impromptu question suggested that he might be persuaded. Sadly, despite Ezra's best efforts, China has since swung further away from tolerance for dissent.

That Ezra could be involved in so many initiatives and still publish groundbreaking books on such a diverse set of topics was astounding. As he got older, it seemed as if Ezra only became busier. Among the fruits of his late-in-life efforts were the National Committee on U.S.-China Relations Public Intellectuals Program and the Mansfield Foundation's U.S.-Japan Network for the Future.

The image of Ezra that stays with me now is from a chance encounter at the Beijing airport near the end of his life. By then I was working for the Congressional Research Service, a unit of the Library of Congress. I was accompanying a delegation of congressional staffers to China, and my group got off the plane feeling groggy after the thirteen-hour flight. In the line at immigration, we found Ezra. He had a walking stick with a fold-down seat and was propped up against it, but was as bright-eyed as ever, showing no signs of fatigue. (If Ezra's high-ranking Chinese contacts had known he was there, they would surely have whisked him through a VIP channel, but Ezra, ever unassuming, ever democratic, never sought special treatment.) I introduced some of the staffers to Ezra. With his trademark earnestness leavened with humor and self-knowledge, Ezra set about doing what he did best: impressing upon a new set of acquaintances the importance of their roles in helping manage the world's most consequential bilateral relationship.

William Overholt

Harvard University

Ezra Vogel was an extraordinary mentor. When he retired, hundreds of his former students came to the celebration. The gala had a day for sociology panels, a day for China specialists, a day for Japan specialists. Most of the leading U.S. journalists on Asia seemed to have been his students. Also numerous were the Japanese and Chinese students whom he had nurtured and organized. Harvard's then-President Derek Bok said he had never seen anything like this outpouring.

Why the enthusiasm? My experience may illuminate it, not because I was special, but because this was archetypical of Ezra's devotion to his students. I came to Harvard to become a mathematical physicist, but in my freshman year I took Ezra's course on Chinese society and found myself enchanted. I majored in Social Studies instead. In my sophomore year, I applied for Ezra's graduate course on Chinese society. Thirty graduate students plus me wanted in, but Ezra could only take ten. Unlike Kissinger, who started by telling all the undergrads to leave, Vogel asked each of us to explain why we wanted the class. I said that Aristotle, Marx, and Weber had all explained persuasively why you couldn't organize peasants into a political force, but Mao had done what they said was impossible. I wanted to understand why the great sociologists were wrong. Ezra accepted me and nine grad students. He liked my paper, so the following year he got me grants to do a senior thesis on why Mao's techniques didn't work in the Philippines. The theoretical work from that paper eventually became my Yale dissertation.

Twenty-five years later, Ezra lectured in Hong Kong, where I was working, and I asked him to critique a short paper I had written on "The Rise of China." I expected him to return it with a flood of red ink. Instead, two letters came. Widener Library wrote that Ezra was making the paper required reading in a course that counted for the Core Curriculum; would I charge royalties? (Of course not.) The deputy head of W. W. Norton publishers wrote that Ezra had shown him the paper; he assumed I would turn it into a book (I had no such plans) and would appreciate it if I would accept the enclosed book contract and check to ensure that Norton could publish it. That book, which came out in ten languages, became the foundation of a second career for me.

Nine years later, when I had tired of investment banking, Ezra brought me back to Harvard and midwifed my transition back to the academic/think-tank world. I took a Distinguished Chair at RAND, then returned to Harvard. In return for all this, Ezra got nothing except my gratitude. Like many others I was his student for a lifetime.

Ezra's retirement party provided one more insight. He was clearly at the height of his powers, so I asked him why on earth he would want to retire. He said, "It's important to give younger people a chance at the big salaries." He happily drove his ancient Toyota while ensuring that the "big salaries" went to younger scholars. Characteristically, he devoted the very substantial royalties from the People's Republic of China's translation of his Deng Xiaoping book to Ohio Wesleyan.

Ezra was an institution builder. He founded Harvard's Asia Center, started the undergraduate concentration in East Asian Studies, organized the Regional Studies East Asia master's degree program, played a crucial role in developing the Fairbank Center for Chinese Studies, and founded the Program on U.S.-Japan Relations. Part of Ezra's institution-building success was his instinct for addressing the right issue at the right time, but much of it was his personal approach. Five years ago he decided that Harvard and the country needed a platform for leading China specialists to address a broad audience. In founding the weekly Critical Issues Confronting China series, which became possibly the most popular weekly public forum at Harvard, he formed a committee of three of us: himself, Prof. William Hsiao of the School of Public Health, and myself. Then he did almost all the work himself, but spread the credit around. Embarrassed by his undeserved generosity, I leaped at any opportunity to help out.

Informally Ezra was a diplomat. He painstakingly cultivated a self-presentation of modesty, professionalism, warmth, and total attentiveness that enabled him to talk with just about anybody about just about anything. Thus, for instance, at the time of the greatest Sino-Japanese antagonism over interpretations of World War II history, he was able to bring leading Chinese and Japanese scholars together in dialogue. Leaders in Japan, China, and South Korea welcomed him and listened. Behind the scenes, he influenced events.

Because of his personal modesty, people who did not know him well may not have perceived his greatness. Because of his eclectic methods and disciplines, in a world of academic hyper-specialization, his contributions were not always fully appreciated. It is therefore imperative for those who understood his reach to ensure that he is remembered.

Karl Eikenberry

Riyadh, Kingdom of Saudi Arabia

As a young U.S. Army captain, I arrived at Harvard University in the fall of 1979 to begin two years of study in the Graduate School of Arts and Sciences East Asia Regional Studies master's degree program. As a military officer selected to become a Foreign Area Officer specializing in China, I was to continue my education after graduating from Harvard in 1981 with two years of immersive Chinese language training at the United Kingdom Ministry of National Defence Chinese Language School in Hong Kong and then at Nanjing University.

The one consistent suggestion I received from the East Asian Studies master's candidates beginning their second year of study was to enroll in Professor Ezra Vogel's course on Communist Chinese society, listed with the Department of Sociology. Those offering this advice were writing on a blank slate—since graduating from the United States Military Academy at West Point in 1973, I had been assigned to hard-charging infantry and ranger units and had few insights into the Harvard faculty. So I dutifully signed up for Professor Vogel's course. As a result, my life's own course changed.

Professor Vogel made sense of the numerous and often contradictory forces at play in China as it transitioned from the Cultural Revolution to its opening under paramount leader Deng Xiaoping. Ezra brilliantly explained these forces—the social continuities and traditions derived from an enduring great civilization; the trauma of nineteenth- and twentieth-century decline and the concomitant humiliation and rising tide of nationalism; and the successes and excesses of Maoist communism. Most importantly, he taught me and my fellow students to be empathetic . . . the necessary starting point of effective diplomacy and a sound national security strategy. I carried Ezra's wisdom with me to later assignments in China, Korea, Afghanistan, NATO, and around the globe.

Due to a shortage of PhD candidates, 1980 proved to be an auspicious year. Professor Vogel invited me to serve as the teaching assistant for his course on Communist Chinese society. Once a week, I would walk to his residence at 14 Sumner Road in Cambridge to spend an hour with an educator who took his mission of teaching seriously and who always stimulated intellectual ferment inside the classroom and beyond. What a role model! He cared so deeply about his students.

My wife Ching and I were blessed over the years by being able to stay in close touch with Ezra and Charlotte, seeing them at the U.S. Embassy Beijing, at the Indo-Pacific Command headquarters in Hawaii, at Harvard and Stanford, in Washington, D.C., in the United Lounge at Narita airport, and in countless other places. I continued to learn from Ezra, both professionally and personally, until his final days.

I have been fortunate over the course of my own life to have had many extraordinary professional opportunities as a soldier, diplomat, and educator. But if you ask me which experiences have proven the most rewarding and which ones I recall most fondly and proudly, at the top of my list is always: "Teaching Assistant for Professor Ezra Vogel, 1980–1981."

Jeff Williams

Harvard Kennedy School

While Ezra Vogel and I had met a few times before, we bonded in 1998 during Harvard President Neil Rudenstine's visit to East Asia. I was a board member of the Taiwan Harvard Club, and Ezra was advising the president on details of the trip. The plan got caught up in political sensitivities between Taiwan and China, resulting in the Taiwan Club—led by a few members who were government officials—threatening to cancel the visit altogether. Ezra and I helped navigate the impasse, focusing on what the best outcome would be for Harvard. Ever since then we stayed in touch. I visited him whenever I returned to Cambridge. Ezra always showed an interest in my work, and we shared a deep concern about Harvard and Harvard's presence in East Asia.

In China Ezra was arguably the best-known and most well-respected among Harvard scholars. A journalist once explained how he had interviewed Ezra for state media at the time he was working in Guangzhou on the Pearl River delta economy. *Japan as Number One* was very well known. Of course, the Deng biography cemented his reputation. I visited a Shanghai bookshop shortly after that book was released to find a ceiling-high display of the Chinese translation.

Yet despite his fame, Ezra was a frugal and unprepossessing man. Some ten years ago my wife Chuang and I were flying back to Boston from China. During a layover in San Francisco Chuang spied Ezra sitting alone in the waiting area. It then emerged that we were on the same flight, but Ezra was sitting in coach while we were in business. Chuang asked him if it wouldn't be more comfortable for him at his age to ride in business class? Ezra replied that yes, he was entitled to ride in business class, but he preferred to reserve the funds to pay his research assistants. Ezra was always thinking about how to improve his research and how to help younger scholars to learn and to gain recognition.

In 2003, as president of the Taiwan Harvard Club, I was preparing a presentation for alumni on the Chinese stele in the Yard, which had been a Tercentenary gift from the club when it was the Harvard Club of the Republic of China in 1936. The stele was showing its years of exposure to

New England weather. I needed a photo of the stele to show its condition and decided at the last minute to ask Ezra to be photographed along with the stele, to add interest and to show scale. He wasn't in, but I left a voice mail asking if he would meet me in the Yard. Ezra called my home to find out what I wanted, but my wife only said she knew I was headed to Widener. With no inkling of what I was up to, Ezra as a true friend hurried over on his bike and joined me for the photo.

Remembering Ezra inevitably calls to mind Ezra on his bike. While living in Beijing around the time of the 2008 Olympics, we met Ezra and Charlotte for dinner in a restaurant inside Ritan Park. At the time, they were in Beijing while he was researching his Deng book. I was alarmed to find that they had ridden bicycles to meet us. I had long before decided that bicycling in Beijing was far too hazardous for mere mortals. But a bicycle was how Ezra got around.

Knowing that I was working in China, Ezra always wanted to know how Harvard was viewed there and was sensitive to Harvard's reputation outside of the U.S. Since I had left my banking job and was consulting in China, Ezra strongly urged me to give back to Harvard by becoming Executive Director of the Harvard Center, Shanghai. I always felt that I represented not only Harvard in China, but Ezra as well, and I kept him informed of goings-on in Shanghai each time I came to campus.

Most recently, Ezra had been working on a paper for the new administration in Washington, laying out recommendations on crafting a solid China policy. He invited me to help by suggesting relevant readings related to business and finance. He read everything I sent him. Ezra and I did not see eye to eye on every issue and as a result had a number of spirited discussions over the phone and via email. Even in disagreement he always listened carefully and respected other viewpoints. In early December 2020 I sent a package of documents to Ezra by email, apologizing for its length. He immediately emailed back, "Yep, a lot of work to do." Sadly the paper was never finished, and the Biden administration was deprived of his wisdom and guidance.

Ezra's passing is a great loss to Harvard and to U.S.-China relations at a critical time.

NINE

Institution Building at Harvard

Dwight Perkins

Harvard University

E zra Vogel and I joined the Harvard faculty at roughly the same time and did a wide range of teaching, research, and administration to-gether continuously right up until his death at age ninety. In the 1960s and for many years thereafter we were both mentored by John Fairbank, even though John was not involved in the formal education require-ments for either of us. In the mid- or late 1960s we were both engaged in broadly similar research on the nature of the Chinese system under Com-munist rule. (Ezra published *Canton under Communism* in 1969, and my *Market Control and Planning in Communist China*, based on my disserta-tion, was published in 1966.)

John Fairbank had created the East Asian Research Center (EARC) in 1955, and it was a key vehicle in his successful effort to build the field of Modern China studies in the United States and elsewhere. By the early 1970s, however, John was about to turn sixty-five, and at Harvard at the time one was not allowed to hold a center directorship or other senior administrative post past the age of sixty-five. John asked Ezra to succeed him as director of the East Asian Research Center in 1973, and he asked me to serve as associate director. Ezra agreed, as did I on the condition that I had a concrete set of responsibilities (which were supervision of the publications program and center liaison to the major East Asian fund drive led by Fairbank and Ed Reischauer, which was then just getting un-derway). Ezra served as director for four years (1973–77) and then con-tinued in other senior administrative roles. I was acting director when Ezra was on leave in the academic year 1975–76, and I moved on to be chairman of the Department of Economics in 1977.

Ezra and I got along well, and I do not remember any incident of any kind where we argued or even disagreed. Ezra was mainly responsi-ble for running the public programs and conferences, and I dealt with

my part. We both had many outside activities, and we often dealt with
Center administrative issues when we were together on planes returning
from a China-related conference or committee meeting. The problem for
the EARC at that time, however, was that it did not have much money.
From its founding in 1955 through to 1973 the Center had been funded
by successive two- or three-year grants from the Ford Foundation (roughly
$300,000 for three years if my memory is correct). The Ford Foundation
in the early 1970s, however, announced that it was no longer going to continue funding of the EARC or China-related programs in the U.S. generally, and they made one last grant, I believe a year or two before Ezra
became director.

Harvard's response to this situation was to authorize John Fairbank
and Ed Reischauer to launch a major fundraising effort for East Asian
Studies, and Jeff Coolidge, who had many years of experience in Korea,
was asked to chair the effort. The fund drive was very successful in raising money for Japan studies (roughly $9 million) and for Korean studies,
but raised only limited funds for China. The Japanese money, however,
was given to create a separate Japan institute (now the Reischauer Institute of Japanese Studies). The Japanese studies faculty had occasionally
expressed resentment that most of the EARC money went to China-
related activities and so were not willing to use the new funds for the
EARC. During my one year as acting director I moved the publications
program out of the EARC and put it under the Council on East Asian
Studies, which included all East Asian faculty. The council at the time
was also headed by Ezra, and Ezra was as much a Japan specialist as a
China specialist, and so the Reischauer Institute then and thereafter supported Japan publications by the publications office.

During his time as director, Ezra substituted his energy and imagination for the lack of funds, and the activities of the center continued as
before. There were lots of speakers and other public activities, but there
was not much funding for recent PhD's to turn their dissertations into
publishable books—something that was central to the Fairbank-led center. For the Harvard community, however, the EARC was as dynamic as
ever, and Ezra deserves nearly all the credit for that. At the same time
that he was heading the EARC, Ezra was also managing the new undergraduate concentration in East Asian Studies. Ezra continued in this role
for all or most of the time it was managed separately from the Depart-

ment of East Asian Languages and Civilizations. Ezra did not just supervise the program. He was the head tutor and ran the program on a day-to-day basis. During his time as director of the EARC this added an important undergraduate component to the EARC, thus broadening the role of the EARC within the Harvard community. Others in this volume will no doubt comment about their own experiences with Ezra in the context of the East Asian Studies concentration, but in my view it was one of Ezra's major achievements and contributions to the university.

Arthur Kleinman

Harvard University

I first saw him at a distance, while walking in Harvard Square near the Coop in the fall of 1970. I had just arrived at Harvard, and Ezra was pointed out to me by my new mentor, Everett Mendelsohn, as someone I definitely had to meet. (I had spent two years in Taiwan doing medical research and was beginning my work in medical anthropology.) But years were to go by before I summoned the courage to reach out and get to know Ezra. Perhaps my problem was the anxiety of influence. I had to formulate my own approach before engaging a senior colleague who had established such an impressive way of engaging China and Japan.

We were colleagues for decades and my daughter was mentored by Ezra in the East Asian Studies concentration. But we really connected during the eight years (2008–16) when I was the director of the Harvard Asia Center. The center had been founded by Ezra, and he also played the central role in creating its endowment from wealthy donors in Hong Kong and Japan. Even though he was retired, Ezra showed up frequently to get the help of Holly Angell, the Asia Center's Director of Programs. She had become something like an informal personal assistant to Ezra even as she carried out her duties at the Center. Loyal, good natured, and deeply caring, Holly graciously accepted this work almost as a second job. I looked the other way and said nothing, since the relationship seemed right to me. Because her office was adjacent to the director's office, I saw Ezra much more frequently than any other Harvard faculty member over those eight years.

Ezra was also a member of a Senior Advisory Committee of distinguished Asianists at Harvard, active and retired, which I had created to
meet once a year over a fancy meal at the Charles Hotel. This committee
gave me an opportunity to present an informal State of the Center report
and receive feedback and sage advice from the likes of Henry Rosovsky,
Amartya Sen, Weiming Tu (before he left for Beida), Rod MacFarquhar,
Dwight Perkins, Homi Bhabha, Steve Owen, Diana Eck, and Liz Perry.
In 2009, I had a real problem to discuss. The then Dean of the Faculty
of Arts and Sciences, in response to a large loss of endowment funds owing to the 2008 financial collapse, began to appropriate leftover funds
from the centers, including the Asia Center, even though those funds were
committed for multi-year programs.

I presented the problem to the Senior Advisors, who lamented and
supported my resistance to this bureaucratic overreach that defied the Asia
Center's charter: the legal status of restricted funds and our supposed financial sovereignty. After a while the conversation began to move on,
but Ezra refused to allow this to happen. At these meetings, Amartya and
Henry tended to dominate discussion, and usually Ezra remained quiet.
But this issue was too close to the bone of what was at stake at the Center.
And Ezra would simply not let it go. Finally, he got the committee to come
up with a resolution to support me. The members would sign a letter that
objected to the dean's actions, and several of them would also visit the
dean to drive home the point: hands off the Asia Center budget.

The visit to the dean did not have an immediate effect, but the next
year, the dean began to relax his incursion into our budget. The biggest
outcome was a rejuvenation of Ezra's engagement with the Asia Center.
He told me that this small battle had made him realize that for all his
influence among China and Japan scholars and his large reputation in
those countries, he had little influence at Harvard. He lamented that from
the time he had first come to Harvard until 2009, Harvard remained a
very America-focused university.

Ezra's rejuvenated work with the Asia Center included a revival of the
Asia Vision 21 meetings in Singapore, Hong Kong, and Cambridge. Those
meetings, which Ezra had initiated but which subsequent directors of
the Asia Center following my tenure decided to end because they were
not considered academic enough, were in my own view quite extraordinary. In a sense they were Ezra and his friends. And what a group of

friends he had! Leading business people, government officials, and academics, particularly from Japan, China, and Southeast Asia, who came together to discuss major political, economic, and social issues affecting U.S.-Asia relations as well as those among Asian nations. These meetings represented a network of over 100 players in the worlds of finance, business, government, and policy whose exchanges, frank and informal, held significance in world affairs. It was as if each of these elite figures had his or her own personal relationship with Ezra. I just marveled at Ezra's ability to encourage conversations that were not easy but important. Ezra had so much more of a presence in Asia than in the U.S. that it could be wrongly assumed that after these meetings, when we returned to Harvard, his influence would be significant. That this was not the case is a tale of the parochial emphasis on domestic interests that really matter at Harvard and in the United States.

The seeming ease with which America has turned so rapidly and so radically to an exaggeratedly negative view of China and a less than fully engaged presence in Asia is a sad sign of the limits of a globalist vision of the world in America and of the influence of even such an illustrious career as that of Ezra Vogel. He never enjoyed, in my view, the influence at his home institution or in his country that he deserved and that he found in Asia. No wonder he continued to travel so frequently to China and Japan in his last years. The right thing for Harvard to do to honor Ezra Vogel would be to name the Asia Center for him and to more substantially support a global approach to world affairs through increased funding for global programs and their students.

William C. Kirby

Harvard University

Ezra Vogel was a force of academic nature. He was busy, always. He was productive. He was active in public affairs as well as in scholarship. He was an optimist in his work and in his life. He was driven to make a difference.

The Ezra Vogel I knew was already a rather famous man when I joined the Harvard faculty in 1992. With scholarship that was expansive and cross-border, he had made his mark in the firsthand study of Japanese society, and then by studying Canton under communism secondhand, from the near abroad of Hong Kong. He returned then to write the blockbuster *Japan as Number One*, before turning for the rest of his career to the study of contemporary China, its leaders, and its relations with its neighbors. At a Harvard that had once prided itself on scholarship and teaching that reached across Asia's borders (for example, the Fairbank, Reischauer, and Craig volumes that found their way into so many American classrooms), Ezra was one of the very few who could actually work seriously as a scholar on either side of the Sea of Japan.

Ezra's vision of dealing with Asia as a whole, beyond the sum of its parts, led me to recruit him to be the first director of our Asia Center. I was then chair of the Council on East Asian Studies, a body about as decisive as an eighteenth-century Polish parliament. As a program, we had slid, seemingly irretrievably, into camps defined by modern nation-states. (Why, after all, should the Japanese and the Chinese get along any better at Harvard than they did in Asia?) The divide between historical and cultural studies and modern social science remained vast. We seized on the opportunity offered by a university capital campaign (this being Harvard, there is almost always one going on) to broach the concept of a new Asia Center that would study and interact with this dynamic region as a whole. Neil Rudenstine, our president, led the effort. But its success depended on getting the right person to run it as founding director. I and others thought of no one but Ezra Vogel.

Ezra, freshly returned from government service, took this on with restless energy and confidence. His tenure began with the Asian financial crisis of 1997. No problem. Partnering with Victor Fung in Hong Kong, he gathered friends and former students (many now in government positions) to set in motion Asia Vision 21, a series of extraordinary gatherings in Asia and at Harvard. He mobilized colleagues within Harvard and across the Pacific to expand our conceptions of "Asia" to South and Southeast Asian realms, and he set the foundation of an Asia Center that, among other things, is today one of the leading publishers of academic scholarship on the region.

His academic center of gravity, however, remained in Northeast Asia, in China and Japan. Ezra had grown up (like everyone else in East Asian Studies at Harvard) in the long shadow of John K. Fairbank. He often remarked that it was no picnic being the first post-Fairbank director of what is today the Fairbank Center. (John K. Fairbank was still very much in the office.) Ezra emulated many of Fairbank's best practices: meeting and hosting students and scholars informally at his home within minutes of his office. Like Fairbank, Ezra was consumed by the relationship between the United States and China.

In the 1990s, in the aftermath of Tiananmen and the shattered hopes of a politically changed China, Ezra aimed to restore a degree of normalcy to Chinese-American relations. He pushed hard—against all manner of opposition and criticism—to invite President Jiang Zemin to Harvard in 1997, filling Sanders Theater with faculty, students, and security details (with very big guns), while protestors raged outside. He made sure that the Q&A, which included discussion of Tiananmen, was open. The security costs alone drained the Fairbank Center budget. But the operation was a diplomatic triumph for Jiang and vindication for Ezra.

In a return visit that Ezra helped arrange the following spring, Neil Rudenstine became the first Harvard president to set foot in mainland China. Neil spoke brilliantly on the values of liberal education at Peking University's centenary. We then met with President Jiang in Mao's old study and bedroom in Zhongnanhai, where the Chairman had lived, worked, and died. It was now Jiang's reception room, with a piano. President Jiang did not play for us, but he did let us know his current favorite song: the theme of the movie *Titanic*.

Ezra believed that if people could talk to each other and actually listen, or read each other's works and actually learn, that understanding of even the toughest issues was possible. That is why he brought Jiang to Harvard. That is why he devoted the next decade of his life to writing a biography of Deng Xiaoping, who oversaw both China's economic reform and its renewed political repression. That was why in later years he arranged a series of Chinese-Japanese dialogues on "facing history," assuming that a history honestly faced might well lead to reconciliation. But it turns out that it is not always true that the more people get to know each other, the more they like each other. Let alone understand each other. For reasons beyond Ezra's control, the embers of enmity between China and Japan remain warm, periodically stoked, more than seventy-five years after the last shot was fired in war.

In his final years, concern with the deterioration of Chinese-American relations became Ezra's overriding passion. He convened conferences and workshops of notables from both countries who were part of the international elite of policy types. He organized public letters and memoranda. He spoke at innumerable panels both in person and, last year, in Zoomland. As China moved "left" under President Xi Jinping and as the United States lurched rightward (and off the edge) under President Donald Trump, Ezra Vogel, a man who believed in his soul that people were fundamentally good and could come to understand one another, was brought not to despair but to a profound disillusionment.

Yet it was in the act of convening—friends and foes, scholars and practitioners, students and alumni, Chinese and Japanese, presidents of countries and presidents of universities, and even humanists and social scientists—that Ezra was in his element. He was an original scholar, a dedicated teacher, a breathless mobilizer, but above all, a convener of talent. His belief in 人才, that talented and good-spirited people could somehow figure everything out, is what I remember most about Ezra Vogel.

Carter J. Eckert

Harvard University

I forget exactly when, but it was surely within the first few weeks of my arrival in Cambridge in the fall of 1985 as a humble instructor in Harvard's Department of East Asian Languages and Civilizations (EALC), a temporary fill-in—or so I thought and expected at the time—for Professor Edward Wagner, who was on sabbatical leave that year. I was barely out of graduate school, still hardly knew anyone in the department or at the university, and suddenly I received a call out of the blue from Ezra, one of the luminaries of Harvard and the East Asia field, whose work I knew well and deeply admired. And he was inviting me to his house for a chat! I put on my best coat and tie—I think it was my *only* coat and tie—and walked over to the big yellow house on Sumner Road with great trepidation. I had barely reached the top of the front porch steps when the door opened and Ezra bounded out, full Ezra-smile in force, and enthusiastically ushered me inside to the living room. After welcoming me to Harvard with great warmth, he got right to his main point: How can we work together to support your scholarship and teaching and develop Korean studies at Harvard? And from that day on over the next thirty-six years, Ezra remained a steadfast mentor, cheerleader, and all-around go-to mensch.

Ezra's reputation in the China and Japan fields is legend, but it is less known that he was also a godfather to Korean studies at Harvard and to the wider Korean studies field. Indeed, one of the things we discussed in that first meeting at his house was the launching of Harvard's first undergraduate junior tutorial on modern Korea. In the process we were able to join together for the first time the two separate and competing undergraduate concentrations on East Asia that incongruously existed at that time (seems so strange now), one in EALC, and the other (East Asian Studies/EAS), which Ezra himself had created and chaired. This was not an ad hoc gesture on Ezra's part. Although he worked on individual countries, mainly China and Japan, his perspective was always a broad transnational and international one, concerned with how those countries resembled, differed, and interacted with each other and with other parts of the world, both in the present and across time. It was thus not surprising that his popular course, which filled the spacious auditorium at 2 Divinity Avenue every year, was a core curriculum offering on the industrial history and development of East Asia as a whole, and that he became the founder and first director of Harvard's Asia Center. And for Ezra, the study of East Asia, whether China or Japan, was inconceivable without a Korea component, something that today seems commonsensical, but at the time was not widely thought about or practiced in or out of academia.

The junior tutorial, like the course on industrial East Asia, was aimed at undergraduates. Many of them went on to illustrious careers in government, journalism, popular culture, or academia, and Ezra kept in close contact with them throughout his life. But both before and after the launching of the Korea junior tutorial, Ezra also took an active role in promoting Korean studies at the graduate and postgraduate levels. He trained generations of scholars, including many from South Korea, among whom were many brilliant young women struggling to break through their country's stifling academic patriarchy. At Harvard he was tireless in supporting Korea-related initiatives, including at the Korea Institute, delivering the Institute's Thirtieth Anniversary Lecture and presiding over numerous colloquia and other events. On one occasion I remember well, when he was feeling quite under the weather from a cold, he still insisted on showing up to introduce a featured speaker, who would otherwise have been most disappointed. He also made numerous trips to Korea for academic meetings and conferences, supporting current and former graduate students working on Korea and lending his many contacts and immense reputation there to hoist the Harvard banner. I participated in one such trip when former Harvard president Neil Rudenstine thanked South Korean president Kim Dae Jung and the Korea Foundation for his country's support of Korean studies at Harvard. While Ezra did not read or speak Korean, he again lent his name, support, and discerning editorship to important publications on Korea, including a pathbreaking conference volume on the Park Chung Hee period, co-edited with Professor Byung-Kook Kim of Korea University.

Ezra always felt that scholars had a responsibility to speak not just to each other but also to educate both government officials and the larger public on important issues and policies. This was one of the reasons he joined President Clinton's National Intelligence Council in the early 1990s, headed at that time by Harvard Kennedy School colleague Joseph Nye. His appointment, as it turned out, coincided with the 1994 North Korean nuclear crisis, in which the U.S. and North Korea came as close as they ever have to open conflict since the end of the Korean War in 1953. He played an important part in helping to defuse the crisis by reaching out for advice and guidance to scholarly colleagues in Korean studies across the globe and summarizing and relaying that information to the Council.

My last memory of Ezra is of his great smiling face on a Zoom gathering to celebrate his ninetieth birthday not long before his unexpected passing. As usual he was full of energy and optimism, thinking ahead to his next books (plural!), including an autobiography, and conveying best wishes and encouragement to all present. Watching him, I felt immense respect and gratitude for all that he had done for Asian (and Korean) studies, and for me personally. I also could not help but remember his ingenious encouragement to me only a few years earlier, when we had both found ourselves working on respective books about Asian developmental dictators, namely, Deng Xiaoping and Park Chung Hee. Ezra was worried that I, as usual, was moving too slowly. In addition to giving me a gentle push by offering to introduce possible editors and presses and to read any chapters I might wish to share with him, he proposed a friendly competition to see who would finish his book first. No surprise who won in the end, but we had great fun pretending spiritedly whenever we met that we were in a real race. Ezra, with his kind and clever ploy, did indeed spur me on to finish the book. He was a champion to the end.

Susan Pharr

Harvard University

Socks flopping in the dryer made steady thuds while I waited for Ezra to return to the kitchen. Minutes before, he had changed the course of my life by asking me, newly arrived at Harvard as a senior faculty member, to succeed him as director of the Harvard Program on U.S.-Japan Relations. The year was 1987. China beckoned, he told me; he was eager to devote more time to writing about the economic transformation occurring under Deng Xiaoping. I would be perfect to succeed him as director, he said. When he returned from taking a phone call elsewhere in his house, I told him that however tempting the invitation, and however much I wanted to accommodate him, becoming director was unthinkable. I had hardly unpacked and knew little of Harvard. I needed to get my feet on the ground. But he parried my doubts, one by one. You'll love it, he told me, and everybody at Harvard needs a base. So, in less time than it took for Ezra's clothes to dry, I was the new director. And Ezra was correct: the fit was right. Years later, the obituary that Steve Vogel wrote for the *Japan Times* told me something I had not known. In his youth, Ezra had learned sales early, from behind the counter of his father's department store in Delaware, Ohio.

Many of the things I associate with Ezra emerged in that early encounter. First, consider the context. Why was this conversation happening in Ezra's kitchen, and why was his laundry a part of the story? As I was soon to learn, Harvard faculty coaxing colleagues into shouldering new responsibilities generally softened them up over a leisurely lunch at the Faculty Club. Ezra, however, had no patience for such rituals. Time was precious to him, and his preferred style was direct and to the point. He willingly heard me out as I rambled on about my doubts, but undoubtedly figured that he might as well multitask.

Also revealed in that early conversation was Ezra's enthusiasm, which was elixir-like and boundless. Ezra took optimism to a new level, beyond the reach of ordinary people. With no hesitation, he moved forward and created his own momentum. He was calling on me to join him in building East Asian studies at Harvard, and he brimmed with confidence that I would embrace the mission.

Finally, there surfaced during the meeting the reality of Ezra's complex set of allegiances. When he stepped down from leading the Program on U.S.-Japan Relations in 1987, many of Ezra's Japanese friends saw it as jilting Japan for China. I confess that as someone eager to see Japanese studies grow at Harvard, I shared their anxiety. I remember once trying to make light of it. Introducing Ezra as a dinner speaker at around that time, I joked that from studying his curriculum vitae, I'd come to see that Ezra either wrote a book on China or married a China specialist every seven years. My jest got a good laugh, including from Ezra, but as I looked around the roomful of Japan specialists, I saw many glum faces. As it turned out, we need not have worried. From his earliest years as a scholar until the final weeks of his life, Ezra was profoundly attached to both Japan and China. When problems came up in Japanese studies or with the Program on U.S.-Japan Relations over the years, he was always ready to listen and brainstorm. We often talked of the challenges Japan faced, and he steadfastly believed that Japan would find solutions. His circle of friends in Japan, already huge, only grew over the years. It stunned and humbled me to realize that he had a parallel universe of Chinese friends. In his final years his interests intertwined. In the months before he died, Ezra told me repeatedly that no task mattered more to him than finding ways to bring the two countries together.

For most people, retirement is a time to ease up and move along at a slower pace. But Ezra, it seemed, hit the accelerator. Retirement was the first chapter in a new book, both figuratively and literally. Of his three most widely read works, two were written in retirement. In addition, his interests were legion. I worked with him closely in one of his endeavors. Over his final decade, we were both senior advisers for the Mansfield Foundation's U.S.-Japan Network for the Future program. The program, focused on building policy expertise among the rising generations of Japan specialists, was a brainchild of Ezra's, and traveling with him from Boston to Washington and Tokyo, I got to know him in a wholly new way. I saw firsthand how seriously he took mentorship, for example. I was also staggered by his energy. I don't think of myself as a slouch, but Ezra's energy level, even as he approached age ninety, took my breath away. One example comes readily to mind. A few years before his death, we were together for an intense multiday schedule of Mansfield activities in Naha, Okinawa. Boarding the plane home, I collapsed into my seat, grateful for a long stretch ahead of uninterrupted sleep. But just as the plane began to pull away from the gate, I heard that unmistakable voice and saw Ezra's face beaming down at me. "Wonderful!" he exclaimed. "We're seatmates! We have a chance to catch up!" And so we did, for the next eighteen hours.

I last heard from Ezra only a few weeks before he died. In the COVID era, he was reaching out, and for someone in his ninety-first year, his email message is remarkable: "I am trying to finish a couple of papers. After I finish, I hope you and I can have a phone conversation when we can talk about the past, present, and future. We have a lot to be thankful for. All the best, Ezra."

Holly Angell

Harvard University

I first met Ezra when I was a graduate student at Harvard wrestling with my master's thesis. He always had time for Harvard students, even if they were not in his fields of expertise—which were extensive. I never forgot that meeting—he provided great advice and insights, pointed out grants I should apply for, and suggested I go to Guangzhou to meet with people he knew who had worked on similar projects.

Cycle forward six years when I started working at the Harvard University Asia Center during Ezra's last year as director, which began a relationship that grew over the next twenty-two years. He continued to involve me in projects after he left the center and always had time to talk. One afternoon, with him and an editor from Harvard University Press,

I spent four hours sorting through hundreds of photographs for his book on Deng Xiaoping. We had a wonderful time. But most of all, I remember Ezra laughing uproariously over some of the images. His laugh—one of the many things I miss.

One morning I stopped by his house—conveniently located a block and a half from my office—to drop off mail. We sat in his front room to catch up. The protests were ongoing in Hong Kong at that time, and I asked him what he thought would happen. He shared various scenarios and his perspective and concerns. As I walked back to my office, I mused about what a remarkable morning I just had—discussing current events in Asia with one of the experts in the field.

I spent another morning listening to an interview with Ezra on a local radio show that was syndicated nationwide. After the initial discussion between Ezra and the host, the telephone lines were open to take questions from the audience—listeners from across the country. Almost everyone who called in was involved in the Asia field in some way, and everyone had had some connection with Ezra—colleagues, former students, journalists, government officials. "Hi Ezra, remember me?" And he did of course. But what stood out was the vast array of fields the audience members represented—in itself a tribute to Ezra. There are numerous ways to be engaged with Asia, and Ezra supported his students, friends, and colleagues in whatever paths their careers took. That generosity of spirit and intellectual scope are some of Ezra's many distinguishing qualities and enduring legacies.

Ezra respected institutions and community. He was a founder of a number of institutions at Harvard, including the Asia Center, and was the creator of that sense of community that I and many others had at the university. Holiday parties at his house, when we would troop over from Coolidge Hall, then home of the international centers, and devour platters of Chinese food. Dinners for speakers at the Critical Issues Confronting China seminars, with guests crowded around his dining room table to talk. Discussion groups with scholars. Birthday parties. Book launch celebrations. And periodically he would chuckle, "We have a nice little community here, don't we?" We did indeed—because of Ezra.

Elizabeth J. Perry

Harvard University

I first met Ezra Vogel in the early 1980s at a dinner party at his home when I was a visiting professor at Harvard for a year. He was one of only two Harvard professors (the other was Tu Weiming) who invited me into their homes that year. We kept in touch, but not until I returned to Harvard in 1997 as a regular member of the faculty did I really get to know Ezra.

Ezra made clear when I was hired back to Harvard that he expected me to succeed him as director of the Fairbank Center. To make the transition as seamless as possible, he was generous in sharing his knowledge and advice. In the interest of collegiality, I complied with the expectation, but on condition that I would serve only a single three-year term. My primary motive for returning to Harvard was to concentrate on research, taking full advantage of the rich resources of the Harvard-Yenching and Fairbank Center library collections, and I did not welcome the prospect of being distracted by administrative responsibilities. Ezra betrayed some disappointment at my lack of enthusiasm for the opportunity he had helped arrange, but in a kindly, avuncular manner indicated his understanding. As a former director, he remained an engaged and supportive mentor (along with Rod MacFarquhar, Philip Kuhn, and Woody Watson), making my own experience as director less onerous and more enjoyable than anticipated. Still, I was anxious to spend maximal time on scholarship, and I did not accept an offer to renew the administrative appointment.

After I had completed my term as Fairbank Center director, Ezra and I continued to meet frequently to talk about ongoing research projects and our shared concern for East Asian studies at Harvard—in particular its library collections. We conversed often over lunch at the Faculty Club; just as often, we chatted over a cup of tea in his living room. So it was nothing out of the ordinary when one day Ezra invited me to afternoon tea at his home to discuss the Harvard-Yenching Library and its parent foundation, the Harvard-Yenching Institute (HYI).

Tea with Ezra always began with his asking about teaching—how were classes going, what new books was I assigning, what issues had especially captured the undergraduates' attention, were the graduate students finding suitable jobs, and so on. We would move on to exchange recent research discoveries, sharing unexpected findings from interviews and documents. Only then did Ezra turn to the topic at hand. In this case, he explained that as a trustee of the Harvard-Yenching Institute he was collecting faculty feedback on the Institute's programs and operations. Tu Weiming would be retiring after thirteen years as HYI director, and the Institute's Board of Trustees was conducting a general review in preparation for a changing of the guard.

Although I was a member of the HYI faculty advisory committee and had conducted interviews for the Institute in Asia, my knowledge of its inner workings was limited. Still, Ezra pressed for my candid impressions. I shared my admiration for the dramatic expansion in partnerships with Chinese universities that had taken place under Tu Weiming's leadership and expressed appreciation for the many wonderful scholars from Asia who came to Harvard each year on HYI fellowships. I praised the amazing holdings of the Harvard-Yenching Library, mostly acquired and owned by the Institute. But I added that I understood there were some serious management issues in the administration of the Institute, and I did not envy what I imagined would be huge headaches awaiting Weiming's successor.

Though Ezra had smiled brightly throughout my recitation of the positive aspects of HYI, he darkened visibly at the mention of problems. Nevertheless, he proceeded to ask for my recommendation of a suitable colleague to serve as the next HYI director. I proposed a couple of senior scholars in the humanities whom I thought might be appropriate. Ezra then mentioned some other names. I shrugged my shoulders. "What's the problem with them?" Ezra asked. "Nothing's wrong with them," I replied, "it's just that the Institute is too valuable a resource to entrust to their care." Ezra broke into a broad grin. "That's a great answer," he said. And he returned the conversation to our earlier discussion of research.

When I got up to leave, I apologized for not being more helpful on the HYI matter. He chuckled in response and said, "You've been extremely helpful." I wasn't sure whether he meant I had persuaded him to nominate one of the people I'd mentioned or had dissuaded him from nominating one of those he had mentioned, but I didn't give it another thought until a week or so later when Peter Geithner, chair of the HYI Board of

Trustees, called to say that the board had voted to offer me the HYI directorship on the nomination of Ezra Vogel and Tu Weiming.

As a social scientist who had made abundantly clear my disinterest in academic administration, it never crossed my mind that I might be a candidate for the directorship of HYI, which I associated with classical sinology. But Ezra would proceed to convince me otherwise. He noted that one of his own graduate advisers, an anthropologist of Japan, had directed HYI for over a decade. Ezra also knew a good deal about my family history, having conducted research for his book on Japan's middle class in the late 1950s when my parents, Episcopal missionaries who had previously taught at St. John's University in Shanghai and were then teaching on the faculty of Rikkyo (St. Paul's) University in Tokyo, were featured prominently in Japanese news stories. Armed with this insider knowledge, he tugged at my heartstrings. Taking on Harvard-Yenching, with its long-standing connection to the Christian colleges of Asia, he argued, would be much more than a gesture of collegiality: it was the perfect way to honor my parents' legacy. Now in my third five-year term as HYI director, I remain ever grateful for Ezra's empathetic insight and encouragement.

Wen-hao Tien

Cambridge, Massachusetts

Professor Ezra Vogel directed three centers at Harvard University: the Asia Center, the Fairbank Center for Chinese Studies, and the Program on U.S.-Japan Relations. I had the great honor of working with Ezra as a program officer in all three centers, from 1996 to 2011.

Ezra played drums when he was a boy. I learned this from his family at his retirement party in 2000. "I wanted to play my drum all day long," Ezra wrote in his diary. From the day I met Ezra in 1996, I heard his deep and unique drumbeat and endeavored to accompany him.

Some of the highlights of the years I worked with him included the many conferences we organized: Ezra's Modern Asia Series, through which he invited creative thinkers from Asia; Asia Vision 21, where Asia's "tomorrow stars" (not yesterday's leaders) met annually, rotating between key cities. We organized visits of the highest-ranking government officials and influential social leaders. I shepherded a steady stream of visiting scholars who came to Harvard for him. I worked well with Ezra due to my understanding of his respect for informal power. I learned it officially, too, in one of my public health classes—the real power in a hospital unit might not reside only with the attending surgeon, but with the senior nurse as well. Work with them! Over the years, I guess I became "that senior nurse" for Ezra until I left my job at the Fairbank Center in 2011 to shift gears and focus on fully encompassing my role as an artist and a mother. I would not see Asia and the world the way I do without Ezra, and I have seen a lot, for which I am eternally grateful.

In 2015, I returned to the work force of Asian studies to become the Assistant Director of Boston University's Center for the Study of Asia, while continuing to be a practicing interdisciplinary artist. These two roles work very well together. As the fields mature, everything is related, and no knowledge is ever wasted. Ezra influenced my work not only concerning Asia, but also as an artist. My MFA thesis, "Navigating a Civic Voice: Between Field and Studio," incorporates both sociology and anthropology methodologies. I often think about the way Ezra studied people. Not only did he pay attention to each individual's personality, he also learned about their personal history and friendship circle. He knew what drove each of them to their goals and aspirations. This way of approaching and relating to people is incredibly effective. I have been applying it to my community story projects. I learned from him that if I am respectful, I can become at least an "accepted outsider."

Ezra accepted Boston University's invitation to speak twice in recent years. For the most recent talk, on October 15, 2019, he discussed his new book, *China and Japan: Facing History.* He arrived early, took a good look at me, and said, "You look very good, very energetic." This moment brought me to tears. I, too, had aged, and motherhood was just so exhausting. Life had not always been fun. But at that moment, I set a goal for myself: "I will always be energetic!" In the middle of his talk, he paused and smiled at me in the audience, declaring, "She is one of us; she is on my team." On my copy of his book, inscribed was, "To Wen Hao, My dear friend and former co-worker, with fond memories, deep respect, and best wishes, Ezra." How I just miss his big hand and kindness when he wrote this.

In the elegant, Victorian, yellow Back Bay lobby, I arranged a surprise reception for him: a clarinet and bass duet playing John Denver's *Country Road*. I figured that because Ezra liked Deng Xiaoping, he would probably share Deng's music taste as well. That night, Ezra talked to every single attending student, especially Chinese and Japanese students. He stayed late and finally left at 9 p.m. to prepare for his West Coast speaking trip the next day. "I want China and Japan to be better friends," he said. That was the last time I saw Ezra.

The sad news of Ezra's death came from a friend in Asia at dawn on the 21st of December, 2020. He had passed away the day before. As the world mourned his death, I felt as if I was being punished. I had planned to write Ezra to see how he was doing during the pandemic, but never did. Coincidentally, that particular night brought the closest great conjunction of Jupiter and Saturn in almost four hundred years. I wonder how people like him were created, and when one would ever meet someone like Ezra again. In the subsequent months since his passing, there has been so much trouble in Asia, including the situation of Taiwan, my native land. I worry about the overwhelming military exercises that may lead to accidents and war. As the domestic hardship from the worst drought in fifty years and the politicized COVID-19 vaccine situation leaves Taiwan without a vaccine strategy, I wish Ezra were here to tell us how to make it better. Instead, I listen to Lo Ta-yu's *Orphan of Asia* (羅大佑 亞細亞的孤兒). In the middle of the song, there is a unique drum accompaniment, duh-DAA, duh-DAA, duh-DAA. I think Ezra would have liked it.

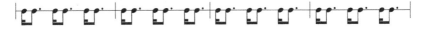

Jin Chen

Fairbank Center for Chinese Studies

I was one of Ezra's last graduate students from the Regional Studies East Asia (RSEA) program before his retirement from Harvard in 2000. I took two courses with him and remember him as a kind professor, always supportive of his students in their pursuit of higher learning.

My close interaction with him began in early 2014, when he hired me as the rapporteur for his weekly talk series Critical Issues Confronting

China. In the following six and a half years, I witnessed firsthand his leadership at work: how he motivated his staff to do their best when increasing their financial compensation was not an option due to a limited budget.

In November 2016, Ezra hosted a Chinese delegation responsible for production of the documentary film, *Deng Goes to Washington*, as a commemoration of Deng Xiaoping's 1979 historic state visit to the U.S. I was asked to be the interpreter for the two main speakers in a panel presentation, and I fumbled with the translation of a few words that I should have readily known. There wasn't as large an audience as we had hoped to attract. Furthermore, I recognized during the event that many of the excerpts selected from the film were not what Ezra had intended to show, which wasted precious meeting time.

Just as I was feeling terrible about this event, on the evening of the same day I received an email from Ezra to his staff members. He thanked us "for making today a success," and "we had no reason to be ashamed." He then moved on to talk about the next speaker's event and solicit our input on how to prepare for it. He knew when to overlook problems and how to keep the team's morale high. In my case, it actually was raised higher than before.

More importantly, Ezra's staunch support for my professional work was tested through trying times. Until the workflow of my summaries was changed in the spring of 2018 in the name of "quality control," and my English writing ability was questioned, I didn't realize that, for the rapporteur job of such a major talk series, being a native English speaker was implicitly expected by some people in Harvard's bureaucracy. While trying to balance conflicting considerations from multiple quarters, Ezra firmly protected my credibility and reaffirmed my contribution and value to his talk series.

I'm not sure if I'm "a mensch" or "a rare talent," as he had said I was, but his faith in me, as shown in those email exchanges, moved me to tears and continues to motivate me to strive to perform better in the future. He epitomized a Chinese maxim on leadership: "If you doubt one's ability, never employ him/her. Once you employ this person, never doubt his/her ability (疑人不用,用人不疑)."

Under Ezra's leadership the talk series became an institution and, year after year, showcased the best minds in China research and attracted a devoted audience. Getting paid for listening and reporting fascinating talks prompted me to comment to Ezra, "I have the best job in the world." He replied without missing a beat, "I have the best rapporteur in the world."

In the fall of 2020, he asked me to work with him after the new year on his next magnum opus, a biography of Hu Yaobang, a top Chinese leader who pushed political system reforms in the 1980s. Ezra explained to me that by January, he would have finished writing policy proposals on U.S.-China relations for the incoming administration in Washington.

His unexpected passing in December 2020 is not only a heavy personal loss to me, but also a grave detriment to what is arguably the most important bilateral relationship in the world at a time when his broad perspective, strategic thinking, and nuanced understanding of China and the U.S. are particularly needed.

Victor K. Fung

Hong Kong, China

Soon after I arrived at Harvard as a graduate student in 1966, the movie everyone was talking about was *A Man for All Seasons,* depicting the sixteenth-century English statesman and philosopher Sir Thomas More, author of *Utopia.* And the newly made professor that students from Asia were hearing about was Ezra Vogel, author of a groundbreaking book on the world of the Japanese "salaryman." Ezra was to be a key influence in my professional life in Hong Kong. I was privileged to spend much time with him as he researched his important work on southern China's reform-driven Pearl River delta economic miracle. That study is among many reasons Ezra remains so highly regarded in China.

But if I must choose just one venture that stands out as the most enjoyable, meaningful, and lasting in my decades-long relationship with Ezra, it has to be Asia Vision 21. I was able to help Ezra conceive this initiative as a way to focus the finest minds on both sides of the Pacific around possibilities, challenges, and prospects for Asia's future. The idea was hatched during brainstorming in an airport lounge in Beijing in March 1998. Then President of Harvard Neil Rudenstine was winding up an inaugural visit to China, accompanied by Ezra (who had recently been appointed founding director of the Harvard Asia Center) and a small Harvard entourage, including myself. The previous fall, President Rudenstine had hosted President Jiang Zemin at Harvard, where the Chinese leader delivered a well-received keynote reflective of those times. President Jiang had warmly reciprocated by hosting us at his Zhongnanhai residence, a rare honor.

Asia in early 1998 was in trouble from the financial crisis that had engulfed the region. During our trip, Ezra and I had hours to exchange thoughts on its severity. We concluded that, even before the "patient" came out of intensive care, we should start thinking about economic reconstruction for the Asian region. As we waited for our flight, I wondered aloud if there was anything Harvard could do to help. President Rudenstine's encouraging response was that Harvard could offer to study the origins of the crisis, which were not well understood at the time; a discussion of actions that could be taken to resolve pressing issues; and thoughts on how to avoid such shocks to Asia's economic and social systems in the future. Ezra took it further, suggesting we convene an annual conference hosted by the Harvard Asia Center, alternating between Cambridge and a major city in Asia. We would invite high-level participants to spend several days together in retreat—away from usual demands—to lend their ideas and voices toward a vision of Asia's post-financial crisis future. Ezra dubbed the initiative "Asia Vision 21" and became its incomparable intellectual leader and driver. My role as co-host was to anchor and underpin, from Hong Kong, our combined efforts on the Asia side.

We agreed that participants should have a perspective reaching beyond any single country of Asia, be willing to put aside historical or national differences so they could think broadly and deeply about growth and development of the wider region, and that they should look further than that moment's front-burner issues. We also agreed that meetings should be held without working media present, so that participants could speak frankly about potentially sensitive issues. Originally envisaged as a three-year research and discussion project, Asia Vision 21 continued beyond Asia's financial crisis. It quickly made its mark as a vibrant, effective new platform for unfettered trans-Pacific dialogue, convening more than fifteen times against an ever-changing regional and global landscape. Helped by Harvard's convening power, its global reputation for political neutrality, and Ezra's personal networks, Asia Vision 21 has been a *Who's Who* of East Asia and the U.S. Participants have included Nobel laureates, scholars and public intellectuals, politicians and diplomats, business leaders, and military officials.[1] Our format has called for inviting some seventy-five participants, large enough to keep each gathering diverse and lively, but not so many as to be unwieldy. We have also invited bright young participants from Asia to share their visions for a region they will one day help to lead.

Ezra instinctively guided conversations toward constructive and positive dialogue. He could see a pathway to win-win solutions in almost any situation. His towering reputation as a scholar, his disarming wisdom, and his personal equanimity made him the ultimate interlocutor between East and West, explaining Asia to Americans and America to Asians. He was too much of a realist to dream of utopia. But Ezra was truly "A Man for Asia's Seasons." Through economic transformations happening at hyperspeed in East Asia, accelerating shifts in great power relations, and rising frictions at the global level, Ezra led us calmly and steadfastly to ever-deeper levels of understanding about the region. He knew its history and societies better than most of us can ever aspire to—including those of us in Asia. Ezra brought all this brilliance and passion to bear on our Asia Vision 21 collaboration. He wholeheartedly took the project under his ample wing, bestowing upon it his insight and gravitas. Something special took off from that airport brainstorming all those years ago. It could not have reached the heights it has without Ezra.

Paul Evans

University of British Columbia

It was a revealing twist of fate that my first conversation with Ezra in 1977 and my last one with him forty-two years later were both about John Fairbank. That 1977 discussion concerned getting access to the records of

---

1. Among Asia Vision 21 participants have been: Nobel laureates Esaki Reona, Amartya Sen, Michael Spence, Joseph Stiglitz; scholars/public intellectuals Stephen Bosworth, Richard Cooper, Gang Fan, Martin Feldstein, Horii Akinari, Kim Byung-Kook, Joseph Nye, Mari Pangestu, Dwight Perkins, Takemi Keizo, Tu Weiming, Wang Gungwu; political/diplomatic leaders Boediono, Han Sung-joo, Kishore Mahbubani, Tharman Shanmugaratnam, Princess Maha Chakri Sirindhorn, Surin Pitsuwan, Yang Jiechi; business leaders Fred Hu, Makihara Minoru, Timothy Ong, Wang Shi, Jaime Zobel de Ayala; military leaders Ashton Carter, Karl Eikenberry, Koda Yoji, Arun Prakash.

the East Asian Research Center, which Fairbank had founded and Ezra was then directing. Fairbank had suggested the plan, the meeting was cordial and brief, and Ezra agreed. But there was a hint of reserve, and he stated that he would not feel comfortable being interviewed about Fairbank. That agreement held during the decade I spent examining the full corpus of Fairbank's professional and private papers, even though Ezra appeared in them at many points, especially in describing how he had been induced into the Asia field and assumed a leadership role in it. Of questions I had many, but I didn't get a chance to ask them until well after Fairbank's death in 1991.

In the late 1990s I came to know Ezra in a different way, when at his invitation I spent two years at Harvard as he led the creation of the Asia Center. He thought it important that the Harvard community and graduate students in particular be better exposed to the new wave of multilateral institutions and the dialogue that was emerging in that hopeful period, which Canada had been active in facilitating. We created a graduate seminar on the state and prospects of multilateral cooperation in Asia. It was impressive how well prepared he was for each session of the class. He did all of the readings (except the more theoretical ones that he found "obtuse"), encouraged me to wear a tie to class ("a senior professor should"), was sharp in judging performance and generous in grading, and advised that the best way to get a seminar rolling was to offer a few minutes on what was most important about the topic and then "let water find its own level."

A decade later I encountered him in a third phase after his retirement, when I assisted in a minor way with the Deng biography and later did the same with what became *China and Japan: Facing History*. On several occasions he and Charlotte welcomed me to their second-floor guest suite and included me in their celebrated breakfast rituals featuring either blueberry pancakes or avocado toast.

We spoke often about developments in Asia, the state of U.S.-China relations, trends in scholarship about China and Japan, the numerous individuals in his trans-Pacific world, and his own writing. Receiving visitors in his home, running a speaker series, and speaking and traveling widely, he was central to national efforts to keep a constructive spirit in U.S. relations with China alive in the past decade. It was difficult not to feel a touch nervous being with him. Open, warm, engaging, kind, and without pretense, he was also so formidable in intellect and purpose that it demanded an on-your-toes presence at all times.

It became clear that he and Fairbank had a great deal in common. Both saw their role as developing Harvard's base for dealing with East Asia, both were institution builders, both were community builders, and both believed that while scholarship and policy making were separate enterprises, academic understanding mattered a great deal and the book was king. Both were also of the same species of American liberal, strong supporters of democratic institutions in the U.S. (and equally frightened by their populist challengers in the 1950s and later, for Ezra, in the Trump era). Yet they both looked at East Asia through a civilizational and historical lens that did not lead to an easy embrace of universal values and their promotion throughout the world.

After finishing the Deng biography, Ezra was stung by reviewers he respected who felt he had not been strong enough in exposing and criticizing Deng for his suppression of human rights during the Tiananmen period in particular. Seeing these events through Deng's eyes was more important to him than critique. But the criticisms pained him and he had in mind a second biography, this time of Hu Yaobang, in which he could evaluate the dynamics of reform inside the Chinese Communist Party.

Our last conversation occurred in late fall 2019 in his basement study on Sumner Road. Thinking about a memoir, he wanted to show me his personal files that were deposited in a score of filing cabinets. We talked about various strategies for using them and he was curious about how I had navigated Fairbank's files for a decade while Fairbank was able to use them in pulling together *Chinabound* in not much more than a year. I asked him why he wanted to do a memoir and hadn't done one earlier. He first gave his standard reply that he'd been too busy. He then added something quite remarkable. "I'm very proud of *China and Japan: Facing History*. It's my best book. With it completed I now feel the equal of Fairbank and Reischauer. Neither of them could have pulled China and Japan together the way that I have. I'm now ready."

Ready, but not able. It remains to be seen how Ezra's story will be written. With his passing comes the end of an era at Harvard that began in the 1930s. Harvard will reinvent itself, but without a great scholar and a generous spirit who so many could call a friend.

Jon D. Mills

Harvard University

I first met Ezra in 1989 at a reception to welcome a group of visiting fellows to the Harvard Program on U.S.-Japan Relations, which Ezra had
co-founded a decade earlier. I had just been hired as the administrator of
the program, and of course I knew who Ezra was because I had read his
works while in college and graduate school. Ezra walked over to where
I was chatting with several fellows and without a hint of pretension introduced himself. For me it was like meeting one of the brightest stars in
a constellation of brilliant scholars, and there he was—modest, open,
and accessible.

I would say that my extended experiences with Ezra, rather than
being notable for one particular memory, consisted of regular or even
daily interactions that were the basis for my respect, admiration, and appreciation for working with and for him. Ezra lived the ethos that students, faculty, and staff are the pillars of a university, and he was engaged
deeply as a thoughtful and helpful guide and adviser mentoring the careers
of young people. My guess is that for most people who knew Ezra well,
it was an accumulation of impressions, events, and kindnesses that meant
the most in their relationship with him.

Ezra, like no other, combined breadth of knowledge with depth of
understanding about people and institutions and how and when they were
interconnected. He would often tell stories that illustrated how well he
knew leading academics, business people, government representatives, and
members of the professions, which lent a depth of understanding to their
significance in the larger scheme of things. For example, he once mentioned an invitation to the White House to meet Bill Clinton early in
the president's first administration. He knew that Clinton would be making a trip to Japan, so he brought along a copy of *Japan as Number One*.
Clinton accepted the gift but, as Ezra explained later with a chuckle, the
president responded that he had received four copies of the book for
Christmas just after he had been elected.

Ezra's facilities with Japanese and Chinese were greater than those of
most people who had studied either of those languages separately, and he
acquired both at an age well beyond what many would have considered

an opportune moment for their scholarship or career. Ezra would routinely greet me warmly in Japanese, greet others in polite Chinese, and greet some with nuances from both in English. He worked at becoming multi-lingual not only because it strengthened his research, but because he knew it also helped widen his perspectives by gaining more than one cultural point of view. In the academic milieu, which is based on finding the truth by stripping away that which is false or unverifiable, Ezra was gentle with criticism. I never heard him say directly that he disagreed with anyone, but rather had a somewhat different opinion or point of view. Other scholars may have disagreed with him at times, but he had no personal antagonists.

Ezra penned several highly acclaimed works, acquired a collection of distinguished awards and honorary degrees, and gave well-received talks all over the globe. Traveling with him in Asia was like accompanying a celebrity. However, Ezra was modest and austere: he lived simply, usually traveled in economy class, and rode a bicycle around campus. He admired the forthright leadership and spartan lifestyle of Doko Toshio, a leading industrialist and head of the hugely influential Keidanren (Japan Business Federation) during Japan's economic rise in the 1970s. When visiting Ezra's home, where he often entertained in a plain drawing room with somewhat mismatched furniture, he was a warm, friendly—and more often than not—amusing conversationalist. Ezra wasn't interested in an individual's status, background, or accomplishments as much as whether he or she had thoughtful ideas and could express them with balance and clarity. Once, while assisting Ezra with organizing one of the annual Asia Vision 21 conferences sponsored by the Harvard Asia Center (another program that Ezra founded and for which I was working at the time), a member of the royal family of the host country expressed an interest in making a presentation to our audience. Ezra wasn't particularly interested unless the royal guest had something worthwhile to say and unless the timing did not interfere with the commitments we had already made to other speakers.

Though Ezra was a clear supporter of democratic candidates and administrations, he was also a pragmatist. He evaluated leaders more by what they did than by what they said. For example, he was a long-term friend of the right-wing, conservative, and incongruously named Liberal Democratic Party (LDP) of Japan. His reasons were simple: the LDP had the support of the people and, more importantly, they could get things done. At Harvard, he favored leaders who brought the university together and were a strong voice for maintaining the university's leadership position in academia. It is hard to imagine Ezra having political views more different than Deng Xiaoping. Yet he admired and respected Deng for his instrumental role in altering the course of Chinese communism and for helping to lift so many from poverty to economic comfort.

My enduring memory of Ezra is that my job at Harvard often was to assist him in his work or to seek his advice to do mine. Ultimately, he did far more for me than I could for him. With that, allow me to conclude this reminiscence with a gentle "goodbye" to Ezra.

Dan Murphy

Harvard University

Over the years I knew Ezra, he often related an anecdote that embodied his approach to life and work. The anecdote was about a compliment he heard delivered to a colleague: the reason the person was so smart was that he could learn something from *anyone*. In his interactions with others, Ezra lived this sentiment. He was equally as magnanimous and attentive interacting with prominent government officials as he was engaging with students and community members in the halls of the university, on the streets of China, or in his own living room. He was the foremost sinologist of our time and a highly regarded figure throughout Asia, yet simultaneously down-to-earth, with a mischievous sense of humor. To me he was a friend, a mentor, a teacher, a scholar, and the consummate cultivator of the China studies community.

There are many amazing stories of Ezra's diplomacy, scholarship, empathy, and mentorship. I recall a dinner with the Chinese ambassador to the United States at which Ezra delivered feedback on the People's Republic of China's (PRC) rhetoric about Japan. Even on this sensitive issue, he put our Chinese friends at ease while firmly delivering his key points.

And yet, I equally remember Ezra for the way he took a deep interest in the work of junior scholars, inquiring about their research with the same curiosity and wisdom with which he engaged the PRC's ambassador. Ezra hosted a weekly seminar series on contemporary China at the

Fairbank Center, and leading scholars readily accepted Ezra's invitation to present their work. Unfailingly, he welcomed and introduced the most junior and most senior lunch attendees with the utmost respect and sincerity. He saw value in the knowledge and perspective each person brought to an issue while being superbly discerning in determining which views to accept as most accurate.

Once, I traveled with Ezra and a dozen China studies scholars to Guang'an, Deng Xiaoping's birthplace. During that trip I learned a lot—both about the respect accorded to Ezra, and about his determination to promote the next generation of China scholars. Due to his work on the definitive biography of Deng, our visit elicited an enthusiastic response. At the exit off the highway a police escort met our van; the local authorities had closed intersections, allowing us to drive into the city unimpeded. Everyone aboard understood this special treatment was out of deference to Ezra. Even so, as we began our meetings Ezra made it clear, with his usual unassuming grace, that one of the mid-career scholars would head the group. It was this person, not Ezra, who took on the ceremonial role of delegation leader. It is as clear now as it was then: Ezra was dedicated to cultivating and supporting the next generation of scholars.

After he passed away, Ezra's family received letters of condolence from heads of state and high-level officials in many Asian countries, as well as from colleagues, students, and friends the world over, some of whom had only met him a handful of times. The level of sadness, respect, and gratitude expressed in these letters, and the range of people who sent them, reflects the way Ezra treated others. He was the type of person you are fortunate to meet a few times in your life. And you are luckier still if—like me—you had the opportunity to watch him work.

When I came to Harvard in 2017, Ezra mentored me. Early on in my tenure he invited me to his house for breakfast. He served me bagels. We looked out the window at his garden as he gave me the lay of the land on Harvard's China studies community. I could always count on him to give me forthright guidance, whether I liked what he had to say or not; his advice was a rare and valuable gift. The remarkable thing is that Ezra made *so many* people feel like I did: that he took an interest in me as a person and in our shared work.

For me, a much smaller and personal story demonstrates Ezra's remarkable humility. Ezra and I had a minor administrative disagreement about six weeks before he passed. Ezra assured me that if—at any time—I felt that the mission of the Fairbank Center for Chinese Studies could be better pursued I should speak up, even if it regarded a decision he had made. Likewise, he was comfortable being just as frank with me. So, in this instance I felt I could tell him, respectfully, that we should change a particular decision he had made. A few days later he unexpectedly wrote to me with the following message:

> You have a fine sense of what it takes for the Fairbank Center to thrive, a sense of responsibility to the mission of the Center. I am very pleased to hear that things are going well with your colleagues.

He was telling *me*, after our minor conflict—and in so many words—that we were all good. I was so incredibly humbled and inspired by his thoughtful response. And I am forever grateful that the small disagreement was resolved before it was too late.

It will not surprise those who knew Ezra to learn that less than two weeks before he passed, he was working on a joint statement between American and Chinese academic institutions intended to improve U.S.-China relations. I believe he wanted desperately for the United States and China to have a productive relationship. For someone with such authority even after his official retirement—I jokingly called him the Honorary President of the Bridge Association (Deng Xiaoping's highest remaining title while he still enjoyed much authority)—Ezra always leveraged his extensive knowledge to pursue interests larger than himself.

When I think of Ezra, I think he would want us to "remember the real work" . . . the real work of studying Greater China, of mentoring and being mentored by friends and colleagues, and of acting with dignity and grace.

I will miss him.

TEN

Institution Building beyond Harvard

Jean Hung

Universities Service Centre

When I heard the news that the Universities Service Centre (USC) was to be closed by my university, my immediate reaction was to email Ezra. He replied right away: "Jean, I would be happy to write a letter if you think it would be helpful. If so, who should I send it to? Ezra." It was mailed on December 16th, 2020, at 1:22 p.m. Noticing that the time was his midnight, I wrote back: "I am sure a letter from you would be of great help. You should go to bed now! Health matters more than anything else." I waited anxiously for the letter that might be able to save the Centre. Four days later the grievous news came. I realized with heartbroken sadness that I would never hear from him again.

The USC was founded in 1963 by a group of American scholars. It was originally located in a two-story European-style building with a nice little garden at 155 Argyle Street in Kowloon, Hong Kong. Ezra was in his early thirties when he arrived. Here, he and Charlotte met and fell in love. Here, Ezra also won the friendship of many outstanding scholars, including Lucien Bianco, who was born in the same year. Above all, this was where he did his fieldwork. He read the newspaper clippings available at USC, trying to find some truth between the lines. Conducting interviews with refugees coming over the border was also a major way to get enough information to finish his first book on China, *Canton under Communism*.

He loved the atmosphere at the Centre: "In the early years, we scholars at the USC were in our 20s and 30s. Professors at our home universities might have had leverage over us as students and junior faculty members, but at the Centre no one had real authority over anyone. We were a band of scholars with no hierarchy." Looking back at the Centre forty years later, he thought very highly of its role: "Where would the study of contemporary China be throughout the past several decades without the work done at the Universities Service Centre? In the 1960s and 1970s, for instance, how much knowledge would we have had about daily life in China without the Centre in Hong Kong?"[1]

When Ezra liked something, he cared for it. He would usually ask himself, what I can do to help? The file of his correspondence with the Centre during the Argyle Street days is the thickest among all the files of that kind. Year after year, the Centre would need to raise funds. Many years later, reading the files, I was deeply touched by the tireless efforts of Ezra and Lucian Pye. The Centre was haunted by the rumor that it was sponsored by the Central Intelligence Agency. It is certainly not true. When Ezra mentioned the Centre's financial straits in his writing or speaking, he never uttered a word about his continuous efforts to help.

After China became accessible to Western scholars in the 1980s, the Centre's mission seemed accomplished, and foundations like Mellon, Carnegie, Luce, and Ford began to withdraw their support. Since Ezra sat on the board of the American Council of Learned Societies, the Centre's management body, he played a pivotal role in persuading the Chinese University to take over the Centre, with a commitment to establishing the best collection on contemporary China and to keeping the Centre open to international scholars. Subsequently he served as the Chairman of the Centre's International Advisory Committee for almost a quarter of a century (1992–2015), visited the Centre numerous times, and gave public lectures and held seminars at the university on various occasions. He also entrusted the publication of the Chinese version of his two magnum opuses, on Deng Xiaoping and on the Sino-Japanese relationship, to the Chinese University Press.

It is part of the mission of USC "to advocate social responsibility of academics." We took that seriously when organizing conferences and seminars, thus inviting scholars from mainland China. Ezra was our model. However, when I got to know him better, I realized that for him, this was not a responsibility or obligation. Rather it came from his personality—he cared.

After the Centre moved to the Chinese University in 1988, I became responsible for the Centre's library collection, premises, and facilities, as

---

1. These and all the following quotations are taken from Professor Vogel's speech at the conference to mark USC's fortieth anniversary, "The First Forty Years of the Universities Service Centre for China Studies."

well as various projects, and Ezra was always very generous with his praise. Though I never felt deserving of his many kind words, together with many other users of the Centre he made my job worthwhile and rewarding. After my retirement, I kept on sending him material which might be of interest, so as to keep in touch. I was no doubt just one of his many friends who were happy to be useful to him in some way. Indeed, we all cared for him.

For more than five decades, Ezra spent a lot of time and effort on an institution far, far away from home, which could not have accrued to his academic credit nor increased his international reputation. He did it simply because he appreciated the Centre and cared about it. Ezra was not just a great scholar, he was a great human being. It distinguished him in the scholarly community.

As he passed away, USC also went into history, almost at exactly the same time. For scholars of China studies the following words of his should be remembered: "Because of what we learned, we could not accept the extreme swings in foreign views of China. When China was the enemy of the West, we could still see that the Chinese were human. When some Westerners were swept away with naive enthusiasm as China began to open, we could not forget that China had serious problems and deficiencies."

Terry Lautz

The Luce Foundation

I first met Ezra and his wife, Charlotte Ikels, nearly forty years ago when they arrived in Hong Kong for several months of research. New Asia College at the Chinese University of Hong Kong—where I was teaching and managing programs for the Yale-China Association—provided them with a flat overlooking Tolo Harbor. Ezra's hugely popular *Japan as Number One: Lessons for America* had been recently published, but he wore his fame lightly. Charlotte and my wife Ellen, both of whom had red hair, stood out in a crowd.

During the following years I saw Ezra from time to time in conjunction with my work at the Luce Foundation and the Harvard-Yenching Institute. But it was in the final decade of his life that we interacted more frequently as advisers to the National Committee on U.S.-China Relations' Public Intellectuals Program (PIP), an initiative for mid-career scholars and other professionals to gain the skills and confidence needed to contribute to wider discussion and debate. Despite many other obligations, Ezra made PIP a priority. He took a personal interest in each of the fellows, no matter their backgrounds or expertise. I marveled at his energy and enthusiasm.

In December 2018, as U.S.-China relations entered a downward spiral, Jan Berris asked Ezra and me to speak with a group of PIP fellows, who were to convene in Washington, D.C., on the politics of China studies. I noted that the current period was not the first time China had been drawn into domestic U.S. politics, be it the Cold War, Vietnam, or Tiananmen. He recalled that John Fairbank, whose loyalty had been questioned during the McCarthy period, advised his students and colleagues to keep a written record of every meeting they had regarding China "for when you're called to testify." Behind Fairbank's dry wit was a serious message: China was a lightning rod, and public education was essential to counter misinformation and misunderstanding. It wasn't enough to remain sitting in the ivory tower.

Ezra accurately predicted that the crisis in U.S.-China relations would get worse before it got better. He also said it would last longer than the "who lost China" debate after the Communist victory in 1949. Still, despite serious challenges and growing constraints on both sides, he believed engagement would continue and was hopeful that the worst outcome could be avoided. It was typical of him to take a long-term view that combined realism and pragmatism with optimism and encouragement. He avoided extremes, always searching for the middle way.

Jan Berris

National Committee on U.S.-China Relations

So many individuals, so many communities, have been enriched by Ezra Vogel's life. One of the latter is the National Committee on U.S.-China Relations' Public Intellectuals Program (PIP), created in 2005 to help upcoming generations of American China specialists broaden their knowledge and equip them to inform policy and public opinion. Though I was fortunate to know Ezra for more than fifty years, it was through working with him so closely on PIP that I came to fully understand his deep humanity.

Changes in recent decades in graduate education, and in the China field in particular, have meant that the younger generations of American China scholars are more narrowly focused on their own disciplines, without the same opportunities for cross-fertilization that benefited older China hands. Thus, one of PIP's goals is to give younger China scholars the chance to develop connections with colleagues in different fields, thereby providing them with a more holistic sense of Greater China and the possibilities for cross-disciplinary collaboration.

The second goal is to give young China specialists with the interest and potential to play significant roles as public intellectuals the tools to be effective: information on how policy is made, media training, introductions to policymakers, etc.

There have been seven cohorts of twenty fellows each since PIP's inception, with the seventh beginning in 2021. Ezra was intimately involved with all of them through 2020. He was one of the first persons we talked to about the concept. To our delight, he was immediately enthusiastic, so much so that we invited him to serve on the advisory committee. Not only did he help shape the program, but he also became an influential force in the lives of PIP fellows.

Ezra was universally admired for his intellect; mastery of Japanese and Chinese; prodigious work ethic; impish, self-deprecating humor; and fierce dedication to helping the governments and people of the three countries he cared about so profoundly to better understand and deal with one another. For me, however, it was his deeply felt concern for and his nurturing of others that was so special.

This was manifested in many ways. First was Ezra's commitment to being there. Despite his very busy schedule (even in retirement), he managed to make it to almost all of the two-per-cohort five-day Washington meetings. Even more impressive, he was the senior public intellectual on one of the two fourteen-day foreign trips for five of the six cohorts—most recently in January 2020, at the age of eighty-nine!

Having Ezra in Washington and with us in the People's Republic of China (PRC), Taiwan, and Hong Kong added a cachet to the program that was priceless, making it much easier to arrange meetings with senior officials wherever we went. Sometimes it was the Chinese who would make the first overture—as was the case when then State Councilor and Politburo member Yang Jiechi, hearing that Ezra was accompanying a group scheduled to meet a vice foreign minister, decided to host the meeting himself—to show his respect for Ezra. Of course, that meant that it became a one-on-one conversation between the two of them, rather than an occasion for the PIP fellows to ask their own questions; but the PIPers didn't mind sacrificing for the chance to participate in a private meeting in Zhongnanhai, listening to the back-and-forth between the two men, and observing how such events play out.

It wasn't only PRC current and past officials—or those in opposition to such officials—who would take notice of Ezra's presence. A meeting with Ma Ying-jeou in Taiwan? No problem. A session with Carrie Lam in Hong Kong? Followed by dinner with Anson Chan? Again, no problem. Everyone, regardless of their political leanings, was eager to break bread with Ezra.

While going anywhere in Greater China with Ezra was amazing, not surprisingly, it was on the two PIP visits to Sichuan (one of which included Deng Xiaoping's birthplace) and the two to Guangzhou where having Ezra along brought terrific and often unexpected perks. Even better was the vicarious thrill PIPers got from seeing people so excited to meet Ezra, to thank him for all he had done for China and the relationship, and to ask him to sign their copies of *Deng Xiaoping and the Transformation of China*. The book would sell out in cities before our arrival, and in 2020 the Shenzhen party secretary was desolate because his staff could scare up only nine copies in the entire city. Ezra graciously signed every one of them (privately grateful that only nine could be found), with a personal message . . . in Chinese.

No matter where we were, however, nor how wonderful the meetings with our Chinese and American interlocutors might be, it was Ezra's interactions with the PIP fellows that most impressed me. He reveled in talking to the groups as a whole—whether seated in a room recounting the history of American China hands or leaning over the back of his seat on a bumpy bus ride to a meeting—giving brief bios of those we would be seeing, suggesting key questions we might ask, and then, back on the bus, rehashing the meeting and discussing the most important takeaways.

Yet most remarkable was the extraordinary individual attention Ezra paid to the fellows. He intentionally sat next to a different person at each meal and on every bus, train, plane, or boat ride, making sure he got to know all of them. He would ask about their backgrounds, current research, relations with their colleagues, and hopes and plans for the future. He made certain that by the end of the two years, he had worked his way through that entire cohort—and he was always available for any PIPer seeking advice or assistance. Ezra could have been using that time to sleep, read, whatever; but the amount of time he spent with each PIP fellow showed them that he truly cared about them—no matter their school, or status, or prospects.

His immigrant parents would have been proud of his fame, but even prouder that he was such a mensch.

Peter Grilli

Japan Society of Boston

Remembering Ezra Vogel, my mind summons forth nothing but superlatives. Of all my academic friends and colleagues, Ezra was the most famous, the most widely read, the one with the broadest intellectual scope, the most internationally acclaimed, and the most modest. I knew him for nearly sixty years, not as well perhaps as his students and disciples, but he left an indelible imprint on my life nonetheless.

I first encountered Ezra at Harvard around 1963 or 1964. I was still an undergraduate, though a bit older than others in my class since I had spent two years away from Cambridge after my sophomore year, studying in Japan, and had just returned to resume my major in Japanese studies as a junior. Ezra had also recently returned to Harvard to begin his tenure as a junior faculty member in sociology. He had just published his first book on Japan, *Japan's New Middle Class,* which I had already read. I was eager to take his course on Japanese society. From his very first lecture in that class, I was struck by the sense of authenticity in his perceptions of Japanese people—a quality that seemed somewhat lacking in my other professors at the time. I myself had grown up in Japan, had lived among Japanese people since the age of five, and had prided myself—unrealistically for my age and inexperience—on having an intuitive understanding of everything Japanese. When other professors spoke about Japan, their comments seemed to me to be somehow detached, at a distance, their perceptions filtered through bookish research and shrouded in scholarly analysis. But when Ezra spoke, his observations about the people I knew so well rang true. Instinctively, I recognized how well he knew Japan and that he knew it directly, from the inside. He spoke about Japanese families that he knew personally. He had not merely encountered them on the dusty shelves of libraries, he had lived with them and had personally experienced almost every aspect of their lives. To me, his words about Japan—written or spoken—were refreshingly true and authentic.

Over the nearly six decades that followed that first class at Harvard in 1964, Ezra and I kept in distant touch. I never took another class with him and never worked closely with him. At Harvard, I majored in Japanese literature, not his fields of sociology or anthropology, and I was never considered one of his students. Later on, I left Cambridge to work in Japan and New York and no longer saw him regularly on campus. Still, I read every one of Ezra's books as they appeared and tried to attend as many of his public lectures as I could. Friends of mine studied under Ezra, and I admired from a distance his extraordinary diligence in helping them find jobs as they ventured out into the "real world" from his classrooms in the academy. Through such friends, who gradually became leading journalists, government officers in the Asia field, or successful business leaders working in Japan or China, I managed to keep in contact with Ezra and he somehow always knew where I was and what I was doing.

In 2000, when I returned to Boston to head the Japan Society of Boston, Ezra was the first friend I turned to for guidance and advice. When I invited him to join the board of the Japan Society, I was thrilled that he accepted immediately—but with one condition. "I'll help you in any ways I can," he told me, "but don't expect me to attend board meetings." Over the next fifteen years, Ezra was absolutely true to his word. On the many occasions when I asked him to give a talk or provide an introduction, he invariably responded positively and generously. But he never once appeared at the Society's regular board meetings.

On one occasion, around 2010, Ezra provided a truly exceptional service for the Japan Society of Boston. A Japanese friend of mine who was a senior executive at Nomura Securities in Tokyo asked if I might arrange for Ezra to speak to a group of Nomura's closest corporate clients. When I asked Ezra to spare an afternoon of his time for this on his next trip to Japan, he agreed immediately and promised to donate to the Society whatever honorarium I might negotiate with Nomura for him. On the appointed day, the Society's Chairman and I accompanied Ezra to the meeting at Nomura's headquarters, and in amazed admiration we observed him address a group of about 250 Japanese business leaders, speaking for nearly ninety minutes, without notes and in fluent Japanese, about current issues in U.S.-Japanese-Chinese relations, followed by another half hour of responses to questions from the audience. It was a virtuoso performance the likes of which I had never seen before!

Such was Ezra Vogel, a *sensei* in the truest and most profound sense of that hallowed (but often abused) term. He was a noble teacher and a committed public intellectual. He inspired his students with his teaching and faithfully nurtured the careers of the best of them long after they left his classroom. In his branch of international relations focused on contemporary Asia, Ezra provided wise counsel to the leaders not only in government but also in nearly every other realm of public activity. His many contributions were as recognized and as appreciated in Washington as they were in Tokyo and Beijing. In large public forums and in small private gatherings in corporate boardrooms or his own living room, he affected the professional work and the inner minds of countless individuals. Throughout my own professional life, I have felt blessed to be touched by Ezra's generous spirit. He will be deeply missed.

John Wheeler

New York City

The inscription in my copy of *Japan as Number One* begins: "To John Wheeler, who could have been co-author." I am still a bit incredulous, but also deeply touched that the author of this now famous, seminal work, Ezra Vogel, had asked me to help in writing it. The offer came when I was in the early phase of an assignment in the Tokyo Bureau of Time-Life Books, fresh out of graduate school. Unfortunately, I was unable to accept, but it was an early manifestation of the very special relationship I was privileged to enjoy with Ezra over the years.

I first encountered Ezra as a graduate student in East Asian Studies and subsequently in the History and East Asian Languages program at Harvard. He quickly became more than a teacher; he was a mentor of the best kind who genuinely cared, providing guidance and advice with insight, compassion, and understanding, all the while giving far too generously of his precious time. Though I was not in sociology and Ezra was not my academic adviser, I frequently turned to him for consultation. And he was always there. One particularly important moment came when I sought his counsel on a critical decision: whether to stay in academia or seek another calling. Perspicacious as always, Ezra was one of the few at the time who stressed the pressing need for American China and Japan specialists to pursue careers not only in academic teaching and research, but also in government, journalism, law, business, nonprofit administration, and other vital professions. His wisdom and vision, not to mention the time he shared and the concern he showed, made a crucial difference in my ultimate career decision.

Ezra remained an invaluable mentor long after I left Harvard, but over the years he also became a colleague in the field of U.S.-Japan relations and, most appreciated, a good friend. He consistently took an interest in how and what I was doing, providing advice and encouragement. He continually nudged me to reach higher, to meet new challenges. And I was not alone. I was constantly amazed at the extraordinary number of students, former students, and colleagues around the world with whom Ezra somehow found the time and energy to keep in touch. I often met him in Tokyo at International House, where we both stayed when visiting Japan. It was common to witness him on his second breakfast with a second student, having had dinner the previous evening with a prominent government minister, Diet member, business executive, or journalist. Ezra's meeting schedule in Japan was always packed with the country's top leaders, but never at the expense of those who, for him and for the future, were the most important.

Ezra's humility is legend. His preference for the modest International House over the luxurious five-star hotels he might have favored as a celebrity in Japan is only one small example of his priorities. Despite his eminence in the academy and in the public forum well beyond it, he was always totally natural, down-to-earth, even self-deprecating. He embodied the meaning of genuine. Notwithstanding the difference in our status and accomplishments, we interacted as equals. During my years at the Japan Society, Ezra's support and counsel were major reasons for whatever success I enjoyed, but more remarkable, at least to me, was that he in turn sought my opinion on various matters of concern to him.

In Ezra's later years, when I visited Cambridge for board meetings and to see my daughter and her family, we met for sushi lunches. (Typical of Ezra, at a dinner he and my daughter once attended in Boston, he made a special effort to introduce himself and greet her.) Our sushi lunches were both substantive and nostalgic—discussing developments in East Asia and reminiscing about people and places. Though physically slower, his acuity, curiosity, and enthusiasm remained in full force. Over one such lunch he animatedly described not one, but two works in progress: a biography of the Chinese reformer Hu Yaobang and a study of the China-Japan relationship in historical context. Ezra had become deeply worried about the serious, dangerous deterioration in China-Japan relations and rightly felt that his expertise on both countries put him in a unique position to offer context and recommendations for improvement. The result was the important volume *China and Japan: Facing History*, which exhibited once again Ezra's uncommon ability to combine academic precision with public policy relevance. The inscription in my copy reads: "To my old old friend John Wheeler." Nothing could make me prouder.

Wang Kaiyuan

Cambridge, Massachusetts

On December 20, 2020, Prof. Ezra Vogel passed away unexpectedly due to a surgical complication. The impact of his sudden death on me was immense because in the 100 days prior to his passing, we had exchanged dozens of emails. Few people probably know that Prof. Ezra Vogel's last social commitment was to take on the position of Chairman of the Board of Directors of the University Forum. He assumed this responsibility amidst the pandemic at the age of ninety.

The story started six years ago. In 2015, several Chinese visiting scholars at Harvard University initiated a biweekly academic salon, which at the time was named the Harvard Salon. Later on, as the Harvard Salon became more influential, Harvard University became involved in its naming, and we accepted the recommendation of Mr. Stephen Kennedy Smith and renamed it the University Forum, which we all agreed was a better fit. In mid-2015, I bought a house at 1709 Cambridge Street, which is across the street from Harvard's Fairbank Center, to serve as the venue of the Forum. Since then, until the outbreak of the pandemic, more than one hundred academic lectures in Chinese had been held at my house, which is only a few houses away from Prof. Vogel's house. We were practically neighbors.

Beginning in 2016, and every year until his passing, Prof. Vogel took an active role in our Forum activities. On November 27, 2016, Prof. Vogel was commentator for Li Shengping's talk on "Hu Yaobang's Political Legacy." On December 22, 2017, he was commentator for Wu Huaizhong's talk on "Japan's China Policy and Japan-China Relations." On November 6, 2018, he was commentator for He Weifang's talk on "The Chinese Factors Behind the Meiji Restoration." On October 26, 2019, he gave a talk on "China-Japan Relations after World War II and the New Imperial Era." On November 7, 2020, he attended the 115th online Forum, "On American Foreign Policy" (presented by Wang Jianwei). After the session, Prof. Vogel wrote to me and told me that he had listened for forty-five minutes.

Prof. Vogel was the first non-Chinese Harvard professor to participate in the Forum and was also the Harvard professor who participated in the most Forum sessions. He was one of the people who gave us so much encouragement during the past five years. Almost every time we saw each other, he would ask after the Forum, indicating his appreciation and support.

Therefore, last year when we were planning to officially register the Forum as an NGO, it was suggested that we invite Prof. Vogel to be the founding Chairman of the Board of Directors. I was happy and worried at the same time. I was very happy with the idea because I had great respect for Prof. Vogel, and he enjoyed a very high reputation in China, Japan, and the United States. Having Prof. Vogel serve as Chairman was very much in line with our aspirations to build an international nonprofit academic platform in pursuit of truth through the discussion of important issues involving China and the world. My worry was that because Prof. Vogel was already ninety years old and we were in the midst of the pandemic, would he be willing to accept our invitation?

I wrote three letters to Prof. Vogel, expounding on the purpose, mission, and governance principles of the University Forum. In the letters, I introduced all the sessions that the Forum had organized over the past five years and discussed our future plans and prospects. I also asked Ms. Nancy Hearst to help coordinate communications between me and Prof. Vogel. Prof. Vogel promptly responded to my letters and requested that we have a face-to-face conversation. We met at 3 p.m. on September 12, 2020, on the deck outside his house. It was a sunny afternoon, and we were both wearing masks, sitting at opposite ends of the table in the open air, six feet apart, and we talked for ninety minutes. Prof. Vogel listened attentively to my thoughts about the University Forum and asked very thoughtful questions. At the end of our conversation, he not only generously accepted my invitation to assume responsibility as Chairman of the Board but also offered great encouragement. We exchanged views on a wide range of issues. He was very humble, taking notes throughout our conversation, and I was deeply moved by his response. Within only a few hours, at 11:55 p.m. that night, he sent me his first email as Chairman of the Board. He was a true practitioner of "never put off till tomorrow what can be done today"! During the following ninety days, we exchanged emails frequently. He worked so efficiently and his mental powers remained undiminished with age. He immediately invited other scholars to serve with him on the board.

His death was a great loss for the University Forum. He was not only an outstanding scholar but also a role model for all. He was very perceptive, with great insights into history and a deep understanding of human nature. He was also very down-to-earth, modest, unassuming, and empathetic. Always adhering to the highest standards, he was never willing to sacrifice his principles.

On January 9, 2021, the University Forum, in cooperation with the U.S.-China Perception Monitor, organized an online memorial service to celebrate the life of Prof. Ezra Vogel. Eighteen scholars from China, the U.S., and Japan shared their memories with more than 500 participants from China, the U.S., and Japan. Prof. Vogel's wife, Prof. Charlotte Ikels, was also present at the service.

I think Prof. Vogel would be very pleased to know that more than 10,000 participants have attended the recent online sessions of the University Forum.

ELEVEN

Shaping Public Policies and Promoting Positive Ties with Asia

Joseph S. Nye

Harvard Kennedy School

Ezra was a great scholar and a great friend, with an insatiable curiosity and an interest in public service. As faculty colleagues at Harvard, he persuaded me to learn more about East Asia, and I followed his advice. I used to joke to him that he was my *sensei*. As a teacher, scholar, adviser, colleague, and public intellectual, Ezra contributed to our national understanding of East Asia in many ways. But he also made an important contribution to public policy during his period in Washington.

In the early 1990s, as American public opinion was turning against Japan and books were published about a coming war with that nation, Ezra, Susan Pharr, and I organized a faculty study group that focused on U.S.-Japan relations and arrived at a much less alarming perspective.

At the beginning of the Clinton administration, when I was invited to chair the National Intelligence Council (which produces intelligence estimates for the President), I asked Ezra to come to Washington to fill the important role of National Intelligence Officer for East Asia. He brought a voice of reason and a tremendous fund of information. I remember attending working meetings in the White House where Ezra and I would shake our heads over the amount of misinformation in the views expressed. But he remained a teacher, always explaining to those who would take the time to listen. American policy gradually moderated, and Ezra played a role in that process.

Ezra traveled frequently to East Asia in his job, and of course he knew everybody and had personal access not available to many officials. I can remember a complaint from one official that Ezra was visiting people at a level that should be reserved for the ambassador. When I had to bring this complaint to his attention, Ezra seemed apologetic but puzzled. I told him not to worry about it and carry on as he wished. But of course, that is what he would have done anyway. Ezra cared about ideas, not protocol. That was part of his greatness, and we are all better off for it.

Graham Allison

Harvard Kennedy School

Ezra was a gentle gentleman: generous to a fault, relentlessly constructive, indomitably optimistic. He was deeply committed to veritas: following the search for truth wherever the evidence and the analysis took him. Almost uniquely among Harvard icons that I've known, he was genuinely modest; indeed, humble. So, a strange and wonderful mixture.

As his son Steven has observed, many memorials include the words "rest in peace." About Ezra it might better be said that he was restless in the search for peace. As he pursued his search for peace, I had the good fortune to work with him on a number of ventures over the decades. I encountered him first as an author, then as a Harvard colleague, and most intensely as a collaborator over his last two years. Sometime in 2018, he persuaded me that he and I should organize a working group of leading faculty members at Harvard to address the issue of the rapid deterioration of relations between China and the U.S. As he put it, we should ask what we can do.

Ezra felt a special burden here because, as a pillar in the Harvard community of scholars, he stood on the shoulders of two giants, John Fairbank and Ed Reischauer. He was a student and colleague of both, and more than any other of their successors, had mastered both languages, both cultures, and both men's perspectives on relations among nations. Like both Fairbank and Reischauer, Ezra believed that serious knowledge of other countries' histories, cultures, and mindsets was fundamental to illuminating challenges the U.S. faced in dealing with them and in offering clues that could, in extreme cases, make the difference between peace and war.

Two snapshots from Ezra's restless pursuit of peace that I saw firsthand may make these generalizations more specific. When our colleague Joe Nye became Chair of the National Intelligence Council in the Clinton administration, he asked Ezra to become the NIO—National Intelligence Officer—for China and East Asia. For those not familiar with what the NIO does, in a nutshell, they are the top analysts in the U.S. intelligence community for their areas of responsibility. Their job is to try to integrate everything that is known—both classified and in open source—about developments and drivers, threats and opportunities, in their area. Needless to say, Ezra's deep base of knowledge, insatiable curiosity, and thoughtful perspective made him a superb NIO.

I saw this firsthand in the preparation for the G7 meeting in Tokyo in July 1993. This could have been a major turning point in establishing a partnership between an emerging Russia that was seeking to make a transition to a market economy-based democracy and the West. Like Ezra, I had joined the Clinton administration, in my case as Assistant Secretary of Defense with lead responsibility for all the nuclear weapons that had been left outside Russia when the Soviet Union collapsed in December 1991. Moreover, having earlier campaigned for what was called a "Grand Bargain," in effect a version of a Marshall Plan for Russia and the fourteen former Soviet states to assist their transitions to market economies and democracies, the G7 meeting offered a golden opportunity for this to become a signature initiative for the Clinton administration. Because President Clinton was concerned about the cost of such an undertaking, given fears about U.S. bond markets, Japan could have been a major source of the money required.

But why would Japan agree to be a major funder? Ezra provided the answer. While Clinton's foreign policy team was thinking about the G7 summit through the lens of international relations, for Japan's Prime Minister Miyazawa, this was first and foremost about his own domestic politics. Struggling to maintain his own position in his party as an election approached, Miyazawa's overriding goal was to be seen in Japan as the host of a visibly successful summit of the leaders of the great democracies. As Ezra's analysis showed, Miyazawa would have done virtually anything within reason that Clinton demanded, including matching a multibillion-dollar pledge from the U.S., as a price for that success. With Ezra's insight, we drafted what I still believe was a winning proposal. Had Clinton followed our recommendation and Miyazawa and Yeltsin accepted it, the course of history might have been altered.

The second example is the joint venture on which Ezra and I were collaborating until the week he died. He was determined that the "Harvard team," as he called it, should try to do something about the deteriorating relationship between the U.S. and China. Though I agreed with his diagnosis of the problem, I pleaded overload. But in his gentle, artful way, Ezra was not to be denied. So after many emails and phone calls and coffees, I agreed to join him as co-chair of a Harvard-wide group from across the university to bring the resources and insights from many faculty members to bear on this issue. This led to our working together intensely every week for the last couple of years.

No one who has been reading what Ezra, I, and others in the group have been writing would be surprised by the big picture in our transition report. It presents three basic propositions. First, fundamental structural realities make an intense rivalry between the U.S. and China inevitable. Second, at the same time, the U.S. and China share a small globe. Each has a robust nuclear arsenal that creates what we Cold Warriors learned to recognize as nuclear MAD, mutual assured destruction. In addition, in the twentieth-first century we now recognize that the U.S. and China live in a small, contained biosphere in which greenhouse gas emissions by anybody impact everybody. Thus we face an analogous climate MAD. Third, this means that we are, as Ezra often put it, condemned to coexist because the alternative to that is co-destruction. If these three propositions define the challenge, then the categorical imperative is to find ways in which the U.S. and China can simultaneously be both fierce competitors, but also thick partners.

I received Ezra's last email ten days before he left us. In it, after giving me an update on an issue on which he was taking the lead, he closed: "I appreciate your willingness to cheer, and I will be in touch soon." So, with gratitude for having had the opportunity to have such a wonderful colleague, I await further guidance.

David Shambaugh

The George Washington University

Ezra and I shared a strong belief in U.S.-China scholarly research exchanges, and particularly the principle of reciprocity. We were both also interested in the study of "elite politics," a sensitive subject not easy to research in China. In this research we each drew on interviews with Chinese historians of Chinese Communist Party (CCP) history (中共党史) and the related (but distinct) subfield of "national history" (国史). In Beijing we were plugged into a network of research institutes in these fields and were both hosted a number of times by the Contemporary China Institute (CCI) (当代中国研究所). This institute was accessible (with difficulty) and could sponsor select foreign researchers owing to its "horizontal" affiliation (快快关系) with the Chinese Academy of Social Sciences, although its "vertical" affiliation (领导关系) was to the CCP Central Committee Party History Leading Group. It was the CCI that sponsored Ezra's research for his monumental Deng Xiaoping biography, as well as the biography on Hu Yaobang that he was working on toward the end of his life.

Ezra and I spoke many times with the CCI leadership (individually and together on occasion) in an effort to progressively push open the bureaucratic doors for foreign scholars to conduct research in these areas. We proposed systematic interviews with retired leaders and senior officials, access to ministerial archives, access to national-level CCP and People's Republic of China government archives (中央档案馆), etc. We also proposed, unsuccessfully, some joint research projects and conferences between Chinese and foreign scholars.

One of the arguments we put forward in these discussions was the openness for Chinese researchers to utilize foreign archives and interview former officials in the United States and many other countries. The CCI leadership listened politely to our entreaties, and they even agreed on the importance of reconstructing such histories, but these conversations nonetheless felt like we were pushing against heavy walls that could not be seen. No real systematic progress was made, but we felt it important to try to broaden the aperture for foreign research access.

These conversations were, of course, private—Ezra knew that was the best way to accomplish something with Chinese bureaucrats. Notes and summaries of the conversations would be taken and circulated within the "system," and perhaps—just perhaps—some bold higher official would see the logic of our arguments and open research doors a crack further. Ezra understood well the sociology of Chinese Leninist bureaucracy.

Ezra's strong belief in scholarly access and reciprocity was exemplified in one other experience that we had together. In 2008 there was growing concern that not only was research access in China seemingly becoming gradually more restrictive across several fields, but certain scholars were now being "blacklisted" from receiving visas and going to China at all. Ezra and I discussed this disturbing trend over a dinner in

Washington, and we wondered what could be done to convey these concerns to the Chinese government *effectively*. We came up with the idea of writing a letter to then Foreign Minister Yang Jiechi (former ambassador to the U.S. and someone we both knew) and having the letter co-signed by a number of leading American China scholars. We worked hard on repeated drafts to balance positive language (to assuage Chinese nationalist sensitivities) while expressing our collective concerns—again classic Ezra: he understood that providing "face" and flattery first would soften a subsequent criticism. But how best to get the letter to Minister Yang, so that he might actually read it? Again, Ezra counseled using private channels—rather than publishing it openly (not Ezra's style).

We made an appointment to see Ambassador Zhou Wenzhong at the Chinese Embassy in Washington. When we sat down over tea, Ezra opened by explaining his belief in the importance of scholarly exchanges between the U.S. and China and the principle of scholarly reciprocity. Ambassador Zhou was welcoming and seemed friendly enough, nodded, and agreed about the value of cultural exchanges. Having opened with a positive, Ezra then zeroed in on the issue of visa bans for certain American scholars and explained that this was a matter of deep concern to the American scholarly community. As a result, a number of leading scholars had written a letter concerning the issue to Foreign Minister Yang, and we were here to ask Ambassador Zhou to privately transfer the letter to Minister Yang. Ezra reached across the table and handed Zhou the letter. As he proceeded to read the letter his face was at first expressionless, but it progressively contracted into a scowl—until he *erupted* in a tirade concerning two names on the letter (Perry Link and Andrew Nathan), his face turning beet red. The ambassador said he certainly would *not* transfer the letter to Yang Jiechi, threw the letter down on the table between us, and stormed out of the room!

Ezra, I, and a junior embassy officer (who was the notetaker) all sat in stunned silence for a minute. Well, what do we do now? I asked Ez, as I reached to pick up the letter. "No," Ezra counseled, "leave it there." So we did. Ezra's assumption was that the junior embassy officer would pick it up and it still might make its way into the "system" back in Beijing. Ezra's calculation was correct. We still do not know if Yang himself received and read it, but within a matter of weeks some of those listed in the letter (plus a few others of whom we were not aware, but unfortunately not Link and Nathan) were contacted by the PRC Embassy and consulates and invited for "tea chats" where they were told to reapply for visas. While by no means complete, some incremental progress was made on individual cases—but, perhaps more importantly, the letter "put down a marker" on the issue. And it was all handled in classic Ezra Vogel fashion, straightforward but private.

Harry Harding and Syaru Shirley Lin

University of Virginia

Shirley may well have met Ezra before Harry did, because Ezra became her mentor in 1986 as soon as she chose East Asian Studies as her concentration as a sophomore at Harvard College. Shirley not only took classes in economics, politics, and sociology as the program required, but also followed Ezra's advice to enroll in foreign language courses, choosing both Japanese and Spanish. Ezra also encouraged her to study and work abroad, which she did in Tokyo, Hong Kong, and Madrid, gaining experiences that shaped both her initial career in investment banking and her subsequent scholarly career.

When Shirley re-entered the academic world as a relatively old junior scholar three decades later, Ezra remained as generous and supportive as ever. When she published *Taiwan's China Dilemma* in 2016, he invited her to give her first book talk at the Fairbank Center and hosted the two of us at his home for dinner with Rod MacFarquhar, who had also been one of Shirley's undergraduate professors. We met Ezra again later that year in Tokyo, where he was enthusiastically speaking in English, Japanese, and Chinese with the participants in the Baixian Foundation's summer exchange program at Waseda University, as always deeply interested in hearing what young people from different countries had to say.

The first time Harry remembers meeting Ezra was in the mid-1990s. Ezra, then on leave from Harvard to serve as a member of the National Intelligence Council, spoke at one of the Washington think tanks, probably Brookings, where he showed himself to be among a very small number of government officials who could speak candidly on sensitive issues without appearing fully scripted or carefully vetted. He offered an insightful analysis of Chinese domestic and foreign policy, then as now a controversial subject, but did so in a casual manner and without a single misstep that might have landed him in trouble if his remarks were leaked to the press.

His experience in government then led him to design a collection of essays, published under the title *Living with China* (1997), about the ways in which the United States and China could manage the growing list of difficult issues that were complicating their relationship as they approached the twenty-first century. This is hardly Ezra's best-known book, but it was the only time Harry had the chance to work directly with him. He remembers how persuasive Ezra was in encouraging him to overcome his initial reluctance to take on the ultrasensitive topic of human rights (mainly through undeserved praise), and then how carefully he helped Harry shape his argument. What made the book particularly important, and should have made it better known, is its premise, extremely prescient for 1997, that the U.S. and China should not necessarily attempt to forge a "constructive strategic partnership," as was their stated goal at the time, nor should the U.S. try to "shape China," as had been the tacit American objective for so many decades, but that the two countries should adopt the more modest goal of learning to live with each other in order to manage, although not necessarily fully resolve, the issues that divided them. Ezra was deeply committed to this vision, and he hoped that his book could point the way toward that more limited but ultimately more realistic objective. This advice remains highly relevant today, when competition, containment, confrontation, and even regime change appear to be the more common, more ambitious, but more risky alternatives.

Both of us fondly recall seeing Ezra attend academic association meetings, diligently taking notes in a small notebook and raising insightful questions of the speakers. Our last experience with Ezra was when Shirley asked him to discuss his latest book, *China and Japan: Facing History*, as the 2020 Coughlin Lecture at the University of Virginia (UVA). Ezra had eagerly accepted the invitation and was planning to travel with Charlotte from Cambridge to Charlottesville. He was excited to revisit UVA after many years and packed his two-day schedule full: he was determined not only to give the lecture itself, but also to join some faculty for dinner the night before and meet with graduate students that afternoon to talk about his research and advise them on theirs. After UVA decided to make the event a virtual one due to the COVID pandemic, Ezra was disappointed that he would not be able to visit Charlottesville and meet us in person. However, he was just as enthusiastic about giving his presentation on Zoom, a technology that he had started to use that summer. He wrote us about how he had embraced Zoom as a very effective medium of communication and instruction. Even in this online setting, Ezra was as energetic and lucid as ever, both in his lecture and in the Q&A session that followed. But unfortunately he spoke only a few days before his tragic passing, so this was almost certainly his last public presentation.

Ezra's extraordinary fifty-seven-year career, bookended by *Japan's New Middle Class* and *China and Japan: Facing History,* spanned the era of the great academic generalists and thoughtful public intellectuals on Asia, from John Fairbank and Lucian Pye to Doak Barnett and Robert Scalapino, before specialization and punditry largely took over the field. Ezra was one of those greats, and he struck us as one of the most insightful, most balanced, and above all the kindest of them all. He served as mentor and model to both of us, as he was for so many others. It was our honor to know him.

Richard Bush

Brookings Institution

Thank you for giving me the opportunity to offer a few thoughts about how Ezra Vogel touched my life (I'll leave it to others to discuss how he shaped the China field). For reasons I will quickly explain, it is fair to say that in the mid-1990s Ezra changed the entire direction of my career, to my great benefit.

I got to know Ezra in the mid-1970s, when he and Andy Nathan arranged opportunities for Harvard and Columbia graduate students to "exchange views" about their doctoral research. Those were very productive sessions, from which I learned a lot. But our paths had already crossed in other, more tangential ways. We happened to have a Methodist connection: my father was a Methodist minister and missionary and Ezra attended Ohio Wesleyan University. One of Ezra's Hong Kong informants for *Canton under Communism* was also very helpful to my father when he was conducting the research for his book, *Religion in Communist China*. *Canton under Communism* came out during my first year of graduate school, and it demonstrated to me that even from outside of China, scholars could say a lot about the country with the right resources, imagination, and effort.

Ezra and I kept in touch during the years that I worked for the Asia Society and the House Foreign Affairs Committee. Our interaction in the aftermath of Tiananmen was particularly important. But the key inflection point for me came in a phone conversation with him in the fall of 1994. Out of the blue, he asked me whether I would be interested in following him as National Intelligence Officer (NIO) for East Asia once he returned to Harvard. As a congressional staffer, I had given no thought to seeking that position, and I probably wasn't even aware that it was coming open. But the idea grew on me, stimulated by his strong desire that a scholar of East Asia succeed him (not an intelligence bureaucrat) and by his support for my candidacy.

As it happened, I did get the NIO job, which liberated me from the increasingly toxic politics of Congress. Following in Ezra's wake as NIO, I deepened my exposure to the intelligence community. That shift later opened opportunities for me as Chairman of the American Institute in Taiwan and then as a scholar at Brookings.

My experience demonstrates one of Ezra's exceptional strengths: always being on the lookout for rising talent (in my case, such talent as I had) and encouraging people to consider new opportunities for growth, both as scholars and as public servants. Our field has flourished as a result, and I am deeply grateful to him for having given me the encouragement that he did over many decades.

Douglas Paal

Carnegie Endowment for International Peace

In some ways, Ezra Vogel was an odd fit when he was chosen by the administration of Bill Clinton to serve as National Intelligence Officer (NIO) for East Asia. He joined his Harvard colleague, newly appointed

National Intelligence Council chair, Joseph S. Nye, Jr., to take on the Asian share of the Council's responsibilities. While always curious about U.S. policy toward the countries he studied and acted as mentor to many who served in the government, including myself, he nonetheless arrived in Washington very much a student himself.

One of his reliable personal qualities, which is evidenced in this volume, was his persistent effort to reach positive appraisals of those whom he taught and with whom he worked. When he arrived in Washington, after the usual vetting and clearance processes, he brought that familiar wide-eyed freshness and optimism to a new set of institutions that was going through substantial change.

Ezra rented a Chevy Chase apartment owned by retired diplomat, China expert, and former ambassador to Burma, Burt Levin and his wife Lily, and commuted back to Cambridge many weekends. In Washington he reached out to familiar faces to interrogate them on process, people, and substance. It was my good luck that he needed people to dine with, and we fell into the habit of going to Washington's University Club, on 16th Street, for Tuesday night buffets. We regularly exchanged views, and I would drop him off in Chevy Chase on our way home.

I left Harvard in 1976 to join the Central Intelligence Agency's Directorate of Intelligence, working on China. By the last year and a half of the Reagan administration, I had migrated to the staff of the National Security Council, with a broader Asian remit. And I stayed on under George H. W. Bush as Senior Director for Asia and the Pacific, under the direction of National Security Adviser Brent Scowcroft. So, by the time Ezra arrived in Washington, I had accumulated some experience with a broad range of intelligence and policy agencies and personnel. Ezra and I had a lot of things to talk about. I was no longer in government and had no continued access to intelligence. Nor did I think I was missing much without it.

The end of the Cold War fed a national hunger for a peace dividend. This led quickly to a considerable downsizing of the defense and intelligence establishments. The previous decade's preoccupation with the rise of Japan was displaced by inattention as Tokyo struggled with economic stagnation. China was in the international doghouse following the Tiananmen suppression of 1989. It was not yet the rising national threat it has since been judged to be. Southeast Asia was attracting investment and attention and had not yet stumbled in the Asian financial crisis.

Thus, when Ezra Vogel became NIO for East Asia, he acquired institutional responsibility to help oversee the priorities for intelligence collection, to coordinate and deconflict, where possible, written intelligence agency judgments for policymakers. In an era of shrinking resources and declining numbers of personnel, this also still entailed some responsibility for identifying coming challenges that needed to be addressed.

In real terms, this meant that thousands of case officers, linguists, and counter-intelligence officials were encouraged to leave, were terminated, or were retracked in their careers. The long-standing practice was not to just cut loose people who had acquired crucial and costly information, but to reassign them and keep them "in the tent" where possible. But in this instance, doing so for everyone was not practicable. What this meant for Ezra was that he had to navigate among senior intelligence officials whose careers had focused on the Soviet Union but were now assigned significant positions around Asia. Moreover, finding new resources was not yet in the cards at that point.

The substance of our dinner meetings therefore boiled down to trying, one, to identify the reliable and less reliable among American resources and that of our foreign partners, and two, the important trends as opposed to the transient concerns of political Washington. Early on, I encouraged Ezra to keep a copy of Machiavelli's *The Prince* close at hand. Washington is not always what it seems.

A major focus of Ezra's work was about how the U.S. was to deal with the government of China. President Clinton won office denouncing the "butchers of Beijing," and at the beginning of 1993 threatened to end Beijing's access to U.S. markets without substantial improvements in China's human rights situation. The Chinese leadership was equally determined not to back down from its hard line on internal dissent. The Chinese essentially signaled to Clinton that he had to choose between human rights or economics, correctly judging that the U.S. business community would put a lot of pressure on the White House to compromise. Ezra was in Washington during this period and provided intelligence inputs into Clinton's eventual reversal of priorities in September 1994, just before the U.S. midterm elections.

Another unsurprising consequence of transplanting Ezra from the liberal environment of Cambridge to the more guarded environs of Washington was that he would not stop being himself. Not long after arriving, he notified his superiors of his intention to take a week's leave. A little early to seek time off, perhaps, but not a deal breaker. But this case was more notable, because he had been privately offered an opportunity to do some interviews in Guangdong, China, where he had done pathbreaking work on the early reforms in the province, published four years earlier as *One Step Ahead in China*. Taking up the offer, he arrived in Guangdong as he had previously, as a scholar, and out of courtesy made contact with the U.S. Consulate General, where unfortunately no official advance word of his visit had been received. Well, ordinarily, this was a trip for which he, as a government officeholder, should have sought formal approval. Discreet communications went back and forth to smooth the bureaucratic wrinkles. But nobody could be really upset. He was being himself.

J. Stapleton Roy

The Wilson Center

Ezra Vogel has a special place in my memory. He personified for me the ideal professor: wise, modest, deeply immersed in his fields of expertise, eager for more knowledge, loyal to friends and colleagues, constantly seeking truth from facts, and considerate of the views of others.

Our paths crossed in three distinct areas: when he was the National Intelligence Officer (NIO) for East Asia during the Clinton administration; during his research for his biography of Deng Xiaoping; and in the course of his persistent efforts to honor my brother David's five-volume translation of a major Ming-dynasty Chinese novel, one of the great classics of Chinese literature.

Ezra's service as National Intelligence Officer for East Asia from 1993 to 1995 overlapped with the final two years of my assignment as U.S. ambassador in Beijing. I had long been aware of Ezra's reputation as an Asian scholar, ever since the publication of his book on *Japan as Number One* in 1979. Rarely have I seen a well-researched scholarly work become the subject of so many lively and controversial discussions among Asia hands both inside and outside the government and among diplomats. I knew he had been a friend of my older brother, David, through their common association with Harvard, where my brother had done his undergraduate and graduate work. However, I had never had the opportunity for extended contact with the distinguished author.

Ezra's service as NIO for East Asia made up for this lost opportunity. Whenever I returned to Washington from Beijing for consultations, I would have long conversations with Ezra on developments in China and more broadly in East Asia as a whole. He was adjusting to the peculiarities of U.S. government procedures, an area where I had over three decades of experience, so we had lots to talk about. I particularly valued his insights on Japan, which always loomed large as a background factor in U.S.-China relations. Through these conversations, we became close friends.

A decade later, following my retirement from the Foreign Service, when Ezra was completing his research on his biography of Deng Xiaoping, he sought me out for several extended conversations about Deng. I was fascinated by the insights he had developed during his research on various aspects of Deng's career, but he deeply regretted that he had never had a personal encounter with Deng. Through my participation in the secret negotiations on establishing U.S.-China diplomatic relations in the fall of 1978, when I was the deputy to Leonard Woodcock, the Chief of the United States Liaison Office in Beijing, I had spent many hours in meetings with Deng. I had also been present at two small lunches hosted by Deng: one for Ambassador Woodcock on his departure from Beijing in February 1981, and one for former U.S. President Gerald Ford, when he visited China a few months later.

Ezra was eager to learn more about Deng's personal characteristics, whereas I was particularly interested in his assessment, based on his extensive research, of political developments in China during the period from 1977 to 1981, when Deng was re-emerging as China's top leader in competition with Hua Guofeng. He was able to provide interpretations that would have been invaluable to those of us in the U.S. Liaison Office and the newly established U.S. embassy when we were reporting on these trends from Beijing.

Years later, when my brother completed his lengthy five-volume translation of *The Plum in the Golden Vase (Jin Ping Mei)*, Ezra was eager to have my brother come to Harvard for a conference on this academic accomplishment. Unfortunately, my brother had been diagnosed with Lou Gehrig's disease (ALS) a month after completing his translation and lacked the energy to make the trip before his death in May 2016. Nevertheless, even though Ezra's area of scholarship was not in Chinese classical literature, he persisted in his belief that Harvard should give due recognition to a signal academic achievement by a Harvard-educated scholar. Through his initiative, Harvard held a daylong conference on December 5, 2019, during which various scholars, including several former students of my brother's, presented papers on various aspects of the *Jin Ping Mei*. I flew to Cambridge for the occasion and stayed with Ezra and his wife. He was an extraordinarily gracious host, for which I was most grateful. I saw no indications at that time that this would be our last chance for the type of extended conversations that had made Ezra such a memorable friend over the years. On one of those evenings, Ezra was visited by a delegation of Japanese scholars, who treated him with the awe reserved for a highly respected elder teacher. My last memory of Ezra is watching with admiration the skillful way he put the delegation at ease while chatting with them in colloquial Japanese. I feel greatly privileged to have known him, both as a scholar and as a fellow Asia hand in the U.S. government.

Andrew M Saidel

Dynamic Strategies Asia

A Japanese proverb says *minoru hodo atama no sagaru inaho ka na*, which translates as "the bough that bears most rice hangs lowest," in other words, the greatest are the humblest. This is how I first met Ezra. In 1990, I was working for a group of Diet members in Tokyo as a policy aide, my first job out of graduate school, and I heard that Ezra Vogel would have breakfast with anyone interesting, whether or not he actually knew them. Never having met him, I could not believe it. He was staying at the International House, and all one had to do was call his assistant and request a slot. So I did. From that meal together sprang a friendship of three decades. Little did we both know that we would end up having lunch together regularly at Central Intelligence Agency headquarters in Langley.

Several years later, Ezra was named National Intelligence Officer for East Asia, collaborating with Joseph Nye on the National Intelligence Council. I was then working for Michael Morell as an analyst in the Office of East Asian Analysis, a fifteen-minute walk from Ezra, desk to desk. We often had lunch together in the cafeteria, our own two-member eating club, sitting in the corner speaking Japanese throughout and having a grand time. Ezra's order never varied; it was always chicken wings.

Ezra Vogel, the dean of Japan scholars, and me, rookie analyst with no title next to my name whatsoever. As long as one had something interesting and new to say or contribute, Ezra was at the table intently listening. The same person who needed no business card at the highest levels in Asia for decades. His scholarship was pathbreaking and his contributions too numerous to count. But I will most remember and cherish the soaring generosity of spirit, his smile as the door opened on Sumner Road, an unanticipated card, the instant response to an email—and that warm spark in his eye each time we met. They engendered more than respect and gratitude.

Sensei. I have never met anyone so deserving of the word.

december

snowflakes warm his brow
to catch the seeker grinning
higashiyama

Gregory F. Treverton

University of Southern California

I had the wonderful good fortune to work with my friend, mentor, and colleague, Joe Nye, as Vice Chair of the National Intelligence Council (NIC) when Joe was named Chair in early 1993. We quickly determined that, given that the NIC was the most outwardly facing element of the

Intelligence community, its National Intelligence Officers (NIOs) should be the best world-class experts we could recruit—from outside government as well as inside. Ezra, the dean of Asian experts who knew both Japan and China, was at the top of our list. We hoped that, given that he had no more worlds to conquer in academia, we might draw on his patriotism and interest in seeing how the other side lived by recruiting him to the NIC. Happily, we could, and he became NIO for East Asia. He was a wonderful model for the other NIOs, always reaching out beyond intelligence and the government, always eager to try new methods or frames of analysis. To be sure, since I didn't want the bureaucracy to get in his way, I did a fair amount of cleaning up litter after him. He had, for instance, been visiting Guangdong regularly for years, and it didn't occur to him that perhaps he might let the Central Intelligence Agency Station Chief in China know he was coming. I could fix that later. What I couldn't do was replace his expertise or enthusiasm, and the last thing I wanted was for those to get constrained by bureaucratic niceties.

What I remember most fondly about Ezra was his dedication to ideas and his humility, which I'll illustrate with a story that is slightly paradoxical. The two of us were having lunch after he had returned from a trip to China with Jim Woolsey, the Director of Central Intelligence and our boss. Ezra, more puzzled than prideful, wondered aloud why people there had wanted to listen to Woolsey rather than him, since he plainly knew so much more about China and the region. His comment issued into an interesting conversation about the numeraire, the most important metric, in various places in the United States. I said that in Washington it was power, and position is a surrogate for power, so those Chinese wanted to talk to power, not to expertise. By contrast, we agreed that for Cambridge the numeraire was ideas (or at least op-eds in the *New York Times*). For New York, it was money, while for Los Angeles it was fame, for which money wasn't a bad way station.

The conversation has stayed with me, for I've lived in all of those places, three of them more than once. What has also stayed with me is Ezra's dedication to ideas—those Chinese should have wanted to question him—and his humility.

Paul Heer

Chicago, Illinois

As a career intelligence analyst at the Central Intelligence Agency (CIA), I first met Ezra Vogel when he ventured into government service as the National Intelligence Officer (NIO) for East Asia from 1993 to 1995 (interrupting his long tenure at Harvard). I was relatively new to the China field, but familiar with his reputation as a scholar and teacher, which deeply impressed me and made me one of his "students" by extension. I came to envy other China scholars and analysts who had known him much longer and had actually been his classroom students over the years. To the best of my recollection, I only interacted with Ezra episodically during his time in government, but our familiarity and friendship continued to grow after he returned to Harvard—partly because he remained a regular consultant for his former colleagues at the CIA, but especially through the occasional crossing of paths and extensive email exchanges among the community of China watchers inside and outside government.

Like most of Ezra's other colleagues, I was always captivated by his graciousness, inquisitiveness, and eagerness to engage with and learn from anyone about China (and the rest of East Asia)—including and especially junior analysts in the Intelligence community. Although his academic reputation and the extensive record of his published work were somewhat intimidating, there was never anything intimidating about Ezra as a person.

In retrospect, my relationship with him seemed to deepen when I followed his career path in the opposite direction: taking a sabbatical from government service to fulfill my ambition as a scholar. I was completing my doctoral degree just as he was returning to Harvard in 1995, so from that point forward we had dual careers—or at least dual identities—in common. This somehow made our exchanges richer and more frequent. I fondly recall one happenstance during this period when we found ourselves on the same flight from Tokyo to Washington; he was seated next to one of my colleagues, who switched places with me for several hours so Ezra and I could have a trans-Pacific conversation about developments in both China and Washington.

For the next twenty years we crossed paths frequently, both in person and online. In 2007, I became the NIO for East Asia—the position Ezra had held a dozen years earlier, thus reinforcing our common bonds. And when I retired from the CIA in 2015 and served for a year as a visiting research fellow at MIT, one of the benefits of the position was the opportunity to interact with Ezra regularly at the Harvard campus in nearby Cambridge. He drew me into his activities and his network there, which was immensely rewarding to a semi-scholar like myself who always had (and still has) more to learn.

But perhaps the most gratifying aspect of my interaction with Ezra during my post-government career was his validation of, and compliments for, my own research and analysis—which he both encouraged and promoted—and his invitations for me to collaborate with him on writing and other projects. We came to realize that we deeply shared many views on the challenges of understanding China—both the need for, and the vital importance of, promoting mutual understanding between the United States and China. This pursuit of U.S.-China mutual understanding was perhaps the core element of Ezra's mission during the last several years of his life, when U.S.-China relations started deteriorating due to mutual suspicion and strategic mistrust. Along with others, I eagerly joined his efforts to try to arrest this trend.

During these last few years of his life, Ezra occasionally expressed to me his pride in being a member of the "NIO Club" and remarked on the contrast between his government and academic experience. He joked in particular about explaining to his fellow scholars what it was like to coordinate an interagency intelligence assessment: "Suppose you were a graduate student working on a PhD thesis and had ten members on your faculty committee, and you had to satisfy all of them to get your thesis accepted." He also observed that, in addition to having held the same NIO position and being both intelligence officers and scholars, we also were both "Midwest boys"—Ezra from central Ohio, and me from eastern Iowa. It was only after he made this remark, and in hindsight, that I came to realize that we really had a special bond of uniquely common experiences. This was comforting to me because it allowed me to overcome my longtime envy of those who had known Ezra for many more years than I had. I now recognized that I had something uniquely in common with him that most of his academic colleagues did not! But more importantly, it was also gratifying to me because it reinforced the great privilege and honor I felt, and still feel, at having gained the friendship and intellectual comradeship of such a brilliant, delightful, and genial man. He will always be one of my heroes.

Michael Eiland

Arlington, Virginia

A little background: Ezra was the National Intelligence Officer (NIO) for East Asia in 1993–95. That made him one of about fifteen NIOs with functional or geographic expertise who comprise the National Intelligence Council (NIC). The NIC is supposed to be above the fray of day-to-day business and completely independent of policymakers. It coordinates the national-level analysis of the various intelligence agencies that make up the intelligence community, from the Central Intelligence Agency to the intelligence arms of the Department of Energy, the military services, the Department of the Treasury, etc.—seventeen agencies in total. The premier products that the NIC produces are National Intelligence Estimates (NIEs) and the Global Trends Report, published every four years for the incoming president. As NIO for East Asia, Ezra was responsible for convening the intelligence experts from all seventeen agencies to produce NIEs concerning Asia on topics of particular interest to high-level policymakers.

The NIO job also calls for some knowledge of bureaucratic procedures within various parts of government. Many, if not most, NIOs come from academia or elsewhere outside government. Although they are each chosen for intellectual accomplishment in their particular fields, they might not have any familiarity with the tribal rituals of government, and specifically of the intelligence agencies. They are therefore assigned deputies who, while they are expected to have demonstrated expertise themselves, can also assist in navigating the bureaucratic shoals. Ezra had three deputies: two who were star analysts of China and me.

Ezra was refreshingly innocent of experience with governmental ways. To the consternation of some of the traditionalists (and to the delight of his three deputies), he would churn out brilliant analyses on his own, without regard to the interagency sausage-making process. NIEs are meticulously sourced and footnoted, referring to documents ranging from super-secret intelligence reports to newspaper articles. Ezra's personal analyses were sourced to, for example, his relationships with an Asian head of state. NIEs have a carefully constructed distribution list; Ezra would send his papers to whomever he thought might benefit from them. It was wonderful.

Not that he ignored the interagency process. Far from it. It is the only way to produce an official, usually classified, NIE. That process could be protracted and painful. It was often frustrating trying to coordinate the judgments of the various agencies. Mass meetings of interagency intelligence representatives to draft an NIE could be tiresome and contentious. The process called for leadership that was patient and open-minded. Who on this earth was more patient and open-minded than Ezra Vogel? I never heard Ezra disagree with an intelligence analyst. He would listen patiently and attentively to a presentation, and at the end, instead of pointing out the flaws, would say, "Another way of looking at this would be. . . ." Thus followed a master class in whatever the subject was. In one meeting, I saw him offer to clear up a disputed point about a certain country by stepping back to his office and calling the foreign minister of that country. The shock and horror around the table was palpable. It just wasn't *done*. (Why not, one might ask.)

Although we were only together at the NIC for one year, we remained in touch, as he typically did with his students (I considered myself his student more than his deputy), and I am proud that I was able to make some minor contribution to his research in later years. That pride comes not from the quality of my contribution, but from the mere fact that I was privileged to be in the orbit of such a giant. Ezra was ever the gentleman, ever the mentor—and ever the friend. As with everyone else contributing to this volume and to countless others not represented here, I miss his friendship and his counsel.

Clyde Prestowitz

Economic Strategy Institute

I first met Ez while serving as Counselor to the Secretary of Commerce and engaging in intense negotiations with Japan on trade issues. Ez kindly encouraged me to write my first book, which was on that negotiating experience. As trade frictions evolved, and particularly as the game changed with the rise of China, our views came to differ sharply, and we did not see or speak with each other for quite some time. We particularly differed on the issue of industrial policy. I thought America needed such a policy, and Ez demurred. A few months before his death, I unexpectedly received a note from him accompanied by an article written by his son that called for an American industrial policy. It led to an exchange between us and a kind of reconciliation. I have wondered if Ez had some premonition of his death. In any case, I am glad we were able to get past our differences before he passed.

TWELVE

Tributes from Asia

Wang Gungwu

National University of Singapore

In January 2020, on the eve of our ninetieth birthdays, we had lunch at Old Peking in Singapore to pre-celebrate. He was three months older and my big brother. I wanted to tell him how much I got out of his new book on 1,500 years of Japanese-Chinese relations. He seemed not to know when to stop getting bolder with each book he wrote. I recalled the first time we met, soon after his *Japan as Number One* was published, after he had leapt from Japan's new middle class to *Canton under Communism*. Not content with that, he went on to the Four Little Dragons and more, and then took on the Deng Xiaoping transformation of the People's Republic of China. Mastering Japanese and then Chinese, he swung from one to the other, daring to lose his hold but always landing on both feet with his audiences cheering him on.

But my most memorable lunch with him was at the Association for Asian Studies annual meeting in Atlanta in 2008. He told me how far he had gone with his study of Deng Xiaoping. He gave me examples of the kinds of documents he managed to find and the people who were happy to answer his questions. I was surprised to learn how far he had gotten. As for the people he interviewed, I was struck by how willing they were to elaborate on the stories that were being told about the man, and the leader, at various stages of his career. He then asked me whether the Mao-Deng transition could be compared to that from Qin Shihuang to the Han founder Liu Bang, and also about other transitions like those of the first two emperors of the Tang, Song, and Ming dynasties. With so much history on the table, I cannot remember what we ate.

Deng Xiaoping as leader was what Ezra wanted to talk about. Why were the Chinese so different from the Japanese where political leadership was concerned? There had been nine prime ministers between Nakasone Yasuhiro and Koizumi Junichiro and, as we sat down for lunch, we were looking at another spell of short-term prime ministers, six as it turned out to be, before Abe's successful second term began in 2012. In comparison, Deng Xiaoping was China's leader from 1978 until his death in 1997, after Mao Zedong acted as Great Helmsman from 1949 until 1976. We did not expect it at the time, but Deng Xiaoping's attempt to limit leadership to two five-year terms was rescinded ten years after our lunch, and Xi Jinping is now free to continue as leader as long as he can.

I did not think that Ezra was expecting me to provide answers. It was one of the puzzling questions he was asking of everyone to see what kinds of responses were forthcoming. But it was a question that pushed deep into the history of the two countries. The Japanese had their unique Imperial House, and their Tennō had godly qualities. The Chinese saw their Sons of Heaven as men, some strong and powerful men with glaring faults. By dynastic standards, only a few families lasted for more than a couple of centuries. I had lost count of those who, at one time or another, had claimed to be emperors, whenever and wherever. But those who acquired real power had the legitimacy to exercise their power unchallenged.

Our conversation was an absorbing one that led us in many directions. I recall that we got on to the word *geming* 革命 that the Japanese had used to translate "revolution," something that the Chinese had been through several times and the Japanese had avoided. The modern Japanese had taken the word from classical Chinese that described the transformative change from the Shang to the Zhou dynasty and applied it to European political revolutions, especially to the English and French, where monarchs lost their heads; but they also applied the word to the American Revolution, where George III was safe and far away in England. That reminded me of how Sun Yat-sen was fascinated when he saw himself described as a revolutionary (*kakumeisha* 革命者) after his dramatic escape from capture in London.

Ezra noted that the word *geming* could not be used for what happened in the Meiji Ishin 维新—restoration, reform, renovation, revolution, we toyed with the words to translate what the Japanese had accomplished. The Chinese, on the other hand, loved *geming* and used it cheerfully until Mao Zedong debased it by his extremist "cultural revolution." We chewed over what Deng Xiaoping had done: reform or transformation? He had not rejected revolution, but appeared to have concluded that Sun Yat-sen's "Revolution has not yet succeeded" 革命尚未成功 had been brought to closure. What had yet to be done was to consolidate it through reform and ensure that the successes could become permanent and progressive.

It was too big a question to answer satisfactorily over lunch. We parted, promising to let each other know if and when the key clue to his question was found and to let the wisps of hope hang in the cool spring Georgia air. Looking back—at another lunch this time in Singapore after he published yet another blockbuster of a book, *China and Japan: Facing History*—I came to think that, over in Atlanta twelve years earlier, Ezra was perhaps already feeling for the stones for a bold historical relook at how the two histories might bring the countries together as modern partners serving a shared world order. I don't think Ezra would have wanted any outcome less than that.

Ban Ki-moon

United Nations

I was incredibly saddened to learn of the passing of Professor Ezra F. Vogel, one of the most esteemed academic experts on East Asian affairs, as well as someone I was lucky enough to learn from during my memorable and transformational time at Harvard University. Not only was Professor Vogel an intellectual giant, he was also a mentor and a friend.

When I arrived in Cambridge in 1983, I quickly realized that my time at the Kennedy School of Government would offer an invaluable opportunity to upgrade my level of intellectual knowledge, which was certainly lacking as a result of my turbulent university days during a period of political upheaval in Korea. At Harvard, I was really fortunate to study under three eminent professors—Professor Vogel, Professor Joseph Nye, and Professor Graham Allison—whom I also considered my mentors. My heart is now heavy knowing that one of my three life-changing mentors is no longer with us.

I met Professor Vogel for the first time at Harvard shortly after I arrived in the early 1980s. I knew that his book, *Japan as Number One*, published in 1979, was already making academic waves and was globally renowned. So, you can imagine my excitement when he invited me to serve as a Special Fellow under him for one year as part of the U.S.-Japan Program. I enthusiastically accepted his offer and was even provided with an office! This opportunity was a great privilege for me to deepen my studies further following my initial one-year scholarship at Harvard, which was funded by the Korean government. However, just five months later, I was asked by then Korean Prime Minister Lho Shinyong to serve as his Senior Secretary for Protocol Affairs. This was an exciting professional honor, but it left me in a difficult position with Professor Vogel since I now had to explain the situation and my deeply apologetic feelings to him. To my surprise, he understood perfectly and wholeheartedly encouraged me to depart Harvard early to assist the Korean Prime Minister and my country. Professor Vogel's generosity, understanding, and support then meant the world to me and continued to characterize my interactions with him over the ensuing decades.

Later, and through my initiative, the Korean government invited Professor Vogel to Seoul, and he had the opportunity to meet with the Korean Prime Minister. During this period he was a distinguished expert on both Japan and China, but not Korea. In fact, this was the main reason why I undertook my own efforts to officially invite him to visit Korea, in order for him to get to know more details about our own unique history, people, and culture.

As the years passed, we remained in touch, and, during my ten-year tenure as United Nations Secretary-General, I was pleased to meet with him several times to exchange views on the geopolitical issues of the day and catch up socially. I have particularly fond memories of the last time we met together—at a Korean restaurant in Boston in 2017—when I was invited by Harvard University to be a Special Fellow following the completion of my decade of service as UN Secretary-General.

Professor Vogel helped enrich and expand East Asian studies in the United States and around the world. Through his research, teaching, and writing, he not only built bridges and enhanced mutual understanding, he also helped nurture the minds of generations of students, colleagues, readers, and friends.

I'm deeply honored and humbled to have counted myself as one of them.

Kishore Mahbubani

National University of Singapore

In 1991/92, I spent a year in Harvard as a fellow at the Center for International Affairs. All I had under my belt was twenty years of experience as a Singapore diplomat. No PhD. No teaching experience. Despite this, Ezra asked me to teach one of his big classes on East Asia when he had to travel overseas for a week. I remember vividly what I did when I walked into the classroom of several hundred students. I took out a stick of chewing gum, unwrapped it, and put it in my mouth. My first question to the class was this: Was I breaking a Singapore law by chewing gum? Most of the class said yes! I told them that the correct answer was no. It is illegal to import chewing gum into Singapore, but not illegal to chew gum.

Ezra Vogel knew Singapore well. He had visited frequently and got to know its leaders very well. He knew that the dominant American view that Singapore was just another typical third world dictatorial state was a caricature of the complex reality of Singapore. Even though it was politically incorrect, especially at the "End of History" moment of 1991, to invite a diplomat from Singapore to challenge the conventional wisdom on Singapore in a Harvard classroom, Ezra was prepared to take the risk. He was a brave scholar, willing to challenge conventional wisdom on East Asia, even at the risk of being vilified for doing so.

He demonstrated this most clearly when he came out with his deep and insightful biography of Deng Xiaoping in 2011. I happened to be at Harvard again soon after the book came out. Some Harvard scholars told me that Ezra Vogel would get into trouble over his biography of Deng. At that time, the only recent event in Chinese history that virtually all Americans remembered was the Tiananmen Massacre of June 1989. The man who ordered the violent crackdown in Tiananmen Square was Deng. To write a biography that drew out the greatness of the man was an act of exceptional political courage.

This was also why Ezra Vogel is widely admired all through East Asia, among both leaders and scholars. They felt that Ezra Vogel understood well the rich complexity of East Asian societies. For example, he regularly met with Mr Lee Kuan Yew, the founding Prime Minister of Singapore. They spent many hours together. Having had these long conversations, Ezra knew well that the man who Lee Kuan Yew admired the most in East Asia was Deng. Indeed, in an interview he gave in 2010, Lee Kuan Yew said publicly, "I would say the greatest [leader I have met] was Deng Xiaoping. At his age, to admit that he was wrong, that all these ideas, Marxism, Leninism, Maoism, they are just not working and have to be abandoned, you need a great man to do that." Sadly, in the West, no leader dared to praise Deng publicly, even though no other leader in history can claim to have improved as many lives as Deng did. Effectively, it was his policies that rescued 800 million people from absolute poverty in China. It was also his policies that had created a middle-class population of 400 million people in China. He did all this by bravely opening up the closed Chinese economy to global competition. As Ezra says in his book, "When Deng became preeminent leader in 1978, China's trade with the world totaled less than $10 billion, within three decades, it had expanded a hundredfold." If Ezra hadn't shown political courage in writing a fair biography of Deng, the world would have been hugely impoverished, as it would not have had the knowledge and insights required to understand the greatest leader of the 20th century.

I also recall vividly a conversation I had with Ezra about Japan. He told me that in the 1970s he used to visit Japan regularly. He also visited Japanese auto factories. Once, after his return, he visited a friend working for General Motors (GM, then the biggest company in the world) as a senior vice president. He told his friend about the new Japanese prowess in automobile manufacturing. His friend was very startled to hear this. He immediately shut the door of his office so that they could speak privately. He told Ezra something along these lines: "Ezra, I know how good the Japanese are. However, if I told my Board and Senior Management this challenging news, GM will not change course. Instead, I will be fired."

History has since shown us what happened to GM after its failure to study and understand the Japanese challenge. It's no longer the biggest and most admired company in the world. Paradoxically, GM is now making more money from China than from the U.S. Yet, GM will not speak out in any way as anti-China sentiment has gained tremendous political momentum in the American body politic, leading to the real danger of an all-out contest between the U.S. and China.

Ezra showed his political courage again in 2019 when he joined a small group of American scholars warning about the dangers of this growing anti-China hysteria in the American body politic. The statement he signed said "a successful U.S. approach to China must focus on creating enduring coalitions with other countries in support of economic and security objectives. It must be based on a realistic appraisal of Chinese perceptions, interests, goals, and behavior; an accurate match of U.S. and allied resources with policy goals and interests; and a rededication of U.S. efforts to strengthen its own capacity to serve as a model for others. Ultimately, the United States' interests are best served by restoring its ability to compete effectively in a changing world and by working alongside other nations and international organizations rather than by promoting a counterproductive effort to undermine and contain China's engagement with the world." This is why Ezra's passing in 2020 was truly untimely: a brave voice like his has never been more needed than now.

He will also be remembered as a great soul, who was exceptionally generous. I have benefited from his generous soul. When he inscribed his book on Deng to me, he wrote, "To my good friend, Kishore Mahbubani, who deep down is a kind wise scholar while on the surface he is a provocateur."

Kevin Rudd

Asia Society

Ezra Vogel was a friend and a colleague—and beyond the conventional meanings associated with both. As a friend, I remember first arriving at Harvard in 2014—my first period of political exile from Australia after having left the prime ministership in that country—only to receive a kind invitation from Ezra and Charlotte to their home in Cambridge. And there Ezra had kindly gathered the entire Harvard community of China scholars under a single roof, where we all ate and drank together well into the evening, the enduring thematic being "whither China." It was a wonderful welcome to Harvard. I can also remember fondly Rod MacFarquhar's attendance that evening. I felt very much as if I was being welcomed to the world's leading university by the world's leading China scholars. It was humbling.

As a colleague, Ezra would always go beyond what was mandated by normal definitions of collegiality. I remember well drafting a paper on Constructive Realism in 2015, which sought to offer a new framework for U.S.-China relations under Xi Jinping and Obama. It formed the basis of my subsequent work on Managed Strategic Competition. But true to his qualities, Ezra, in response to a short cover note to himself and many other colleagues asking for any feedback, then provided the longest response I've ever received to any piece I've ever circulated on the Middle Kingdom. Ezra's note started with, "I assume you sent this because you welcomed constructive comments." It's at that point where you quietly draw in a breath as you consider what is to follow. In Ezra's case there followed fifty points—all sharp and excellent. This was then followed by his trademark decency: "Please take the length of my comments as a sign of respect for the seriousness of your efforts." In one of his last (and shortest) emails to me, in late 2020, he simply wrote: "Kevin, I agree with all of your points. Work to do. Best, Ezra."

I remember having long conversations with Ezra not just about his seminal work on Deng Xiaoping, but also his incomplete work on Hu Yaobang. Both men were objects of deep intellectual fascination on Ezra's part as he sought to make sense of China's transformation after the killing fields of the Cultural Revolution. But I uniquely remember his work on trying to make sense of the history and future of China-Japan relations. It's rare to find a sinologist with such a simultaneous depth of expertise in the study of the language, literature, and history of Japan. His deep personal burden was how to interpret and reinterpret the troubled (and at times felicitous) history of these two great civilizations and their dealings with each other in a manner that would chart a different course for the future. His work on that relationship—his last major work—is a final testament not just to the depth of his scholarship, but also to the depth of the moral framework he brought to his academic study. I remember Ezra as a wonderful human being. I remember him wearing his French beret, riding his bicycle around the Cambridge campus at the tender age of eighty-seven. His Chinese name, as many of you know, is Fu Gaoyi—Gaoyi is a hallowed Chinese given name. In one rendering it is interpreted as meaning righteousness. There is another meaning, however, which I think goes to the soul of Ezra's character. *Yi* also means decency. And when I think of Ezra Vogel I think foremost of a genuinely decent human being, kind and considerate toward his fellow human beings, deeply intellectually curious, and with a profound ethical commitment to the cause of peace.

Yasushi Akashi

Kyoto International Conference Center

I am still overwhelmed by the news of Ezra Vogel's passing in December 2020 at the age of ninety. He was only two months older than me. I am one of many who are filled with indescribable sorrow by his departure from our midst. Ezra is well known in Japan as the author of *Japan as Number One: Lessons for America*. I often saw him surrounded by his friends and admirers who assembled together at the news of his Tokyo visits. The scene evoked in me the image of a paternalistic, kind teacher in feudal Japan. For his younger disciples and students, Ezra was certainly much more than just another Harvard professor. I used to see him frequently at the Columbia University faculty seminar on modern Japan in the 1960s and 1970s, when Japan specialists on the East Coast gathered in Butler Hall once a month to exchange views on different aspects of modern Japan. At the time, I was a young UN official doing my PhD at Columbia, enjoying the company of Ezra, James Morley, and many other scholars. Gerald Curtis also joined the membership later.

More recently, I saw Ezra Vogel often at the International House of Japan in Tokyo. The founding of the International House was first envisioned by John D. Rockefeller III and Shigeharu Matsumoto at the third conference of the Institute of Pacific Relations held in Kyoto in 1929; it was eventually established in 1952.

As Chairman of the International House, I invited Ezra to speak in the fall of 2012, when I organized a series of international symposia to commemorate its sixtieth anniversary. I asked him to discuss the image of Japan in the world from different perspectives. Obviously, U.S.-Japan relations constituted one such focus, and Ezra was my choice to introduce that subject. I was glad that every remark he made had the imprint of his characteristic thinking. He emphasized the very strong impact that General MacArthur's occupation, backed by over 400,000 troops, had made on remaking a new Japan. Ezra stressed how deep the impact of the occupation had been due to the determination on the American side and the receptivity of many Japanese. I agreed completely with Ezra regarding the enduring U.S. imprint on Japan, which is demonstrated by the emotional attachment of many Japanese today to the postwar Constitution and its spirit.

Ezra never ceased discussing Japan and the United States and their special relationship. He was also quite unique among experts in that he brought in China and the Chinese people whenever he discussed East Asia as a whole. Ezra told the Chinese that postwar Japan was so imbued with the spirit of democracy and human rights that there should not be any basic barrier to achieving mutual understanding among the Americans, the Chinese, and the Japanese. Furthermore, Ezra felt that the territorial issue between Tokyo and Beijing over the Senkaku Islands would eventually be resolved in the spirit of Deng Xiaoping, who came to Japan in 1978, carrying with him the signed text of the Japan-China Treaty of Peace and Friendship. At a press conference in Tokyo, Deng Xiaoping said that there was no other choice but to shelve the dispute over the Senkaku Islands until future generations in China and Japan would be able to develop the mutual tolerance and wisdom to resolve the delicate territorial issue to their mutual satisfaction. I see in this suggestion profound pragmatism and realism for both countries, where the thorny issue of the Senkaku Islands was thought of as a formidable irritant, but as something not as vital as other, greater issues. In my view, Ezra was right to tell the Japanese and Chinese that they should be extremely careful not to fall into serious nationalism and instead should strive together in the spirit of cohabitation and cooperation as good neighbors.

In a world which keeps changing, amazing new issues make their appearance. We will be confronted by the emergence of new deadly diseases as well as other grave problems. We are, however, bound together to discover innovative solutions to them. Northeast Asia, which has more people than any other part of our planet, is no exception to this general rule. Ezra Vogel's simple yet profound advice to all of us is that the United States, China, and Japan, the three large pillars of the Pacific, will be able to overcome all possible conflicts with each other and meet any major challenges they face in the remainder of the twenty-first century.

Han Seung-soo

Seoul, Korea

My relationship with Ezra goes back to 1985, when I spent a year in the Department of Economics at Harvard University as a Senior Fulbright Scholar while on my sabbatical from Seoul National University. Although I had heard long before of his reputation as an eminent scholar of East Asia, it was not until my stay at Harvard that I finally met him. By that time, he had already gained worldwide renown with his monumental book in 1979, *Japan as Number One: Lessons for America.* While I was in Cambridge, I was busy meeting with Japan specialists, including Haru Matsukata Reischauer, who happened to be the cousin of one of my closest Japanese friends.

Later, in 1993 when I went to Washington, D.C., to serve as the Korean ambassador to the United States, we met again and began to consolidate our close and long-lasting friendship. Ezra was then serving as the National Intelligence Officer for East Asia, and his years at the National Intelligence Council (NIC) more or less coincided with my term of office in Washington, D.C. Coming from academia, we quickly forged a bond that soon developed into a lifelong friendship.

Whenever he was invited to the Korean ambassador's residence, my wife, Soja, would always ask him to sit beside her, as they had so many things to talk and argue about. Ezra liked Lee Eo-ryung, one of Korea's best literary critics and the author who in 1982 wrote the Japanese best-seller entitled, in English translation, the *Miniaturization-Oriented Japanese.* Soja would always jokingly ask Ezra when he would write a book on Korea with equally perceptive observations.

It was very unusual for a Harvard professor to be appointed to work at the NIC, but I believe that Ezra's profound expertise and comprehensive knowledge of East Asia made Joseph Nye, Jr., then the NIC Chair and also a Harvard faculty member, encourage him to join the organization. It was a time of nuclear crisis, when tension between the U.S.

and North Korea heightened with North Korea's announcement of withdrawal from the Non-Proliferation Treaty in March 1993. I am sure that Ezra fulfilled the role better than anyone else could have during this particularly delicate time in the U.S.-North Korea relationship.

By the time I was appointed Foreign Minister in early 2001, Ezra had returned to Cambridge and had published *Is Japan Still Number One?* and *The Golden Age of the U.S.-China-Japan Triangle, 1972–1989.* Combined with his practical experience in government, his studies and works on East Asia had become even more profound and insightful.

During my service as the UN President of the 56th Session of the General Assembly and later as Prime Minister of the Republic of Korea, we continued our strong relationship of mutual support and respect. Although we did not meet often, I always knew that I had a good friend in Cambridge to count on when I needed advice and assistance.

Sometime after I retired from public service, I was invited by the Harvard Kennedy School to give a public lecture. I gave the speech on the subject of "Improving the Trilateral Relations among China, Japan, and Korea—A Building Block Approach," in October 2015. Hearing of my forthcoming visit to Cambridge, Ezra kindly invited me to also give a talk of my choice at the Asia Center, where I delivered a speech entitled "Sustainable Development in a Carbon-Constrained World." While I knew it was not the kind of subject he necessarily enjoyed listening to, he stayed until the end. It was a rather cold day for October. After the speech all of us, including a group of young Chinese friends from Shanghai who traveled all the way to listen to my speech in Cambridge, were invited to tea at his house. He was the most hospitable and cordial host, and these Chinese friends, when later informed of his untimely passing, sent their deepest condolences.

Ezra was a gracious friend who also wrote very warm and kind words for the 2015 published collection of the speeches I gave during my years of public service, *Here for Global Good.* Although he was famous in our part of the world, particularly for his bestseller *Japan as Number One*, he had extensive knowledge of East Asian history, politics, and culture in general. He wrote excellent biographies of prominent figures such as Deng Xiaoping and Park Chung Hee, describing their lives and contributions in *Deng Xiaoping and the Transformation of China* (2011) and *The Park Chung Hee Era: The Transformation of South Korea* (2011). I remember him somewhere mentioning the four remarkable, transformative Asian leaders in the twentieth century: Mustafa Kemal Ataturk of Turkey, Deng Xiaoping of China, Park Chung Hee of Korea, and Lee Kwan Yew of Singapore. How perceptive and insightful he was!

At a time when the relationship between two great powers in the world, the United States and China, is rapidly deteriorating and the danger of the Thucydides Trap is even being raised, Ezra Vogel, a man of great scholastic achievement and shrewd insights as well as a fundamentally decent disposition and genuine commitment, is truly needed on both sides of the Pacific. I am sure we will miss him more and more as time goes on.

Yoichi Funabashi

Asahi Shimbun

It was in China in 1981 that I first listened to a speech by Ezra Vogel. At that time I was *Asahi Shimbun*'s Beijing correspondent and was attending a special event at the Chinese People's Political Consultative Conference (CPPCC). Ezra had been invited to give a keynote speech on Japan, which he delivered entirely in Chinese before an audience of about 2,000 people, all clad in Mao suits. During his speech, Ezra talked about how well prepared Japan was for the increasingly globalized economy. He astutely drew attention to Japan's *zonghe shangshe* (general trading firms such as Mitsubishi, Mitsui, and Itochu) and their acumen for networking and global business. He noted that their employees were very familiar with local cultures and had a strong command of local languages, asserting that this was the model China should look to for its open door and drive for reform, ushered in by the comeback of Deng Xiaoping. Ezra had just published his bestselling book, *Japan as Number One*, in 1979, and the Chinese also came to be intensely interested in Japan's developmental model. On that occasion, I was seated in the auditorium next to Keizo Takemi, then a young China scholar and TV commentator, now a member of the Japanese House of Councillors. We had been invited to the speech by Ezra, and both of us left feeling extremely impressed with his fluent command of Chinese and his deep grasp of Japanese organizational culture and Japanese society. We benefited greatly from Ezra's profound insights on Sino-Japanese predicaments.

Throughout the years, my connection with Ezra continued. When I was living in Foxhole Crescent in Washington, D.C., as bureau chief of the *Asahi Shimbun*, I had a monthly lunch with Ezra at my home. Ezra at that time was an analyst for East Asia with the National Intelligence Council (NIC), when Joe Nye was chairman. Over lunch we found that we shared views on matters both contemporary and historical. One deep concern we shared was about the prospects for the U.S.-Japan alliance after the Cold War ended. We felt that the clear direction of the alliance during the Cold War era had started to blur with the advent of the Clinton administration, when the "It's the economy, stupid" mantra began to influence U.S. national security policy and alliances. Joe Nye started an initiative to redefine and reaffirm the U.S.-Japan alliance, with much support from Ezra Vogel's expertise and intellect. A couple of years later I published the book *Alliance Adrift* on the new challenges of the alliance. Perhaps Ezra felt a bit unhappy because I focused excessively on Joe Nye and didn't pay sufficient attention to Ezra's role, but nonetheless he was incredibly generous to share his insights and thoughts with me. We talked a lot about historical issues and shared deep concerns about Japan's relationship with neighboring countries throughout history. When I was invited by Dick Solomon, President of the United States Institute of Peace, to write about Japan's historical issues and edit the book *Reconciliation in the Asia-Pacific*, Ezra kindly wrote a foreword for the book. In it, he noted that "some potentially valuable elements of a reconciliation process can also be provided by outsiders. For instance, outsiders such as Americans can convene meetings and facilitate discussions that enable the parties to a dispute to adopt a more objective tone than they employ in purely bilateral encounters." This, in fact, had been his ongoing and lifelong noble cause—to promote the reconciliation process between Japan and China—and we greatly appreciated his efforts toward that goal. He will be eternally missed as a true, honest broker and a symbol of an era where the U.S. was trusted to play a role in ameliorating tensions between Japan and China.

Two years ago, I happened to come across Ezra at the International House of Japan. At this point, Ezra had just finished his new book, *China and Japan: Facing History*. Ever ready to start a new project, he told me that his next ambition was to write about the life and history of Hu Yaobang, who was tragically purged and eventually died after being expelled from leadership in the late 1980s. Hu has always been special to me. Early in the morning in May 1980, as Prime Minister Hua Guofeng left for his trip to Belgrade to attend the state funeral of Marshal Tito, some foreign correspondents and I were invited to see him off at the Beijing airport (yes, that old shabby one), side by side with members of the Standing Committee of the Chinese Communist Party (CCP). After the plane had already vanished into the clouds, the small gentleman next to me was still waving. I suddenly realized that this was Hu Yaobang, General Secretary of the CCP. He smiled at me, then asked whether I had some time. Unable to find an open room in the airport to chat in, we sat on a bench, and he started to talk about his dream project: a massive exchange program for youth from both Japan and China. When I mentioned this to Ezra, he started to take notes, but I unfortunately had a previous engagement and had to excuse myself. He asked me to tell him more of the story next time. That was the last conversation I had with Ezra.

If only Ezra could have finished his book about this most humanistic and compassionate leader of the CCP. It was a fitting topic for Ezra. Hu's days as the top official of the party were the golden years of the postwar Japan-China relationship. Indeed, Ezra's beautiful speech to the Chinese elite at the CPPCC was at the apex of those days. We had been lucky to meet at a pivotal point in history, a moment of great growth and positive change. There were blue skies in autumn as we looked out over the past forty years. In the auditorium, we had shared an extraordinary moment together, Ezra and myself.

Makoto Iokibe

Public University of Hyōgo

I first studied overseas at Harvard University for two years, beginning in 1977. My stay was made possible by Professor Ezra Vogel, then the director of the East Asian Research Center at the university. Three years before, I had had the opportunity to visit the United States for a month and had spent my last week at the National Archives, collecting a large number of original documents about the U.S. occupation of Japan.

When I called on Professor Reischauer at Harvard with the materials I had found, he was very pleased and introduced me to many people. In gratitude for having been given access to an office and a secretary, I set up a series of seminars related to U.S.-Japan relations, where Japanese and American researchers in various fields could get to know each other. From that time on, I had close ties with Professor Vogel for over forty years.

Professor Vogel was full of curiosity and had a strong interest in people. At the same time, he had a sense of big-picture issues. He studied sociology under Talcott Parsons and received his PhD in 1958, then made the pioneering move of choosing Asia as the focus of his research. With Professor Reischauer leading Japanese studies at Harvard and Professor John Fairbank focusing on China, Professor Vogel was undoubtedly stimulated by the intellectual fertility of Asian studies at Harvard. Back then, however, the U.S. had no diplomatic relations with the People's Republic of China, and Japan had not entered its rapid economic growth period. Instead, the driving force behind Professor Vogel's ascent as an internationally indispensable figure was most likely his unwavering conviction that Asia would be a new frontier for the United States and the world.

The decision to focus on Japan was wise. During the 1960s, the country achieved miraculously high economic growth. Japan resurfaced after the 1973 oil crisis with many technological innovations. Its industrial competitiveness rose sharply, and its exports of home appliances and automobiles flooded the U.S. market. It was during this period that Professor Vogel wrote *Japan as Number One: Lessons for America*. Based on sociological methodology, the book analyzed the structural factors that propelled Japan's economic development and the value systems that were responsible. He had the talent and the will to write clearly and persuasively, and the book became a bestseller in Japan. Rather than aiming to praise Japan, Professor Vogel wanted his own country to learn the secrets of Japan's strength and to overcome challenges without sinking into easy and tasteless Japan-bashing.

With the end of the Cold War, some argued that the Japan-U.S. alliance was no longer necessary. However, it soon became clear that North

Korea and China could pose new threats. Secretary of Defense William Perry of the Clinton administration called on Assistant Secretary of Defense Joseph Nye to formulate a new Asian policy. Then came the Nye Initiative of 1995, which was intended to build a new regional order in Asia with the commitment of 100,000 U.S. troops and the Japan-U.S. alliance as its backbone. Several months before the initiative's announcement, the Higuchi Report, presenting Japan's options for national security and diplomacy, was issued in Japan under the direction of Prime Minister Morihiro Hosokawa. To coordinate the two post–Cold War strategies, from 1993 through 1995 Professor Vogel traveled frequently between Japan and the United States as the National Intelligence Officer for East Asia under Joseph Nye. The "reset" of bilateral relations after the end of the Cold War was significant for the Japan-U.S. alliance and has survived to this day.

My second stint at Harvard was in 2002. This time, I took part in a joint research project at the Harvard-Yenching Institute, having been invited by Professor Akira Iriye. With Professor Iriye serving as the moderator and Professor Vogel in attendance, the monthly sessions on the history of postwar Japan's foreign relations attracted many young researchers and graduate students. Some participants said that they had never seen professors teach so many sessions without pay. During this time, the "Vogel *juku*," study and discussion meetings of Japanese students, generously guided by Professor Vogel, was born.

Professor Vogel's book, *Deng Xiaoping and the Transformation of China*, was published in 2011. It was an epoch-making work that explained how a new China was born after the internal conflicts following the Communist revolution. With the publication of this book, Professor Vogel became the only American to publish bestsellers in both Japan and China. He strongly encouraged a good bilateral relationship between the two countries, saying, "I consider myself to be on the side of both Japan and China." With this goal in mind, he published *China and Japan: Facing History* in 2019. Even in his final years, Professor Vogel continued to be an ardent researcher of Asian relations. When I asked him to be the keynote speaker at an international symposium in Kumamoto in 2015, he came all the way from the U.S. to discuss the rise of China and the regional order in the Asia-Pacific region. Professor Vogel was determined that confrontation and war with China was the worst option. His position was to search for a way of coexisting with China. He also voiced expectations for the role Japan could play, given its knowledge of both the United States and China.

Many of Professor Vogel's colleagues probably had come to think of him as immortal. His demise in December 2020 was a very sad shock to us all.

Alexander Lukin, with Vladimir Lukin

National Research University Higher School of Economics, Moscow

Professor Vogel was not a Russia specialist, but he always had an interest in our country and was very enthusiastic about collaborating with Russia's orientalists. He was not only a pillar of American oriental studies, but also an important link in the relationship between Soviet (Russian) and American professional colleagues, which was particularly important during the most difficult moments of the U.S.-Soviet confrontation and in recent times, when relations between our two countries had deteriorated again. As far as our family was concerned, he was also a guiding light and an example of academic objectivity, displaying admirable personal qualities. Ezra met my father, Vladimir Lukin, in 1981 when, at the height of Soviet communism's period of "stagnation," he came to the Soviet Union at the invitation of Yevgeny Primakov, as part of a group of Asia specialists headed by Robert Scalapino. Ezra wrote about this visit himself in a short article published in 2018 in a book marking the eightieth birthday of my father, whom he referred to as his "Russian colleague and friend," which was a great honor. At the time future foreign minister and premier Primakov was Director of the Russian Academy of Science's Institute of Oriental Studies and, despite the difficulties at the end of Brezhnev's time in power, organized a conference to discuss Asian issues with the Americans. Afterward, the participants traveled to Tashkent to take part in another conference on East Asia.

The name Vogel was, of course, well known to Russian experts at the time. Despite censorship and ordinary people's inability to purchase books published abroad, specialists were able to keep abreast of professional literature either through special library departments or through receiving books as gifts from colleagues when meeting personally at conferences akin to the abovementioned events. Ezra Vogel's 1979 book, *Japan as Number One: Lessons for America,* was discussed broadly throughout the world, including in Russia. It has been on our bookshelves at home ever since then. During the perestroika years, my father became a politician and was elected to Russia's Supreme Soviet (parliament) in the country's first free elections, and then in 1992, immediately after the fall of the USSR, President Yeltsin appointed him as Russia's ambassador to the U.S. The job of the first ambassador from a democratic Russia was not a simple one: he needed to transform the Soviet image of a "Mr. Nyet" into that of a normal person. For this, his old connections with fellow academics such as Ezra were very helpful. Professor Vogel had moved to Washington and worked for a while for the government as National Intelligence Officer for East Asia. But as he himself wrote, he and my father would meet in those days "more as friends than as representatives of governments."

Subsequently, I took the lead in this friendship with Professor Vogel. We met when I was at Harvard for the 1997–98 year, working in a post-doctoral role at the Kennedy School. We maintained constant contact from that moment on. In 2004, I invited him to take part in the 3rd Russian International Studies Association Convention, which was held at the Moscow State Institute of International Relations (MGIMO). There, he gave a talk at the Asia-Pacific session on triangular relations between the U.S., China, and Japan. On that occasion, my father and I organized a dinner for guests from various countries at one of Moscow's Chinese restaurants, and I enjoyed talking to Ezra in an informal setting.

Ezra twice invited me to speak at seminars he ran at the Fairbank Center. The first time was in winter 2016, and following my talk, we visited his home before walking around the campus. I remember that everything was covered in snow, with Cambridge looking almost like Moscow. On the second occasion in March 2020, however, the trip fell through due to the coronavirus pandemic, and the talk and discussion had to be held a little later online. In April 2020, I invited him to be the inaugural speaker at our Eurasian Online Seminar, which we organized at the Higher School of Economics in order to maintain contact with leading specialists on international affairs during the pandemic, when conditions made meeting in person impossible. He gave a talk on his research concerning the history of, and prospects for, Sino-Japanese relations. There were no indications of any trouble ahead: in spite of Ezra's advanced years, he was very active to his final days, constantly traveling and giving talks. The last time that we "met" online was on 1 December during the Beijing Xiangshan Forum, a high-powered conference organized by the Chinese military, at which Ezra, as always, called upon China and the U.S. to make reciprocal compromises and improve relations. Shortly afterward came the sad news of his death.

Ezra's passing represents a big loss to the world of academia and to us personally. Professor Vogel was an outstanding orientalist, having known two Asian countries—China and Japan—intimately. His books shall remain highly important in this area of academia for a long time. He gained popularity in many countries. In China, he is known by his Chinese name, Fu Gaoyi, and his biography of Deng Xiaoping has been translated into Chinese and is known by every educated Chinese person. He was well known in Japan as well, and his books have been read by oriental studies students in Russia. Now, when remembering him, one feels the importance of all of these achievements. But that is not the main issue here. The main thing is that he was a wonderful person—kind, considerate, always willing to help and to offer advice to anyone, even the youngest of colleagues. At a very advanced age, he maintained his optimism and an amazing amount of faith in mankind and in human goodness. He believed that people strive for the best in everything—be it in one's private life or in politics and international relations—and that this will ultimately make all of our lives better.

Yuan Ming

Peking University

Prof. Ezra Vogel was a man of enlightenment: erudite and tolerant, aspiring to wisdom and pursuing truth. In his writings and in his deeds, he exemplified the brightest qualities of the human spirit and those of a contemporary *junzi*.

My first encounter with Ezra was back in the late fall of 1983 in Cambridge, Massachusetts. Mr. Xiang Ziming, then Chairman of the Peking University Council, had been invited to visit Harvard, and I was his interpreter. Our first campus moment saw the welcoming sign of the national flag of China hung in the bright autumn sunshine. After a meeting with John K. Fairbank, we were introduced at the office door of a local resident, and there Ezra Vogel opened his arms and greeted us with *huanying* (欢迎) in a slightly accented Chinese. Those words ushered in the beginnings of our lasting friendship of thirty-seven years.

Our first encounter, however, had wider significance beyond personal amity. In broader terms, that visit, together with other thriving activities of academic exchange, started a new journey of joint efforts between the two oldest institutions of higher learning in China and the United States. In fostering these efforts, Prof. Vogel was a central figure and assumed an active role. For brevity's sake, from my personal experience I will mention just two examples of the energy he invested toward those noble aims.

In 1998, Ezra was invited to attend the 100th anniversary of Peking University (PKU). For the past decade, he had witnessed new obstacles emerge in the stable bilateral relations he had helped to painstakingly construct. In a flash of inspiration, he reached out to both Professor Tanaka Akihiro of Tokyo University and me, to join him in his new research project to revive the impetus for improving relations between the United States and China and also with Japan. The project was called "Ha-Bei-Dong," "Ha" for Harvard, "Bei" for PKU, and "Dong" for Tokyo University. Two workshops were organized, in Tokyo in 1999 and in Cambridge in 2000, respectively, followed by the publication of a volume titled *The Golden Age of the U.S.-China-Japan Triangle, 1972–1989*. The purposes of the project and the book were, as Ezra noted in his introduction, to re-examine "the patterns of cooperation developed during the period of 1972–1989, when the U.S., China, and Japan enjoyed positive relations with each other," and to see if relations going forward could re-capture some of the magic.

In the early spring of 2001, the National Committee on U.S.-China Relations organized a team to visit China. In Washington, the Republican administration had replaced the Clinton team. Concerned people on both sides felt the imperatives of avoiding mutual misunderstanding, which might navigate into the wrong waters. The group was well received in Beijing. In addition to the meetings with the Chinese leaders, Henry Kissinger, William Perry, Ezra Vogel, and the others had one more highlight at Peking University. It was a face-to-face dialogue—a lively meeting between senior Americans and young Chinese students. In a particularly thoughtful exchange, Ezra humbly noted that "For countries that we (Americans) don't have that much historical contact with, we tend to have more extreme reactions from one time to another. China is one of those countries. Because we have relatively little contact with China, our public opinion tends to go from one extreme to the other much more easily."

Ezra dedicated his life's work to moderating the excesses of those reactions, and to keeping relations on track in spite of misunderstandings and differences. His life, therefore, remains a testament to the possibility of successful cross-cultural exchange within a world full of complexities. By his example, Ezra gives us the confidence to continue to honor his legacy and never give up even in the face of strong headwinds.

I present one last personal anecdote that captures the spirit and depth of Ezra's unwavering commitment to that calling. Ezra was eighty-five in 2015 when he made a field study in Sichuan to collect materials for his new book. Unexpectedly he had to receive an emergency medical treatment because of a relapse in one of his medical conditions. Two weeks later, when he returned to Beijing, Ezra recounted this extraordinary experience to me. He just walked into a local clinic, pulled out his phone, and showed the doctors what treatment he needed. Given his advanced age, some of the doctors were nervous to operate on him. Ezra looked into their eyes, smiled, and said, "I trust you." The surgery went without a hitch.

In human affairs, as Ezra demonstrated fruitfully, "trust" is the ingredient necessary to overcome many difficult problems. May we remember that and him.

Xia Shuzhang and Florence Xia

Sun Yat-sen University

I am extremely disheartened that Professor Vogel has passed away. Not only was he my dearest friend for decades, he was also our country's old friend, a best friend. When my wife and I came to Harvard as visiting professors in the 1980s, he graciously opened his door and took us in. He paid countless visits to China, and he specifically did extensive study and research on the culture of Guangzhou. He also gave speeches at many cities in China. Back in the 1980s, he resided at Sun Yat-Sen University for an extensive period. He had a soft spot for China, and he would always criticize the American politicians who had insulted China. I will miss him very dearly, as he was my, and our country's, dear old friend.

FLORENCE XIA'S MEMORIES
OF PROFESSOR VOGEL

My grandfather, Xia Shuzhang, has always recalled his time at Harvard fondly, and he always talked about Professor Vogel reverently. When I decided to attend Boston College for graduate school, he insisted I visit Professor Vogel and Dr. Ikels first thing when I arrived in Boston. I will always remember my grandfather and Professor Vogel talking about the origin of Professor Vogel's Chinese name, 傅高义, the support and respect they had for each other, and their lifelong friendship. Although I met Professor Vogel only a handful of times, I felt like I had always known him through my grandfather. At ninety years young, he has left us too early. He will be missed dearly, and may he rest in peace.

Lu Mai, with a Contribution by Vice Premier Liu He

China Development Research Foundation

I've known Professor Vogel since the 1990s, when I went to the Harvard Kennedy School. The last time I saw him was at his home near campus in 2018. Ezra made me a cup of tea, and our conversation began with his books about China. I told him that his book *One Step Ahead in China: Guangdong under Reform*, published in 1989, was a vivid record of China's reforms in the 1980s. I read it at the Hong Kong Polytechnic University in 1993, and it was inspiring. Unfortunately, not many people in

China knew about it. The book was not as famous as *Deng Xiaoping and the Transformation of China*. Ezra was very happy to hear my comments. He went to the bookshelf and took a copy of his book, published in 1991 by the Guangdong Publishing House in Chinese, signed it, and gave it to me.

Ezra had been studying Guangdong as a means of exploring and understanding China since the 1960s. His profound and detailed description of the counties and cities in Guangdong greatly impressed me. From the reform of the rural areas to the establishment of special economic zones, from the reorganization of the state-owned economy to the transformation from the collective to the individual economy, Ezra's depiction of the reforms in Guangdong was real and three-dimensional. It was the epitome of China's economic and social exploration, development, and ongoing innovation.

Ezra was actually invited by the Guangdong provincial government to write the book *One Step Ahead in China*. In the 1980s, when Guangdong and Massachusetts began to establish friendly relationships, Ezra met with Liang Lingguang, Zhu Senlin, and Yang Li, the then governor and vice governors of Guangdong, respectively. At that time Guangdong officials believed having a foreigner come to Guangdong and write stories about its social and economic transformation would help attract foreign investments. In retrospect, Ezra saw it as a perfect match between him and the Guangdong officials: "I was like 'I am not dangerous, I am a scholar, and I will try to be objective.' They said, 'Great, let's try to tell the world what we've done from an objective perspective.' So, I came to Guangdong, stayed there, and visited more than 70 counties. They didn't even ask for my draft before publication."

One Step Ahead in China is a truthful account of Guangdong's reform and opening up, and Ezra formed great friendships with Chinese officials during his stay there. To Ezra, these Chinese government officials did not seem like part of a totalitarian bureaucracy. They were not closed-minded or arrogant. On the contrary, they had an open, pragmatic, and enthusiastic approach to promoting China's reform and opening up. Over the past forty years, they greatly contributed to China's economic transformation and social development. In the decades that followed and until his death, Ezra was outspoken in his praise of "the remarkable contribution of that generation of officials to China's development." For the past four decades, since the U.S and China established diplomatic relations, I've met many scholars like Ezra who are passionate and friendly to China. There have also been many talented government officials like Liang Lingguang and Zhu Senlin who are willing to open their arms and minds and learn from the United States. These respectful people comprise a vital part of U.S-China relations.

Since 2002, the China's Leaders in Development Executive Program has been held at the Kennedy School at Harvard. The China Development Research Foundation was the coordinator from the Chinese side. Each year, Ezra came to lecture Chinese government officials. With the help of our friends in the United States, China has continued to embark on the path of reform and opening up.

Ezra noticed subtle changes in China-U.S. relations a few years ago. He once reminded me: "China is a very large country with a large population. I hope the Chinese can understand if the West has concerns about China's growth." When Ezra's death was announced in December 2020, I was as shocked and then as deeply regretful as everyone else.

In 1993, I had accompanied Liu He (who was then working at the State Planning Commission) to visit Professor Vogel at his home, where Ezra received us warmly. Liu He went on to study at the Kennedy School and is now China's Vice Premier. After learning about the terrible news of Ezra's passing away, Vice Premier Liu He said to me, "It is a great loss that a scholar like Vogel passed away. Vogel was not only a respected scholar, but also a good friend of China. His profound knowledge and research on China's reform and opening up, especially on Deng Xiaoping, had an important impact on the world. The world now faces a series of challenges that call for greater understanding and new cooperation between China and the United States. And we are placing our hopes on the rising generation and the young."

I believe that, among the next generation of officials and scholars, there will be young people with the same vision, who will pass on the friendship between our two countries with an open and rational mind. I will always remember Ezra Vogel as an old friend and share his hope for the bright future of China-U.S. relations.

Chan Heng Chee

Ministry of Foreign Affairs, Singapore

I first met Ezra Vogel in Singapore in the wake of his celebrity as author of *Japan as Number One: Lessons for America*. It must have been 1980 or 1981. I was asked to do a TV interview with him on his book for Singapore Broadcasting Corporation (SBC). Ezra had an enormous impact on Singapore and then Prime Minister Lee Kuan Yew. He was invited to visit Singapore to have discussions with our bureaucrats at a time when they were thinking of restructuring the economy. He met Lee Kuan Yew on nearly all of these visits.

At that time Singapore was grappling with the issue of how a country could maintain its growth trajectory with practically no natural resources. If Lee Kuan Yew was thinking of Japan, the publication of Ezra's book in 1979 confirmed for him and many Asian leaders that Japan could be their model for economic success. In 1980 at a National Day Rally (the Singapore equivalent of the State of the Union address), Prime Minister Lee focused his speech on "Productivity" and highlighted what made the Japanese such a world-beating success. He noted their work culture and attitudes and Japanese organization and management. He admired the Japanese for conceptualizing "forward engineering" to counter Western criticism of the "reverse engineering" basis of their economic success and for pushing the "creative knowledge industries" in the eighties, long before the world was taken over by technological disruption and the digital economy.

So I met Ezra Vogel, this famous towering academic. I was a nervous young political scientist from the National University of Singapore. I must have looked even younger to Ezra, for it is hard to tell the age of Chinese women even though Ezra had spent time in China. As he said to me later, he was feeling relaxed in his chair when the shoot started, but when I began fielding my questions one by one, he sat up a little straighter because he thought, "This is serious." That was so like Ezra, to show such kindness and encouragement to a younger academic. He had done these interviews multiple times. It was my first TV interview in conversation with a distinguished personality. We became good friends after that and kept in touch.

I visited Ezra Vogel in Cambridge a few times and met his wife, Charlotte Ikels, on one of those visits. Her research was based in Hong Kong, and as my family came from Guangdong Province and Hong Kong, we had a rather nice conversation, partly in Cantonese. I was struck on these visits by how close and generous Ezra was to his graduate students. In the middle of the conversation, Ezra would suddenly stop and say he just remembered he needed to check if his Chinese graduate student could get into the house.

It was during my appointment as Singapore's ambassador to the United States that I had the opportunity to see Ezra Vogel again and again since I held the post for sixteen years and was nearly "dean of the diplomatic corps." I remember meeting Ezra just before I left for Washington to take up the post. We may have met in Singapore or perhaps at a conference or meeting in the United States. Ezra gave me an introduction to Fred Hiatt, who in 1996 had just joined the editorial board of the *Washington Post*, clearly a person of importance to a foreign ambassador. Fred Hiatt later became editor of the editorial page in 2000. I had many interesting breakfasts with Fred, in which we discussed and argued about political developments in my region. We remained good friends and were in touch until his recent passing.

This time, meeting Ezra again, we had a new dimension to our talks. Ezra had served on the National Intelligence Council under the Clinton administration in 1993–95. We were both academics and were also active in helping shape policy in a direct way. It was the experience and the scholar's perspective. After I made a trip to Harvard again and had lunch at the Faculty Club, I had given Ezra an open invitation to stay at the residence as my guest when he visited Washington, D.C. Ezra took up the invitation a few times. His visits were always short, usually one or two evenings in town for meetings. I made sure I would have dinner with him on one of those evenings. It was a treat for me. It was speaking the academic language again and hearing the voice and views of an erudite, humane, and wise man. Usually, I was the one asking questions about new writings or thinking on political issues I was following. Or it could be Japan, China, or the United States. Sometimes, it was a theoretical discussion, playing with concepts, which I missed in the daily business of diplomacy. I found Ezra a great source when it came to identifying younger scholars emerging in the field, whether it was on China or Southeast Asia.

The last time I saw Ezra was on his visit to Singapore in January 2020. He had come to attend a Middle East Institute Conference in the National University of Singapore. I had not seen him since 2012, which was when I left my post in Washington. We met for breakfast on January 18. He was looking a little frail but as intellectually alert as ever. We spent a great deal of time talking about Hong Kong, the United States, and China. His departure was too sudden. I remember I gasped at the news of his death, but I cannot recall if I read it in an email from a friend or in the newspapers. I look back and am so grateful to have had those hours of conversation with him. I will miss the mentor, the man, and the idea of Ezra Vogel—the renowned, unassuming, thoroughly scholarly, kind, and generous human being, a model for us all.

Zhou Xiaohong

Nanjing University

My first encounter with Ezra Vogel was in April 1999. I was a visiting scholar at the Fairbank Center, but I had arrived mid-semester, so I was unable to find lodging. Luckily I was invited to stay with Professor Elizabeth Perry at her home until I could secure a place of my own. Every morning, weather permitting, Liz would walk her dog Randall at Fresh Pond, northwest of Cambridge, and I would accompany them on occasion. One day, enroute to Fresh Pond, we happened upon Ezra Vogel and his wife, Charlotte Ikels, out jogging, and we stopped to chat. From that moment on, I had a series of warm exchanges with this wonderful human being.

Professor Vogel was nearly seventy when I met him. The place where we encountered the joggers was four or five miles from their house on Sumner Road, so they would have covered ten miles at least that morning. This shows how energetic they were. In autumn of that year, Professor Li Dahua and I attended a seminar on China taught by Professor Vogel. It was his final semester teaching. He officially retired in July the next year, so we might have been among his last students!

As a sociologist, I often knocked on Professor Vogel's door on Sumner Road and on the door of Professor Daniel Bell on Francis Avenue not far away, or made an appointment with Ezra to have a drink at the Yen-ching Restaurant in Harvard Square. I was writing *The History and Systems of Western Sociology* (2002) at that time. What intrigued me the most was not the research on China and Japan in which Professor Vogel special-ized, but the history of Harvard sociology, especially the work of Talcott Parsons, who ruled an empire of structural functionalism. Ezra took Pro-fessor Parsons's course in American social research as a graduate student, which not only prompted him to make sociology his career, but also shaped his initial research on Chinese society, using his teacher's ideas about social equilibrium.

To help me better understand Parsons's sociology, Ezra sent me a book he had treasured for many years, *Invitation to Talcott Parsons's Theory* (Lackey, 1987). Before Parsons's retirement in 1973, his structural func-tionalism theory began to lose influence under continuous criticism from scholars like C. Wright Mills, Ralf Dahrendorf, and Alvin Gouldner. Ac-cording to Richard Madsen, the most eloquent graduate students of that period scrambled to satirize Parsons. Then George Homans, Chair of the Department of Social Relations in the early 1970s, changed the "Depart-ment of Social Relations" to the "Department of Sociology," with social anthropology, social psychology, and clinical psychology moved out into the Department of Anthropology and the Department of Psychology, re-spectively. The empire that Parsons had presided over collapsed in the blink of an eye. Ezra told me that Parsons, who had just retired, regu-larly went to the reorganized sociology department to collect his mail, where he would pound on the floor with his cane and complain about Homans, frightening the administrative staff into silence.

I returned to China in May 2000, so I was unable to attend Ezra's retirement party scheduled for that July. Although I left Harvard, my ex-changes with Ezra were not interrupted. Two years later, on the occasion of centennial celebrations for Nanjing University, I invited Ezra to cele-brate with us. I had just become head of the Department of Sociology. Ezra sat in my office and joked, "Xiaohong, is your position at the division-head level (of the Chinese civil service)? I have served at the (higher) deputy bureau director level!" He was referring to being treated almost as deputy director of the Guangdong Economic Commission in 1988, while Ezra and Charlotte were living in Guangzhou.

Shortly after Ezra retired, he began to hone his Chinese. Every Tuesday and Thursday afternoon he studied with a Chinese tutor. I did not know the reason at the time, but admired him for continuing to learn into his seventies. Later, I learned that he had started a new project: it took ten years for him to research and write the more than 700 pages of *Deng Xiaoping and the Transformation of China*. Polishing his Chinese allowed him to conduct interviews directly, which enabled him to collect more extensive firsthand materials. In January 2013, the People's Republic of China translation of this book, *The Deng Xiaoping Era*, was published. By the time I visited Harvard in October of that year, half a million copies had been sold. When I went to see him, he told me that he had donated the royalties of ¥600,000 to his alma mater, Ohio Wesleyan University. I asked curiously, "Why didn't you donate them to Harvard?" He answered bluntly, "Oh, they are not short of money."

Perhaps because of this meeting, a few years later as I was on my way to Brown University to lecture on the Chinese middle class, Ezra commissioned me to translate his first book, *Japan's New Middle Class* (1963) into Chinese. As I had already translated C. Wright Mills's *White Collar: The American Middle Classes* (1951), I paid attention to the points of similarity and difference in these two works. Both scholars had identified radical and comparable changes caused by rapid industrialization. However, as an ardent proponent of left-wing ideology, Mills concentrated more on the emergence of the middle class and how rapid growth alleviated the Western world's earlier dissatisfaction with capitalism. He disdained the conservative posture of the American middle class. On the other hand, as a researcher on social transformations in East Asia, Ezra was gratified to see how the emergence of the new middle class had alleviated the severe impact of modernization on traditional Japanese society. I suspect that the subsequent popularity of this book in China also alleviated the internal anxiety of the Chinese middle class about the profound social changes they were experiencing. The moderation and understanding in this book accords with Ezra Vogel's image in Chinese scholarship as a "good gentleman."

Seio Nakajima

Waseda University

During an upper-division economic sociology lecture at the University of Tokyo, Professor Ken'ichi Tominaga mentioned Ezra Vogel as one of the sociologists who had examined Japan's industrialization since the Meiji Restoration. During office hours, Professor Tominaga told me that when he was studying in the United States from 1968 to 1969, he came to know Professor Vogel at Harvard, and that he would ask questions about Talcott Parsons. In turn, Professor Vogel would ask questions about Japanese society. This was my first indirect encounter with Professor Vogel.

In the fall of 1996, the opportunity came for me to actually study with Professor Vogel as a student in the Regional Studies East Asia program at Harvard University. Aside from the substantive academic interactions I had with him, one thing that struck me was his extraordinary ability for intercultural communication. He sometimes spoke with me in Japanese. I had known a good number of non-native speakers who spoke Japanese fluently. But I had not seen anyone whose mannerisms—bodily gestures, facial expressions, and other non-linguistic cues—felt so naturally "Japanese." He looked Japanese when he spoke the language.

After a year of study at Harvard, I decided to pursue a doctorate in the United States, and I chose the University of California-Berkeley's Sociology Department. There I met three people closely related to Professor Vogel. One was Professor Robert Bellah. Due to student office space limitations at Berkeley in those days I, together with a few other grad students, was assigned Professor Bellah's office; as emeritus Professor Bellah wasn't using his office very much. Fortunately, I got to meet Professor Bellah a few times a year and was able to have casual chats with him. At one of the meetings, I had a chance to introduce myself as a student from Japan working on issues related to contemporary China. He immediately asked me if I knew Ezra Vogel. I told Professor Bellah that I had studied with him for one year. Professor Bellah looked very satisfied to hear that, told me that he was rethinking issues concerning Japan after a long hiatus, and shared with me a manuscript on Japanese society that he was working on.

Another important person I met at Berkeley was Professor Thomas Gold, a leading sociologist working on China and Taiwan and one of the China-focused sociologists Professor Vogel had nurtured at Harvard. Professor Gold became one of my dissertation committee members. Then there's Professor Steven Vogel—Professor Ezra Vogel's son—who moved from Harvard to Berkeley when I was a few years into my graduate study. I got to interact with him in some of the workshops and study groups I attended, as my dissertation on the Chinese film industry overlapped with Professor Steven Vogel's expertise in industrial policy.

After finishing my PhD, I got a job in the Department of Sociology at the University of Hawai'i at Mānoa and started teaching there in the fall of 2007. Once more, I met a member of the "Vogel clan"—Professor Patricia Steinhoff, one of the leading sociologists of Japan whom Professor Vogel had mentored at Harvard. Patricia Steinhoff was also teaching in the Hawai'i Department of Sociology.

In February 2013, my father Mineo Nakajima, who was a China scholar and translated Professor Vogel's *One Step Ahead in China* (1989) into Japanese (the translation was published in 1991), passed away suddenly and very unexpectedly. Many people sent me condolence messages but one of the warmest and most memorable was the one sent by Professor Ezra Vogel, just a few days after my father's death was announced.

Commencing in April 2014, I began teaching at the Graduate School of Asia-Pacific Studies, Waseda University. Every summer after that, Professor Vogel invited me for lunch or coffee at the International House of Japan (Kokusai Bunkakaikan) during his yearly visit to Tokyo. There are two things I particularly remember. One is that unlike our past conversations, which focused on issues related either to Japan or China separately, most of our conversations concentrated on how we could improve Japan-China relations. For example, at one meeting he asked me for information on past attempts by Japanese and Chinese production companies to co-produce films or TV programs. Via email I sent him a list of such projects as well as academic works examining the relations between Japanese and Chinese media. He followed through and asked me further questions for clarification. Second, when I met Professor Vogel at International House, I was always introduced to senior scholars who worked on related topics or from whom I might be able to learn academically and professionally. Professor Vogel scheduled meetings with people in Japan back to back, partly of course because he was busy. But it also seems that he was intentionally scheduling these meetings so he could connect me to other people. In the last several years of my meetings with him at International House, I was introduced to senior scholars, including Professor Hiroshi Ishida, Professor Akira Iriye, and Professor Robert Cole, who were either living in or visiting Tokyo.

At my last meeting with Professor Vogel in the summer of 2018, I asked him to write a letter of recommendation for my membership application to International House. He kindly accepted and wrote down his words on the form while sipping a glass of Coca-Cola (I think that was his favorite drink during Japan's hot summer). As the application needed two recommenders, I thought about another person who might be able to write the recommendation. Professor Steinhoff came to mind, so I asked her to write it during one of her visits to Japan. She also kindly accepted. And as I mentioned, Professor Steinhoff was a student of Professor Vogel. It seems that wherever I go, I encounter traces of Professor Vogel in my life.

Keizo Takemi

House of Councillors, Japan

I first met Professor Vogel when I was a graduate student at Keio University. At that time, my father, who was the President of the Japan Medical Association, was thinking about establishing an international health program at the Harvard School of Public Health. Professor Vogel gave my father very good advice on the establishment of the program.

Many years later, after I had been unsuccessful in the House of Councillors election at the age of fifty-seven, I spent two years as a fellow at the Harvard School of Public Health. At that time, I joined the "Vogel *juku*" for young researchers studying in the Boston area, hosted by Professor Vogel at his home. As I was already older, Professor Vogel said to me, "Since you are so senior, it is difficult for you to be a member of the Vogel *juku*. However, you may join as an observer!" From that point on he became a mentor to me and opened my eyes to many things during the wide-ranging discussions he hosted. For that, I am sincerely grateful to him.

THIRTEEN

What Made Ezra Vogel So Special?

Michael Dukakis

Northeastern University

We've lost a very special guy. We first met when I came back from Korea to go to law school and he was a graduate student. Many years later he did something very special for Kitty and me. We decided while I was governor to do a trip to China and Japan in 1985, and Ezra volunteered to come with us and be our translator. How he became so fluent in Chinese and Japanese is beyond me, but he was a very special part of the trip. He was not only a great traveling companion and constant fund of knowledge, but he was a superb interpreter. And above all, a great human being, one of the best in every respect.

Perry Link

Riverside, California

Ezra was gentle. Agreeable, considerate, humble, a good listener, and famous enough to wear a stuffed shirt but utterly lacking any desire to do so. He shook hands limply, and at first might give you the impression of "soft." But the Chinese idiom 外圓內方, that is, "round outside and right-angled inside," is more like it. He was rigorous inside. In the spring semester of 1966 I had a tutorial with him on Mondays from 4 p.m. to 4:30 p.m. We started every Monday at exactly 4 and he dismissed me at precisely 4:30. No wobble. The purpose of the rigor was as much to discipline himself, I felt, as to train me.

His use of language was the same: on the surface were plain, simple words that a high school student could follow, but inside was packed content that experts envied. Later, as I moved into literary studies and had to cope with the discourse of constructed subjectivity and its imbricated topoi (in short, with emptiness), the plunk-plunk-plunk of Ezra's style, each meek word carrying its own freight, became a model.

In the early 2010s, on a visit by Ezra to California, Dick Madsen, Paul Pickowicz, and I invited him to dinner. He started bemoaning the way young sociologists became overjoyed when they found huge data sets at hospitals, police departments, or wherever. Working out one's theoretical contribution had become essential for professional advancement, and it had become a real coup to lay hands on a stash of fresh data that one could use to illustrate one's point. "What's wrong with that?" we asked Ezra. "Intellectually, it's upside down," he said. "You learn from your data; you don't teach it." A provocative view, trenchantly put. Here, too, was rigor inside softness.

Rigorous never meant brittle or narrow. Ezra's expansive intellect was the very opposite of that, as this book amply shows. I want to point out his political breadth. He was strongly supportive of me from my undergraduate years on, even though we both knew that my views of the Chinese Communist Party (CCP) came to diverge sharply from his. (In brief: I see Deng Xiaoping less as a beneficent "architect" of reform from the top down and more as a savvy ship captain who kept the CCP boat on top of a sea of demands for reform that pushed from the bottom up.) I once visited Congress to testify about Confucius Institutes and was very harsh on the CCP (properly, of course). I denounced, among other things, its practice of spending billions of yuan to promote its image around the world while kids in the hills of Guizhou still didn't have desks and blackboards. A couple of weeks later I got an email from Ezra. He told me he had seen my testimony and liked it. I wrote back that he didn't have to be polite. He is my dear teacher and I his ever-grateful student, and it's OK if we disagree on some questions. He wrote back quickly: "No, no, no, I really *do* like your testimony." I had been wrong to guess that he was being polite. His broad intellect could take in a wide range of viewpoints and think about all of them. This ability also allowed him space to tell me, with nothing but kind intentions, when I had gone astray. When Andy Nathan and I edited *The Tiananmen Papers*, he told me I shouldn't be so confident of the "compiler" of the papers until I got to the bottom of who he was.

The last time I saw Ezra was in June 2017 when my family and I were visiting Cambridge on our way back from a short stay in Maine. My wife Tong Yi had served as an assistant to Wei Jingsheng during Wei's seven-month respite from prison in 1994, and for that offense she had spent two and a half years in a labor camp. She knew about Ezra because of the Deng Xiaoping book. She loathed Deng, and so, at first, I was swimming upstream in getting her to understand my affection for Ezra. We were walking near Sumner Road when I pointed to number 14. "See that house? That's where Ezra Vogel lives." "Let's go!" she said. I had to say "no, we can't just crash in uninvited. We can send an email first." But it's not easy to stop an ex-convict with an idea. Tong Yi walked straight to the house and knocked on the door. Ezra and Charlotte were at home, were extremely warm, asked us in, and gave us tea—using about an hour, right in the middle of Ezra's work day. He was doing his China-Japan book at the time and explained that he wanted to do a Hu Yaobang book next. In his mid-eighties, he had two more books in mind—Hu Yaobang and his own memoirs.

My peppery spouse put the key question, "Why do you do this? Why are you working so hard even at your age?" Any other person might have taken this as a rhetorical question and given a pro forma answer. Not Ezra. He took it as a serious question that deserved a responsible reply. Visibly, he started introspecting: WHY do I do this? After a moment or two he was talking about his hometown in Ohio, where his parents had made him feel that it was his duty to be "a good boy." He grew up, he said, always wanting to be a good boy for them. They died, but the habit had become rooted in his character. His duty to parents just shifted to be a general duty toward the world. He was still trying to be "a good boy," he said. This reminded me of the late-Ming ideal of *tongxin* 童心, "the child-like heart." A person who has such a heart grows old while preserving the sincerity of a child's outlook. *Tongxin* is not the same as naiveté. The person absorbs experience and strife while maintaining pellucid authenticity. The trait is truly rare, but Ezra had it.

Joseph Schmelzeis

Tokyo, Japan

Ezra had a keen sense of justice and would act upon it. As I had been a teaching fellow and kept in regular contact for thirty years, I guess he was proud when I was nominated to serve in a senior position in the U.S.

Embassy in Tokyo. The position required a high-level security clearance, and at one point it looked like the clearance might not be issued because bureaucratic standard operating procedures somehow equated my living overseas for a long time with a lack of loyalty to the United States (ironic that Foreign Service officers sign up specifically to live overseas and often seek repeated assignments to Japan). This seemingly arbitrary slur on my patriotism stung, in particular, because I was nominated by an Eagle Scout and am an Eagle Scout myself and could possibly be denied the opportunity to serve my country.

I shared this information with Ezra. It was 9 p.m. Cambridge time when he learned it. He was clearly indignant. He spent the next five hours drafting a lengthy character reference for me, citing our long relationship and his work for the National Intelligence Council. It was 2 a.m. his time when I received an email from him with the letter attached. That led to a chain of events where sixteen others wrote similar letters—and ultimately the clearance was granted. Had he not stood up for me I doubt I would have been able to serve.

Yuen Yuen Ang

Singapore

Professor Ezra Vogel was kind, generous, humble, erudite, and above all, wise. He understood life, though he never preached about it. He shared his wisdom almost accidentally, through passing comments that he probably did not think would leave a deep impression on the countless people who crossed paths with him—like myself.

One piece of wisdom I learned was about having a long-term perspective. When I told him that the Chinese-language version of my book could not be published, he replied that in the 1970s the same had happened to his book, *Canton under Communism*, which was finally released in Chinese forty years later. In an email, he wrote: "When I was young I was upset that it was not published. As I matured, I grew more philosophical and was finally amused when it was published."

He also imparted wisdom on fame. Professor Vogel told me that he became famous at the age of 49. In thirty seconds, he did an impersonation of how people treated him with skepticism before that, and how they swooned around him after he became famous. Unfortunately, I am not able to capture this impersonation in words, but it was at once hilarious and profound. What struck me most was the lightness with which he talked about fame. He acknowledged that it had practical benefits, but he was not attached to it, nor was he defined by it. Perhaps that is why he could joke about success in a casual conversation. He applied the same light touch of amusement in his comments about failures in life.

I once heard that humility comes from wisdom, from understanding the nature of life and one's place in it. This sounds abstract, but Professor Vogel showed through his words and his actions how it manifests in reality. Everywhere he went, he shone and inspired—simply by being himself. I am immeasurably fortunate to have learned from him.

Wenjuan Jia

Shanghai University

News of the passing of Harvard Professor Ezra F. Vogel was met with shock and sadness in China. Media outlets and academics alike posted memorials and retrospectives praising his wisdom and thanking him for helping the outside world better understand their country.

But Ezra Vogel was more than just the former director of Harvard's Fairbank Center for Chinese Studies, the author of masterworks like *Deng Xiaoping and the Transformation of China*, or a torchbearer for Sino-U.S. studies. To me, and other students like me, he was "Grandpa Fu," that much-loved professor who, every month, invited students and researchers from China to his home to eat dumplings and chat.

From 2011 to 2012, I was a visiting fellow at the Harvard-Yenching Institute. The winter nights in Cambridge are always bitter cold, but once a month, no matter how freezing cold it was, I would rush out the door and head to the professor's residential neighborhood. Sometimes I'd get a little lost in front of so many similar-looking buildings not far from William James Hall, but never for long. That's because the door to one was always open; its warm porch light and the smell of food being cooked within called to me, as if to say: "This is the place!" "This" was the home of

Professor Vogel, whose dinner and study group on China studies, organized with Professor Martin Whyte, was a long-standing tradition at
Harvard. I can't even begin to imagine how many Chinese students or
visiting scholars to the university spent time in that house over the years.

Professor Vogel's concern and care for young scholars was widely
known throughout the academic world. We showed up to his door brim-
ming with dreams and ambition—and no idea if we were supposed to
take our shoes off before entering his home. Yet we were always warmly
ushered in by him and his wife (our shoes still firmly on our feet). We
would carefully place our bags on the floor of his bedroom, and then we'd
join the line for a sumptuous buffet.

Over dinner, Professor Vogel became Grandpa Fu. Back then, his
magisterial *Deng Xiaoping and the Transformation of China* had just been
published, and he had a copy displayed prominently on the bookshelf in
his living room. He explained to a rapt audience how he had toiled for a
decade to write the book, how he'd gotten those who knew Deng best to
open up, and the difficulties he'd faced during its translation and publication processes. We laughed often while we ate, then crammed into the
kitchen and clumsily helped load the dishwasher.

I still remember how, at the first dinner after the 2011 Christmas vacation, I had the chance to talk about a paper I'd written, "Labor Enthusiasm and Deception." As an assignment for one of Professor Whyte's
courses, I'd explored how people's enthusiasm for production in the early
days of the People's Republic of China devolved into deception, abuse of
power for personal gain, and discontent during the Great Leap Forward
of 1958 to 1962.

Some of those attending the dinner didn't know much about that
period in Chinese history and frequently cut in with questions. For example, when I mentioned that southern Guangdong province had "launched
a satellite" during its steel production campaign, someone interrupted
me to ask: "What do you mean 'launched a satellite?' How could factories
have satellites?" Quick as a flash, Professor Vogel explained that "to
launch a satellite" means "to boast or exaggerate." Although the country's
factories could not produce large amounts of steel, managers declared
higher output anyway to pander to their superiors. In this way, production gains suddenly appeared stratospheric—just like a satellite being launched into space. The discussion over dinner that evening was

lively and lasted late into the night. I can still remember Professor Vogel smiling amiably, while Professor Whyte furrowed his brow, as was his habit. The advice they gave me was consistent and to the point, and my article was published later that year in the tenth edition of the Chinese journal, *Open Times*.

It's been eight years since I left Cambridge. Originally, I had meant to come back in 2020. I'd organized a panel session for the 2020 conference of the Association for Asian Studies, which was to be held in Boston in March, and had applied to return to the Harvard-Yenching Institute as a visiting professor. I'd already made up my mind that I simply had to see Professor Vogel again and attend another of his dinners. Then the coronavirus came and put an end to all my plans. Now, during yet another cold winter, comes the devastating news of Professor Vogel's sudden passing.

Sometimes I look back at my year in Cambridge and how, whether we realized it or not, we were witnessing the end of an era, the long twentieth century. We seem set to return to the political lines and ideological confrontation of the Cold War era. China and the United States face many of the same challenges: the myopia of financial capitalism, the hollow prosperity generated by abstract economic development, environmental collapse spurred on by global warming, precarious work for the many and the concentration of wealth for the few, and the crisis of an aging society.

Professor Vogel argued that, although the U.S. was a leading party to the Cold War, American China-watchers were never among the country's Cold Warriors. Whether during the McCarthyism of the 1950s or the frequent frictions of the past four years, Professor Vogel's actions consistently promoted dialogue between the two nations. The dinner parties he organized at his home are a testament to this. Now he's gone, but the light in front of his house will always shine on in our hearts.

Wenying Shi

Mililani, Hawaii

I first met Professor Vogel in Guangzhou in 1998, my second year working as a Chinese teacher at South China Normal University. Before summer break started, I received my new assignment, tutoring Professor Fu Gaoyi, a famous China expert from Harvard University, for two months. I had never heard of Fu Gaoyi before and wondered whether he was a Chinese American since he had a very authentic Chinese name. My school considered it a great honor to host him and his wife, Professor Ikels, an anthropologist researching the living conditions of the elderly in Guangdong that summer, so they put them up in the best suite in the guest house on campus.

I still remember our first meeting. When I knocked on the door, it swung open immediately, and there was Fu Gaoyi, medium to slim build, balding on the crown, a warm and cheerful voice, and a friendly face with smiling eyes. He spoke Chinese quite fluently with a faint foreign accent and consciously emphasized the pronunciations of certain consonants. He shook his head and cried out, "Ai ya!" like a Chinese person whenever he made a mistake. I learned that his first Chinese teacher was Zhao Ru-lan, daughter of the renowned linguist Zhao Yuanren. He even read novels by Lao She, which was very impressive. Time flew by, and we both enjoyed the class. I owed the success of our first meeting to my ignorance. Had I known that Professor Vogel was a prolific scholar and an influential figure in the East Asian social and political realms before I met him, I might have been starstruck and unable to be myself around him.

When Professor Vogel hired me to teach him Chinese at the Fairbank Center, I brought him a novel to study, *Lai Lai Wang Wang* (*Comes and Goes*), by Chi Li. Every day, we read the book together for three hours. He read a couple of sentences or a short paragraph first and then translated sentence by sentence into English. He used his mechanical pencil to mark every mispronounced tone or syllable and write down the English translation for every unknown word. By the time we finished the book, he had filled every page with squiggles and words between the lines and margins. He asked me to record the book so that he could listen to it whenever he had time. He truly appreciated Chi Li's book and sang praises of her clever and incisive depictions of characters' internal activities and social relationships in the 1980s, when China just started opening up. He often reviewed *Lai Lai Wang Wang* and even recommended it for his wife to use as study material.

I think he loved the book because he was genuinely interested in understanding people. He was also a great storyteller. He could remember thousands of people's names and anecdotes about them. He also had this innate optimism toward humanity. He often mentioned that he was the son of a small town and felt lucky that everybody treated him kindly; therefore, he believed in giving back to the community and helping as many people as possible. His small-town sentiment resonated with me because I was from a small town as well, and I believed people were born good and generally had good intentions. Trust might be the most dangerous approach to building a business relationship, but it is the only way to have a meaningful friendship.

Professor Vogel and I became cross-generational friends, and we maintained this friendship for over two decades. We became like family; he regarded me as his Chinese daughter, and I thought of him as my American father. Professor Vogel supported all the major decisions I made in life, and not just through words. Once, he handwrote a letter in Chinese to my parents expressing his appreciation for my work ethic and character. He hoped that his name and influence would be a bonus point for my career development. I looked up to him as my role model. He was the epitome of a lifelong learner. His humility kept him going on his long journey to learn Chinese.

After I moved to Hawaii in 2003, we kept in close touch by email and had classes via telephone and Skype when he needed help with his Chinese. In April 2020, when the pandemic grew increasingly grim in the U.S., I emailed Professor Vogel to check in on him. He immediately wrote back saying he and his wife were healthy and still walking or cycling every day. He mentioned that his new book on China and Japan was published and wanted to send me a copy. Then, he said that he would like to practice speaking Chinese with me once a week via Zoom, since he might have opportunities to go to Taiwan to promote his new book. Professor Vogel never failed to surprise me. He wasn't tech-savvy, but he learned to use Zoom to hold seminars and give talks at age ninety. How cool is that! We met online at 11 a.m. Hawaii time every Saturday for an hour for the next eight months. He read and translated articles that he wrote for various occasions and practiced lectures. I was envious of his enthusiasm and energy level. He didn't seem to slow down a bit compared to twenty years earlier. On December 19, 2020, we were supposed to translate the second segment of a monograph on China from 1949 to 2019 that he recently wrote for a history class. However, he didn't show up for the meeting. Then, the next day, sad news arrived—Professor Vogel had passed away.

Like a candle, Professor Vogel burned brilliantly, and his light reached numerous lives worldwide. I was extremely fortunate to have had the opportunity to work closely with him and witness his charisma. I sincerely believe that learning made him happy, and I am honored to have been of some help to him on his extraordinary journey.

Su Wei

Yale University

In the spring of 2000 I went to a cocktail party at Harvard held in honor of Ezra Vogel's retirement. Present at the party were numerous former students, many of them now eminent scholars in their own right or leaders in other fields. When he saw me, Professor Vogel gave me a hug and introduced me to the other guests by saying, "And here is Su Wei, my Chinese son." Hearing those words, I started to tear up, and I explained to the other guests that my own father had just passed away. With a lump in my throat I said to Ezra, "And you—you're my American father." After that, whenever we met, Ezra and I would embrace and laughingly call each other "father" and "son."

In 1980, as the policy of reform and opening was just beginning and a new era was blossoming, foreign professors began showing up on China's university campuses. The first foreign face to appear at mine, Sun Yat-sen University in Guangzhou, was that of Ezra's former student, Perry Link, who had come to do research into contemporary Chinese fiction. A copy of the student literary magazine I edited happened to fall into Perry's hands, and he invited me and several other student editors to visit him in the little brick house where the university had put him up on campus. It was there that I had my first-ever conversation with a foreigner, and it wasn't long before we were inviting Perry over to our dorm rooms and sitting crowded together cross-legged, having long conversations over tea.

For this reason Ezra remembers me as one of the few students bold enough to interact with foreigners when he came to Sun Yat-sen University that summer as a visiting scholar. Perry had to leave for a research trip to Beijing, and it was to me that he entrusted the task of helping his former teacher and his wife navigate life on campus. We got along well, and when the summer was over, Ezra sat me down for a serious chat. "You should come study in the United States," he told me. "Apply to Harvard! I'll write you a recommendation letter." I was astonished. "But my English is terrible," I protested. Ezra gave me two boxes of blank cassette tapes and took me over to the School of Foreign Languages, where he introduced me to a Canadian teacher whom he prevailed upon to tutor me in English. When Perry came back from Beijing, he had a suggestion for me: Rather than apply to Harvard, which required a high TOEFL score, I should come to UCLA, where Perry was a professor. UCLA's language programs didn't accept the TOEFL, and instead would require me to pass their own test after I was admitted. This would give me a nice, flexible buffer period in which to beef up my English.

"Study in the U.S.?" "Recommendations from two American professors?" To people around me this sounded like an unbelievable windfall. But the idea set off a storm of emotions within me. I was just in the throes of my tumultuous first college-era romance, and I had just published my first novel in a prestigious literary journal. My dreams of love and literary fame seemed about to come true, and the dream of studying abroad had never penetrated my consciousness. Yet now, with a simple nod of assent, the then-unimaginable dream of studying in the U.S. could, just as easily as that, become my reality. "Why not?" friends and family members asked me. "What are you waiting for?" Finally, I bit my lip and made my decision: *Yes, I'll do it.*

In the spring of 1982 I left for UCLA, where I earned my master's degree. After that I took Ezra up on his invitation and went to Harvard as a visiting scholar, where I lived for two and half years in Ezra's home while serving as a research assistant at the Harvard-Yenching Institute. We spent our days side by side, and at least once a week Ezra would invite various Chinese students and scholars at Harvard to a "Chinese dinner" where we would only speak Chinese at the table. Some people who went on to become big names in the business world, such as economists Fan Gang and Qian Yingyi and financier Cai Jinyong, were frequent guests at Ezra's "Chinese dinners." While I was living there, Ezra also put up some eminent house guests, such as Kim Dae-jung, who would later become South Korea's president and who was then in political exile in the United States.

After I left Harvard in 1986, Ezra's home became a regular pied-à-terre for intellectuals visiting from China, and many famous writers and scholars stayed at his house. I have no doubt that Ezra's deep understanding of and love for China, and his ability to produce such rigorous, valuable scholarship, came in great part from his having had so many Chinese friends—from his having taken under his wing so many "Chinese sons and daughters" like myself. He once confided in me that he felt most Western sinologists were in the habit of regarding China from an outsider's perspective, and that those who were able to truly understand China as an insider would—to "see China from a Chinese point of view"—were few and far between. This was the area toward which he most wanted to direct his efforts in the future. That Ezra Vogel's work has been acclaimed both within and outside of China, and that it has come so close to capturing real historical truths, must be due to his having consulted and interacted with such a wide network of Chinese friends and acquaintances in order to understand his primary sources—in other words, to his novel approach of attempting to inhabit a "Chinese point of view."

(Translated and adapted by Austin Woerner)

Martin K. Whyte

Harvard University

I am fortunate to have had a history with Ezra Vogel stretching over fifty-five years, starting in 1965 as a student in Harvard's Russian Studies MA program, when I enrolled in his course on Contemporary Chinese Society. With Ezra's encouragement and advice, I eventually migrated into sociology and Chinese studies, becoming his first China sociology doctoral student. Our relationship continued over the years, up through my return to Harvard as professor of sociology (2000–2015) and beyond. At the ninetieth birthday Zoom celebration for Ezra in July 2020, I quipped, "Ezra Vogel has been the most important person in my life except for my immediate family, and some members of my family I am not so sure about." But the countless kindnesses and generosities I received from Ezra over the years were not because I was special, as the many reminiscences in this volume attest. Ezra treated countless others, high and low, in the same friendly, unpretentious, and generous fashion, and working on this volume in his honor has made me puzzle over what made him special in so many ways, but in particular in his generosity and support for so many others.

In the social sciences there are influential "social exchange" theories that describe how societies are knit together by social relationships based upon norms of reciprocity, with individuals doing things for others in the expectation that the favors will be returned, sooner or perhaps later. And in societies like China and Japan we learn of the importance of 关系 (*guanxi*; *kankei* in Japanese), a cultural near-obsession with cultivating ties with individuals who may bring you future benefits. Yet the amazing thing about Ezra was that he devoted extraordinary time and effort to getting to know people and offering them advice and assistance, without any expectation, or often even the possibility, that he would benefit in return. What made him behave in such an unusual way? I don't have any convincing explanation, but I suspect that his family background and roots in a small town in Ohio impelled him to be so generous. I think Ezra found being embedded in a wide-ranging network of colleagues, former students, and friends (with a Christmas card list that grew to more than 600 names) provided such strong intrinsic satisfaction to Ezra that he never had any concern for reciprocity.

Even though I was not in any way special as a recipient of Ezra's generosity, let me mention some of my personal experiences in this regard, focusing on the period after I returned to Harvard to join the faculty. And just to be clear, even though I returned in 2000, the same year Ezra retired, I was not his replacement, as he was, of course, irreplaceable.

My family did not move to Massachusetts until 2002, so initially I commuted to Boston once a week. Ezra facilitated things by renting me his third-floor furnished apartment at a bargain rent. Furthermore, at least once on each visit, Ezra would invite me downstairs and make breakfast so that we could catch up, making my commutes more pleasant.

From 2000 onward, even though Ezra had retired from teaching, he and I held monthly China sociology dinner meetings to which graduate students and visiting scholars were invited. Throughout, these dinners were held at 14 Sumner Road, with take-out Chinese food provided for the eight to fifteen attending, with one of the participants (or a visiting China sociology researcher, or Ezra, or myself) giving an after-dinner talk. Several essays in this volume (e.g., by Yun Zhou, Jia Wenjuan) describe these dinner meetings fondly. I feel they contributed as much to the training of sociology doctoral students as the China seminars I taught. What the students and scholars attending did not realize was the over-the-top efforts Ezra made to make the China sociology dinners successful. Not only were they held in his home, but he always did the ordering of the take-out food, often driving to pick up our meal himself. My role in the proceedings was decidedly secondary. I split the cost of the food with Ezra (we paid out of pocket). I helped move chairs into the dining room and set the table, heated tea-kettles, and greeted participants at the door. After dinner I helped clear the table, moved chairs into the living room, and prepared to chair the session jointly with Ezra. Despite our age difference, in these sessions Ezra remained alert and asked insightful questions until the end of the evening, while I sometimes struggled to stay awake and alert.

After I retired and moved away, I continued to return to Cambridge to meet with students. Each time I would contact Ezra, and he would always invite me to stay in his second-floor guest room, where numerous others in this volume have been guests. And as before, Ezra and Charlotte would invite me to have breakfast with them during my stay. Sometimes I would arrive bearing a bottle of wine or a box of chocolates. But I always felt such gifts were trifles, given the incredible hospitality I always received from Ezra and Charlotte.

I never could have repaid in any substantial way the generosity and support I received from Ezra over the decades. So I will have to rationalize my lack of reciprocity with the hope that, together with so many others, I added to the intrinsic satisfactions he gained from his impressive social network. As I mourn his loss, I will always happily recall the scene at one of the last breakfasts we shared. I was dressed in street clothes, sitting at the kitchen table drinking coffee, and Ezra was in his breakfast cooking attire—pajamas, slippers, bathrobe, and knit sleeping cap—leaning over the stove and masterfully cooking his famous blueberry pancakes.

Author Index

Harvard East Asian Monographs
(most recent titles)